Derrida and the Future of Literature

SUNY series,

Intersections: Philosophy and Critical Theory

Rodolphe Gasché, editor

Derrida and the Future of Literature

Joseph G. Kronick

STATE UNIVERSITY OF NEW YORK PRESS

Chapter 2 is a revision of an essay originally published as "Edmond Jabès and the Poetry of the Jewish Unhappy Consciousness," *MLN,* vol. 106/N. 5 (Dec. 1991): 967–996. Reprinted by permission of Johns Hopkins University Press.

Production by Ruth Fisher
Marketing by Dana E. Yanulavich

Published by
State University of New York Press, Albany

For information, address State University of New York Press,
State University Plaza, Albany, NY 12246

Library of Congress Cataloging-in-Publication-Data
Kronick, Joseph G.
   Derrida and the future of literature / Joseph G. Kronick.
      p.   cm.—(SUNY series, intersections—philosophy and critical theory)
   Includes bibliographical references and index.
   ISBN 0–7914–4335–3 (alk. paper).—ISBN 0–7914–4336–1 (pbk. : alk. paper)
      1. Derrida, Jacques—Contributions in criticism. 2. Literature—History and criticism—Theory, etc. 3. Politics and literature. 4. Democracy. I. Title.   II. Series: Intersections (Albany, N.Y.)
PN75.D45K76   1999
801'.95'092—dc21   99-14975
                                                        CIP

10 9 8 7 6 5 4 3 2 1

For my grandparents,

Max and Rose Steinberg

Que *Je* soit un autre, voilà l'une des trouvailles récentes de l'homme à propos de lui-même, pour se rendre la vie difficile, pour s'inquiéter.

—Francis Ponge

la littérature m'a toujours paru inacceptable, le scandale, la faute morale par excellence, et comme une carte postale qui voudrait se faire valoir pour autre chose, pour une vraie lettre à qui on ferait passer la censure ou la douane, une imposture pour se dédouaner de tout.

(literature has always appeared unacceptable to me, a scandal, the moral fault *par excellence*, and like a post card seeking to pass itself as something else, as a true letter that would have to pass through the censor or customs, an imposture in order to get rid of the duties on everything.)

—Jacques Derrida

Contents

Acknowledgments

Portions of this book were presented at various conferences, and I would like to thank those people who gave me the opportunity to speak: Stephen Barker, Sandor Goodheart, Adelaide Russo, and Krzysztof Ziarek. Grants from the Louisiana State University Office of Research, the Manship Fellowship, and the Center for French and Francophone Studies allowed me to work on this project. I am grateful for the careful scrutiny given my manuscript by Rodolphe Gasché and the other readers for SUNY Press. My thanks also goes to Lisa Forte Doyle, Ruth Fisher, and James Peltz of SUNY Press, and to Sarah Benoit, Gale Carrithers, Jr., and Bainard Cowan. Harro Stammerjohnann graciously answered my questions concerning translations. Mark Bauerlein read portions of the manuscript and gave good advice at crucial times. I am especially grateful to Henry Sussman without whose support and counsel I probably never would have been able to complete this work. It is a pleasure to acknowledge my debt to him.

Abbreviations of Derrida's Works

FRENCH TEXTS

DG   *De la grammatologie.* Paris: Minuit, 1967.

DM   "Donner la mort." In *L'éthique du don: Jacques Derrida et la pensée du don.* Paris: Métailié-Transition, 1992.

DT   *Donner le temps. 1. La fausse monnaie.* Paris: Galilée, 1991.

ED   *L'écriture et la différence.* 1967; rpr. Paris: Seuil, 1979.

G   *Glas.* Paris: Galilée, 1974.

LOG   *L'origine de la géométrie, de Husserl. Introduction et traduction.* Paris: PUF, 1962.

Pass   *Passions.* Paris: Galilée, 1993.

Parages   *Parages.* Paris: Galilée, 1986.

PdS   *Points de suspension: Entretiens.* Ed. Elisabeth Weber. Paris: Galilée, 1992.

Psyché   *Psyché: Inventions de l'autre.* Paris: Galilée, 1987.

S   *Schibboleth, pour Paul Celan.* Paris: Galilée, 1986.

TA   "D'un ton apocalyptique adopté naguère en philosophie." In *Les fins de l'homme: à partir du travail de Jacques Derrida.* Paris: Galilée, 1981.

UG   *Ulysse gramophone: Deux mots pour Joyce.* Paris: Galilée, 1987.

ENGLISH TRANSLATIONS

Aporias   *Aporias: Dying-awaiting (one another at) the "limits of truth."* Trans. Thomas Dutoit. Stanford: Stanford University Press, 1993.

AT   "On a Newly Arisen Apocalyptic Tone in Philosophy."
          Trans. John P. Leavey, Jr. In *Raising the Tone of
          Philosophy: Late Essays by Immanuel Kant,
          Transformative Critique by Jacques Derrida*. Ed. Peter
          Fenves. Baltimore: Johns Hopkins University Press,
          1993.
BL   "Before the Law." Trans. Avital Ronnell and Christine
          Roulston. In *Acts of Literature*. Ed. Derek Attridge. New
          York: Routledge, 1992.
C   *Cinders*. Trans. Ned Lukacher. Lincoln: University of
          Nebraska Press, 1991.
D   *Dissemination*. Trans. Barabara Johnson. Chicago:
          University of Chicago Press, 1981.
EO   *The Ear of the Other: Otobiography, Transference,
          Translation*. English edition ed. Christie McDonald.
          Trans. Peggy Kamuf. Lincoln: University of Nebraska
          Press, 1988.
FL   "Force of Law: The 'Mystical Foundation of Authority.'"
          Trans. Mary Quaintance. *Cardozo Law Review* 11
          (July/Aug. 1990): 919-1045.
Glas-E   *Glas*. Trans. John P. Leavey, Jr. and Richard Rand.
          Lincoln: University of Nebraska Press, 1986.
GT   *Given Time: I. Counterfeit Money*. Trans. Peggy Kamuf.
          Chicago: University of Chicago Press, 1993.
IOG   *Edmund Husserl's "Origin of Geometry": An
          Introduction*. Trans. John P. Leavey, Jr. Stony Brook,
          N.Y.: Nicholas Hays. Ltd., 1978.
LI   *Limited Inc*. Ed. Gerald Graff. Trans. Samuel Weber,
          with Jeffrey Mehlman. Lincoln: University of Nebraska
          Press, 1988.
M   *Margins of Philosophy*. Trans. Alan Bass. Chicago:
          University of Chicago Press, 1982.
Mem   *Memoires for Paul de Man*. Rev. ed. Trans. Cecile
          Lindsay, et al. New York: Columbia University Press,
          1989.
NA   "No Apocalypse, Not Now (full speed ahead, seven
          missles, seven missives)." Trans. Catherine Porter and
          Philip Lewis. *Diacritics* 14 (Summer 1984): 20-31.
OG   *Of Grammatology*. Trans. Gayatri Spivak. Baltimore:
          Johns Hopkins University Press, 1976.

Derek Attridge and Daniel Ferrer. Cambridge University Press, 1984.

UGE   "Ulysses Gramophone: Hear Say Yes in Joyce." Trans. Derek Attridge. In *Acts of Literature*. Ed. Derek Attridge. London: Routledge, 1992.

VR   "The Villanova Roundtable: A Conversation with Jacques Derrida." In *Deconstruction in a Nutshell*. Ed. with a commentary by John Caputo. New York: Fordham University Press, 1997.

WD   *Writing and Difference*. Trans. Alan Bass. Chicago: University of Chicago Press, 1978.

Note: Where English versions are not cited in the text, the translations are my own.

Introduction

On the Secret

I begin with a secret and a confession—but not my own. The confession is Derrida's, and it is hardly a secret. He has a "taste (probably unconditional) for literature, more precisely for literary writing" (*ON*, 27). This public confession would appear to be unnecessary. Derrida and deconstruction have been, in America at least, linked to literature from the beginning. The debates surrounding him typically turn upon the very question of literature and its place in his writings.[1] This book attempts to situate "literature" in Derrida's thought, which is something quite different from applying deconstruction to literary texts or interpreting his writings as literary.[2] From the start, I need to point out that "literature" or "literary writing" is frequently used by Derrida in a sense quite different from our conventional notion of literature. I am not offering a study of deconstructive "methodology" nor an essay in literary criticism but a reading of "literature" in the texts of Derrida. By this, I do not mean that his writings, particularly in works like *Glas* or *The Post Card*, are more literary than philosophical, nor do I wish to be understood to be suggesting that literature as such is a questioning or deconstruction of philosophical categories—we will see that there is no literature *as such*. I propose instead that literature is not only something other than belles lettres or even those modes of writing we designate as poetry, fiction, and drama, but literature, or what Derrida prefers to call "literary writing," is what haunts experience. "There is no—hardly any, ever so little—literature; that in any event there is no essence of literature, no truth of literature, no literary-being or being-literary of literature" (*D*, 223). "Literature," in this notorious declaration, is not: it is not an entity nor does it subsist in the identity of its historical being. The spectral quality of literature—its being a specter—means that it is not an existent or being nor a localizable remains or archive but belongs to a future, the promise that

1

returns to haunt the present. Spectrality evokes both a temporal anachrony—the time is out of joint—and the dispropriation of identity, the non-contemporaneity of the living present. Literature shares with the specter an undecidable relation between body and spirit, or, to put it in more familiar terms, materiality and ideality. If one follows Husserl, literature, like all arts, is a particular type of thing that embodies an ideality, or what he calls an "irreal objectivity." For instance, we can burn a copy of Goethe's *Faust*, but in doing so we have not destroyed his *Faust*, merely a copy or instantiation of it.[3] For Derrida, however, the spectrality of literature invokes a certain anachrony, a disruption of linear time. The condition of the "presence" of both ghosts and literature is their living on, *survie*. Derrida has called this the repetition that is older than presence. I refer here to that which has the structure of a repetition and a first time, something like a specter:

> the specter is a paradoxical incorporation, the becoming-body, a certain phenomenal and carnal form of the spirit. It becomes, rather, some "thing" that remains difficult to name: neither soul nor body, and both one and the other. For it is flesh and phenomenality that give to the spirit its spectral apparition, but which disappear right away in the apparition, in the very coming of the *revenant* or the return of the specter. There is something disappeared, departed in the apparition itself as reapparition of the departed (*SM*, 6).

As a specter, literature is neither spirit nor body and both at the same time, which makes it difficult to name.

"Literature" is but a provisional "name" for that which takes place each time there is some trace. "Trace" designates a minimum structure of referral; it is the relation to otherness by which self-identity is maintained. Without this relation to the other, there could be no identity, but as the presence of writing or absence in speech suggests, identity from the beginning is always carried away from itself, differing from and deferring itself. What happens between presence and absence *"maintains itself* with some ghost" (*SM*, xi). *"Without this non-contemporaneity with itself of the living present*, without that which secretly unhinges it," without this specter, there would be nothing to come (*SM*, xix). The possibility of a future hinges upon the lure of otherness. In Derrida's idiom of the specter, the opening of the future to the return of the past, a *revenant*, is the possibility of ethics. Therefore, to speak of "literature" in Derrida demands that one speak of many things—for example, the law, the gift, the other, singularity, secrets, nuclear catastrophe, apocalypse, God—but hardly about literature, or poetry and fiction in any case.

Derrida's passion for literature must be seen as a passion for something to come, an impossible something, which he frequently calls "justice" or "democracy." Although not unrelated to an Enlightenment tradition that links literature in its conventional sense to freedom, Derrida's "literature" must be thought of as a quasi-transcendental condition for the coming of the other. Derrida's "to come" (*l'à venir*) is not the future as a modality of the present but describes the general structure of experience. To the extent that the affirmation of the other is a promise before speech, literature is invariably linked to ethics. It is an experience of writing: "To recognize writing in speech, that is to say *différance* and the absence of speech, is to begin to think the lure. There is no ethics without the presence *of the other* but also, and consequently, without absence, dissimulation, detour, *différance*, writing. The arche-writing is the origin of morality as of immorality. The nonethical opening of ethics" (*OG*, 139–40).

This does not simply mean that literature has the potential to open us to other aspects of existence that in our everyday lives we are unwilling or unable to confront—although the fact that it can do this is certainly important for Derrida—but "literature" names this possibility wherein the undecidable relation to the other might occur, and it does not necessarily happen when we read poetry and fiction. The experience of the other is not a matter of spirit nor of other people. The other as "spirit," the other spirit, has no content of its own but must parasitically "attach" itself to a body or, as Derrida says, it is the being that "gives the spirit its spiritual apparition" (*SM*, 6). This does not mean that literature is the body of the other, but there is literature wherever there is a trace, which is what makes literature so difficult to name, or so difficult a name for what haunts us.

Derrida's confession has something of the quality of a specter: it blurs the distinction between what is visible and invisible, between what has been and what is to come. What need is there for revealing a secret that is, by common understanding, no secret at all? The secret, however, does not belong to a strictly private domain but is something that keeps itself, offers itself, as in a confession that is no more public than it is private, an opposition that Derrida says does not apply to his work. The paradox of the secret is that it constitutes itself by putting something in reserve, by making something disappear, as when Derrida declares he likes literature and readers think he likes "literature," whereas he likes something about it that is difficult to name.[4] We conventionally think of a secret as the holding back from utterance or appearance that which is essentially recognizable or public; that is, a secret is thought to be essentially phenomenolizable or a not yet visible phenomenon. Derrida's secret is more radical; it cannot be said to belong to anyone or to any place.

There is something like a secret every time, which is to say, everywhere, there is writing. It is a matter of passion, Derrida's passion, perhaps. Derrida's secret is not some idea or word waiting to be discovered. I have no secrets to reveal; the secret does not consist in keeping back or holding in reserve something that would finally explain, expose, demystify Derrida's corpus.[5] Such a hope, or suspicion that there is a secret to disclose, proves the secret to have been linked to representation and consciousness. The secret as the keeping-for-oneself what one already knows constitutes a denial of the secret *as such* "because it appears to itself in order to be what it is" (*HAS*, 25). The secret, then, does not belong to the topos of place, the space of memory, but is an *atopos*; it is already a sharing—with myself who is not one insofar as I must differ from myself to share and dissimulate the secret. It presupposes, as Derrida says, "the space of a promised speech, that is to say, a trace to which the affirmation is not symmetrical" (*HAS*, 18). The secret describes a certain experience of writing, or what one calls "literature": "What one calls poetry or literature, art itself (let us not distinguish them for the moment), in other words a certain experience of language, of the mark or of the trait *as such*, is nothing perhaps but an intense familiarity with the ineluctable originarity of the specter. One can naturally translate it into the ineluctable loss of the origin" (*SPC*, 58). What one calls literature is at work everywhere a secret inscribes itself within iterability, when it shows that there is something not shown, an event that is to come.

Derrida's writings on the secret, passion, denegation, mourning, apophatic discourse, and the specter weave themselves around a discourse on negative theology and the (im)possibility of the unnameable. The strategy of evading is attested to in his essay "How to Avoid Speaking," where he says that the talk of a God who is beyond Being and more than Being is the very rhetoric of apophasis; not speaking of that which escapes presence remains a modality of speech.[6] All speech implies a promise that escapes presence. I cannot avoid speaking because even before I open my mouth, I have been seized, engaged by, a promise (*HAS*, 14). The motif of the promise before speech, a promise that seizes the *I*, belongs to the anachrony of the address to the other. Alterity, as Derrida has said from the beginning, is the condition for presence, the present, and presentation (see *SP*, 65). In his analysis of negative theology and the name, he distinguishes deconstruction from theology, negative and other, on the grounds that theology is a heterological discourse of that which is beyond Being, God, whereas deconstruction annuls all anthropomorphisms of the other and speaks instead of what has already taken place, or started without us or is before us or is always already past—in other words, of the writing of writing or of the trace or *différance* that exceeds the oppositions of infinite and finite. But Derrida asks, what "if God was an *effect of the trace*? If the idea of divine presence (life, existence, parousia, etc.), if the name of God was but the movement of erasure of the trace in presence" (*WD*, 108)? God is the name of the absolute revelation, the erasure of the trace in presence. "To say that God is the effect of the trace means that God *as* God is dependent on a structure of referral that, as such, ceaselessly refers to an Other, away from itself, so as to have itself no *as such*." If, as Gasché goes on to say, "God is the *exemplary* revelation" of the quasi-transcendentals of trace,[7] difference, etc., then I suggest that literature, which is "exemplary of what happens everywhere, each time there is some trace" (*ON*, 143, n. 14), is the experience of what resists absolute totality— that is, the experience of what can never be the object of any experience, a specter, for example, or a secret.

I do not say this to exalt literature above philosophy and certainly not to claim that Derrida's writings are more literary than philosophical. First, it must be said that "literature," as I am using the term here, does not refer to belles lettres. Therefore, it is a mistake to argue that his texts since *Glas* are literary as opposed to philosophical. Secondly, Derrida's "literature" must be distinguished from Heidegger's "poetry" or *Dichtung*. Although Heidegger also enlarges upon the conventional meaning of poetry, his notion of *poiesis* as the setting up of the world and the happening of truth belongs to a thinking of mimesis as positioning or installation. As a setting forth, *poiesis* belongs to a metaphysics of subjectivity.[8] To the extent that literary writing is to be thought of as an act or experience and not as language, it is distinct from a Heideggerean project of thinking the mode of being of *Dichtung*.[9] At issue is not so much whether Derrida dissociates literature from the Heideggerean question of truth but his notion that literature "'is' the place or experience of this 'trouble'" that we have with the essence of language, with the question of (essence, truth, language) (*SIL*, 48).

This brings us to the question of mimesis, which is a question of literature, a double question, if you will. In "The Double Session," Derrida writes, "the whole history of the interpretation of the arts of letters has moved and been transformed within the diverse logical possibilities opened up by the concept of *mimêsis*" (*D*, 187). The question of literature, he suggests, has been a question folded between truth and the question *what is?* Considered under the general interpretation of truth as *adequatio*, mimesis has been interpreted according to a logic of resemblance between an original and its copy, but even this overly simplified version succumbs to repetition, the doubling that displaces the "original." This displacement reminds us of Plato's attack on the poets and the secondary status of mimetic arts to philosophical truth. Repeatability, however, is already inscribed within the original if it is to be open to the possibility of imitation. Philippe Lacoue-Labarthe exposes an unthought mimetologism in Heidegger's concept of world. There would be no *techne*, no bringing forth of beings out of concealment, if *physis* or world were not already an "original *mimeme*."[10] Mimetic doubling removes or displaces the origin. The very possibility of poetic unconcealment rests upon an "originary" repetition. In a provocative discussion of Heidegger's poetics, John Sallis writes, "truth is nothing apart from its coming to be established in a being. It is not as though there is, first, difference, which then comes to be mediated; rather, difference first occurs precisely at the site of the happening of truth. The return is necessary for truth."[11] Sallis concludes, art would be the mimesis of truth, a mimesis that sets truth into the work. Consequently, it is an error to say Derrida's "literature" resembles Heidegger's *Dichtung*. Such an interpretation ignores Derrida's reinscription of Being as text and his consistent questioning of Heidegger's characterization of thinking as gathering (*Versammlung*).[12] For Heidegger, the setting of truth in the work accords with Being as appropriation (*Ereignis*).

In "The Origin of the Work of Art," Heidegger says, "Truth happens only by establishing itself in the conflict and sphere opened up by truth itself. Because truth is the opposition of clearing and concealing, there belongs to it what is here to be called establishing." In other words, truth does not occur apart from beings or descend from beyond, but is the single event of clearing and concealing that takes place in the work of art. Heidegger calls this the rift (*Der Riss*) between world and earth, which is not a severing but a drawing together.[13] "World" is the specific mode of openness that belongs to human beings in their historical relation. "Earth" is what the Greeks called *physis*, the place where beings are located. The site of this conflict is the rift, which brings together into a unity clearing and concealing. Truth establishes itself in a being in such a way that what is "brought forth, the rift, entrusts itself to the self-secluding factor that juts up in the Open."[14] The work of art brings forth truth in the conflict between concealedness and unconcealedness, which means that truth's being set in place in the work is simultaneously a retrait or withdrawal of truth.

A good deal of attention has been given to the place of "The Origin of the Work of Art" in the so-called "reversal" in Heidegger's thought in which he turned from the existential inquiry into Dasein as the locus of the truth of Being to raise the question of the meaning of Being itself. The happening of truth, the unconcealment of Being, belongs to the double movement of the sending withdrawal of Being. The arrival of Being in beings is simultaneously a withdrawal of Being. The temporal character of the happening of truth, the concurrent concealment and unconcealment of Being, is the destining of Being (*Seinsgeschick*).[15] This all too brief discussion should, at the least, indicate that Heidegger's turn to poetry continues his inquiry into the question of Being and the determination of Being as finitude. The thinking of Being in terms of temporality and as historicity determines Being as destining, the sending that holds itself back in favor of the "discernibility of the gift."[16] In *Identity and Difference*, Heidegger explains how whenever we come to the place where we would represent difference (between Being and beings), we "find that Being and beings in their difference are already there." He goes on to say how representational thinking is so structured as to "insert the difference ahead of time between beings and Being."[17] The effort to think more originally this difference requires the step back (*der Schritt zurück*) from what is unthought, the difference between Being and beings, to what gives us thought, the oblivion of the difference.[18] The oblivion belongs to the difference because Being is never separable from its dissimulation. Being is nothing apart from this withholding of itself in its coming forth or sending. Because the original event of metaphysics is the forgetting of Being, thinking is not an act of recovery but belongs to this withdrawal of Being as the destiny of Being.

Insofar as mimesis is a doubling that conceals what it would disclose, Heidegger's thought remains bound by an unquestioned mimetologism.[19] Although he rejects the Platonic concept of mimesis as the doubling of a pre-existent Idea, his determination of truth as Being, which is nothing apart from its sending withdrawal, is mimetic. Although we should not confuse Heidegger's concept of the dissimulation of Being with a notion of the copy, we can say that insofar as art is the happening or event of truth, it is the mimesis of Being.[20] Nevertheless, Being is not something that stands behind or is the ground of beings, but Being enters into or gives itself in the sending withdrawal of Being. Being is not realized in the present or in the presence of what is but keeps itself or withdraws in the sending of the gift.

We can distinguish Derrida's "literary writing" from Heidegger's *Dichtung* in several ways. We can first note the difference between Heidegger's Being as withdrawal and Derrida's text as the re-mark of the fold, what he calls its "differential-supplementary structure" (*D*, 270). Whereas *Dichtung* concerns the presentation of truth *as such*, Derrida's *retrait*, or re-mark, accounts for the *as*-structure of appearing in terms of what does not properly belong to the thing.[21] This issue has been dealt with by Gasché,[22] so I would merely like to point out that Derrida explicitly evokes Heidegger in his notion of the text: "If there were no fold, or if the fold had a limit somewhere—a limit other than itself as a mark, margin, or march (threshold, limit, or border)—there would be no text. But if the text does not, to the letter, exist, then *there is* perhaps a text. A text one must make tracks with" (*D*, 270). The notion of the fold, which he comes to in a reading of Mallarmé's "Mimique," upsets any determination of the text on the basis of the dyadic pairs form and meaning, inside and outside, identity and difference. The fold and related effects suspend any possibility of totalization or resolution of the text in self-reflexivity. There can be no phenomenon of the text; the text never appears as such. Heidegger's investigation into the donative character of Being, on the other hand, still remains bound by mimetism, even if Being does not precede beings and truth does not precede art. Insofar as Dasein is the site of Being (referring now to *Being and Time*) and art the site of truth, a determination of mimesis by phenomenalism still operates in Heidegger's thought.

Although Heidegger breaks from the Platonic concept of mimesis as imitation, his thinking of *poiesis* as bringing-forth (*Hervor-bringen*) conforms to a Platonic interpretation of mimesis as a displacement of Being by what is not, which is no longer an interpretation of mimesis as *adequatio* but as the mimesis of Being, the repetition and disclosure of Being in the withdrawal of the gift.[23] This is the concept of mimesis as installation (*Stellung*), which is simultaneously a disinstallation, the "'inadequation' of the aletheic withdrawal in regard to any opposition between the adequate and the in-adequate, between presence and absence, etc."[24] This reading of Heidegger resembles Derrida's, who finds in Heidegger's *Geshick des Seins* "a structure as yet innocent of representation," a preontological sending that issues forth only in sending-back: "it issues forth only on the basis of the other, the other in itself without itself." In Derrida's reading, the sending withdrawal of Being, the *Geschick des Seins*, is menaced by a divisibility that is the condition of the gift, the *envoi* of Being. It is only on the basis of *renvois* (back-references), which are not transcendental conditions, that there can be the "chance" of "history, meaning, presence, truth, language, theme, thesis." These *renvois* do not belong to metaphysics because they do not originate in the question of Being. They constitute the law, Derrida says, which "has often been considered as that which puts things in place . . . in other words what governs the order of representation," but "manages to do no more than transgress the figure of all possible representation" (*SOR*, 136–37). The *renvois* are the conditions of possibility and impossibility of representation. They remind us that as much as Heidegger's thinking remains within metaphysics there co-exists in it the possibility of another thinking at the margins of Being, a possibility we find in his reading of Plato on mimesis.

What I propose in this book is that just as Derrida's concept of writing is neither phonetic transcription nor linear notation but the movement of *différance* and text is not a book but a name for what reinscribes the question of Being, so literary writing is neither literariness nor belles lettres, nor even necessarily books or those genres we designate as "literature." And although it must be read with and against those concepts that traditionally determine what is literature—mimesis, representation, self-reflexivity, writing, metaphor, etc.—literature is the remarking of institutionality in general. As Derrida has explained in a number of essays, literature, in its conventional sense, is a recent invention tied to law, copyright, and other legal and societal institutions. In another sense, literature is the reserve or remainder that cannot be taken up or totalized within its institution. This is why literature is said to be exemplary of what happens each time there is some trace. As trace, literature remarks a relation to an outside, an absolute past or remainder, which, like a secret, cannot be re-presented in a present but holds in a reserve a promise, a future that is to come, an *à-venir* ("to come").[25] While this means that I am concerned with how deconstruction asks us to rethink literature in its conventional sense, I am more intent upon demonstrating that literary writing is to be understood in conjunction with Derrida's notions of singularity, responsibility, the law, destruction, invention, and time.

What is literature? It does not necessarily have anything whatsoever to do with "great books," aesthetic beauty, fiction, poetry, or other constitutive genres of what is called "literature" but has something to do with performativity and the irruptive force of all founding origins. Derrida says, "Something of literature will have begun when it is not possible to decide whether, when I speak of something, I am indeed speaking of something (of the thing itself, this one, for itself) or if I am giving an example, an example of something or an example of the fact that I can speak of something" (*ON*, 142–43, n. 14). When we speak of examples, as when we speak of an example of literature, we think of it as it is without making it an object, as when we offer an example of the novel in order to think the novel as such rather than this particular novel. The example of the example can go on and on; there are only examples but the example, as such, is impossible, just as the law as such is impossible. Whenever we ask what something is: what is literature? What is the law? What is . . . ? We are speaking of exemplariness, which is to say, of singularity and generality. When we hold up something to be an example, we imply it is its own commentary, it reveals in itself what it is (an example of). If you want an example of the, novel, take *Tristram Shandy*. The example, then, is at once singular and general. There is nothing like the example, and the example stands in place of everything it would exemplify. The more a novel, such as *Tristram Shandy*, is said to be unique, the more it exemplifies the novel.[26] What then is so exemplary about literature? It re-marks the impossibility of the example to be an example of itself, which is to say it re-marks the impossibility of singularity to be absolutely singular; there are no examples and there are only examples. The law is at once unique and universal. Not to understand this is to have trouble with literature.

Literature witnesses the undecidability between the singular and the general, the impossibility of the law to be the law or, as in Freud's fable of the origin of the law given in *Totem and Taboo*, the passage from *physis* to *nomos*.[27] It re-marks the non-coincidence, the non-identity, of judgment and the law that makes judgment necessary and a failure—but that is the power of judgment; it only succeeds if it fails. The impossibility of judgment to succeed, to be a founding act, is the possibility of fresh judgments. Literature, more than other disciplines, bears witness to this undecidable relation between singularity and generality, judgment and the law. This is not, however, an exclusive property of literature, but literature exemplifies the status of any discipline to be present to itself in its founding act: this aporia of the law, this law of the law "thou shalt not approach the origin of *différance*" is what distinguishes literature. The aporia of the law—we have only examples of the law but never the law itself—appears in the impossibility of writing a narrative of the origin of the law. Literature bears witness to this secret: there are no examples and there are only examples. This is literature's secret: the possibility of law is its impurity, its iterability. Because there can be no pure law, no pure singularity, literature can say anything without touching upon the secret.

I am not done with the secret. I quoted above Derrida's comment that literature is exemplary of what happens wherever there is some trace (see *ON*, 143, n. 14). John Caputo writes, "Literature is the name of the trace and the text, which for Derrida implies 'the unlimited right to ask questions.'"[28] For Caputo, literature belongs to the open-ended questioning of the secret, which is nothing itself, or hardly anything, but is what permits the possibility of a future. Consequently, literature in his reading is assimilated to the messianic theme of the future as what is foreign or heterogeneous to knowledge. This non-knowledge is not ignorance but something more originary than experience or knowledge; it is the ethico-political imperative to respond to the call "come!" Derrida's passion for literature is a passion that "keeps the future open by the passion of its love, its messianic yearning for what is 'to come.'"[29] And if the messianic tone has not already made clear that literature's secret is the secret of faith, Caputo writes, "'God' is the name of a question not an answer, of an errancy not a destination . . . to whom one prays."[30]

Although I find much to agree with in Caputo's powerful book and will turn to the themes of apocalypse and messianism in my last two chapters, I find his analysis of the name of God as the name for the secret without truth, the name of passion—that is, of love and suffering—a little too theological. As "the name of the structural secret or limit, the secret without truth,"[31] God is the name for absolute *différance*, the possibility for what is—and Derrida does say that in the beginning there is *différance*, the structure of referral and deferral that is the enabling and disabling condition of thought. As the secret without truth, God stands in place as the impossible possibility, the name for a desired and unforeseeable future, what can go by the name of "justice." Throughout Caputo's book there resonates the question, what is the love of God but the love of justice? Again, I find his argument compelling, but it raises the question, if God is not a being or the name for Being, does God remain without attributes if, as Caputo says, He is an "*addressee*"? As the name for the secret without secret, the passion of life/death, God, says Caputo, "is the most powerful deconstructive name we can invoke"; it is what disseminates truth.[32] In truth's place, in place of truth, we have the *viens*, the justice to come. The risk that lies in this formulation is not that it turns God into a predicable being but in its speaking of God as truth without Truth, it transforms God into a master name for passion and whatever trembles in the possibility/impossibility of its "is."[33]

The danger, as Caputo acknowledges and risks, lies in the task of thinking religion without religion, of thinking "deconstruction *as* religion."[34] This is to make deconstruction a heterological discourse, a discourse of the purely Other precisely because God is the name for the quasi-transcendental, and it obscures the notion that God, as an *"effect of the trace"* (*WD*, 108), is an example of the unthought.[35] That is, if thinking is, as Heidegger said, the thinking of difference between Being and beings, then Derrida's inquiry into conditions of possibility and impossibility leads him to the unthought, which means that our limits in knowing God lie not in an infinite deferral of the justice to come or in the unrepresentable as such but in the structural limits of thought itself, which are encountered in the quasi-transcendentals of *différance*, trace, writing, iterability. As the *tout autre*, God is the name of the wholly other and hence substitutable for every other. In arguing that God is the example of the other, Caputo restores analogical thinking wherein God is every other, which is to say His name is infinitely substitutable or translatable. The exemplariness of God lies, therefore, in His being the name of every other, and every other is the example of God.[36]

Caputo, in saying the name of God is the name for the impossible, makes God "the exemplary revelation . . . of the trace because he is the *One* absolute Other, compared with the plural characteristics of the trace." In "God, for Example," Gasché argues that the thinking of God as example is consistent with onto-theological tradition. Being is the fundamental characteristic of God, but so long as God is, Being is anterior to Him. "Since Being is only the Being *of* beings and nothing else, nothing, indeed outside of beings, there is not even, as Derrida remarks, 'a *distinction* in the usual sense of the word between Being and the existent'" (*WD*, 138). Being is without relation to beings, just as "beings have no relation to Being, since Being is nothing else than that beings are." The question, then, is how is God linked to Being if the thinking of Being is not relational? "From the perspective of the thinking of Being, to think God is to think Him *as* the figure of the unthought of Being." Citing Derrida's first essay on Emmanuel Levinas, "Violence and Metaphysics," Gasché proceeds to analyze Derrida's remark, "The thought of Being is what permits us to say . . . 'God, for example.' That is, to *think* God as what he is without making him an object" (*WD*, 318, n. 78). We can think God as example because "the thinking of Being, precisely because it does not substitute Being for God, can think God as the example par excellence of a mode of thought oblivious to difference. God *as* the metaphysical name for Being is primarily an excellent example of the unthought."[37] That is to say, if God is (substituted for) Being, then he is all beings, which is pantheism. To think Him as example, however, is to think in a mode that is without analogy, exemplarity. What is God an example of but of God?

Gasché's argument, following Derrida, is that there is nothing blasphemous in thinking God as example, and indeed, within onto-theology, the thinking of God is precisely the thinking of the unthought insofar as thinking, as Heidegger says, is always the thinking of difference (between Being and beings). As the name for the unthought, God is the example of the thought oblivious to difference. This is, then, a non-relational, an-analogical thinking. Gasché goes on to demonstrate that Derrida "makes room for God, so to speak," in calling Him the "endless referral to Other that all attempts to think a positive infinity and full presence must meet." Hence, the thinking of God "is not possible without the trace." As an effect of the trace, "God *as* God is dependent on a structure of referral that, as such, ceaselessly refers to an Other, away from itself, so as to have itself no *as such*."[38] As trace, God is the possibility of the example, but as the exemplary example, He is what cannot be exemplified—no other example can serve to render Him. He is the example of "the non-exemplifiable structure that constitutes the structure of the example."[39] The trace, as the relation to the other, opens the possibility for God as its self-exemplification, an impossible task according to the logic of the example. The thought of the trace as the retained mark of the other distinguishes philosophy from theology's dream of a pure heterology (see *WD*, 151).[40] In this way, deconstruction resists the temptation of the thought of the absolutely Other.

Caputo would keep God, as the *tout autre*, alive by giving up the dream "of an alterity that is not somehow or other inscribed within the trace."[41] This dream of the impossible is the dream of

God as the example of the trace, which is to say that God has the impossible task of exemplifying the trace that precedes him. Caputo, then, is close to Gasché and disavows negative theology to the extent that it would be a dream of being "outside the play of traces," but in a gesture that has become familiar since Derrida, he does not so much reject negative theology as he subjects it to a thinking that allows for the play of the trace and *différance*. Yet his reading of the example as the endless substitutability of names takes on the glimmer of *parousia*. He writes, "God is the exemplar of every 'other,' the other is the exemplar of God. When John says 'God is love,' 'love' exemplifies what 'God' means, but it is also true that 'God' exemplifies what 'love' means. Is God an example of justice, or justice of God? Does it matter?"[42] Perhaps it does, for if every other is, as he says, the exemplar of God, the wholly other, then there can be no difference, as Derrida says of Levinas, "between a claimed generality of ethics that would need to be sacrificed in sacrifice, and the faith that turns towards God alone, as wholly other, turning away from human duty. But since Levinas also wants to distinguish between the infinite alterity of God and the 'same' infinite alterity of every human, or of the other in general," he cannot determine the limits between the ethical and the religious (*GD*, 84). The generality of ethics, according to Kierkegaard, impels the sacrifice of my singularity insofar as it involves me in a universal concept and, hence, substitutability.[43] To be responsible, I must sacrifice ethics and be "irresponsible" (*GD*, 61). This is why Abraham, according to Kierkegaard, does not speak; absolute responsibility to God cannot be externalized, or else it becomes universalized ethics.

Derrida's analysis uncovers an aporia in Kierkegaard's distinction between religion and ethics.[44] Abraham's decision—in the instant God stops him, he has fulfilled the command as if he "had *already* killed Isaac" (*GD*, 72)—binds him to the absolute other and binds him in his absolute singularity to the other as other. But there are others, Derrida says, innumerable others, whom I must sacrifice every time I respond to the other. "The simple concepts of alterity and of singularity constitute the concept of duty as much as that of responsibility. As a result, the concepts of responsibility, of decision, or of duty, are condemned a priori to paradox, scandal, and aporia. Paradox, scandal, and aporia are themselves nothing other than sacrifice, the revelation of conceptual thinking at its

limit, at its death and finitude" (*GD*, 68). Metaphysics would dis-
avow time by setting an opposition between the eternal, which is
here the ethical, and the transitory, the act. The aporetic decision—all decisions are aporetic—involves the instant, an irreducible experience of time wherein the paradox or scandal consists
in a single act or entity, here the sacrifice of Isaac: Abraham cannot respond to the call of the other, God, without sacrificing other
others. The experience of the sacrifice is the experience of an aporia, that is, of the impassable (the original meaning of "aporia")
limit of conceptual thinking.[45] The absolute singularity that binds
me to others is a universal responsibility, the ethical, that I must
sacrifice in the name of responsibility: "I am responsible to any one
(that is to say to any other) only by failing in my responsibility to
all others, to the ethical or political generality. And I can never justify this sacrifice" (*GD*, 70). There can be no law governing the
decision; it cannot, in other words, be reduced to a history that
could account for it. The decision is necessary *and* is unjustifiable,
responsible (to the wholly other) and irresponsible (to the wholly
other), as every decision must be. Derrida uncovers an aporia that
not only makes it impossible to distinguish between "the infinite
alterity of God and that of every other human," but uncovers the
irreducible incoherence of responsibility, which does not stop it
from "'functioning'" (*GD*, 84).

Caputo's God is not the God of onto-theology, but as wholly
other, He is the example of justice, which always commands a
responsibility to the singular other, another human being. To be
brief, his Other is a human other, which is closer to Levinas than
to Derrida. When Caputo asserts that deconstruction as religion is
a pact with the unrepresentable, a justice to come,[46] he no longer
"holds desire in suspense" (*ON*, 85), which is to say, he would
figure alterity as the Other. To think alterity *as* the Other is to
think it as a mode of Being. The re-mark, the supplementary trait
that allows us to determine something *as* something, does not
belong to what it marks. Timothy Clark writes that the re-mark
signals a break with Heidegger's *Dichtung*,[47] and we can add from
our look at the analogical thinking of God as example that it also
marks the difference between Being and text. The "as-structure" of
the understanding is taken up in section 31 of *Being and Time*,
where Heidegger says that, along with state-of-mind, understanding "is *one* of the existential structures in which the Being of the

'there' maintains itself."[48] States-of-mind and understanding characterize the primordial disclosedness of the *there* of Dasein, its Being-in-the-world. Interpreted according to the primordial temporality that temporalizes itself as the future, Dasein is equiprimordially its "there." "If it lacks its 'there,' it is not factically the entity which is essentially Dasein; indeed, it is not this entity at all. *Dasein is its disclosedness.*" This means "that the Being which is an issue for this entity in its very Being is to be its 'there.'" [49] As the "there" of Dasein, Being is veiled in the "whence" and "whither" of Dasein's "that it is." Being can be known only in its dissimulation and deferral in Dasein.[50] Because Being is nothing outside beings, the as-structure articulates the world *as* a world for that being which understands, Dasein. Hence, the *as-structure* assures us that there is a world, and without the articulation of the *as*, there is no "there" of Dasein.[51] Being is nothing in itself but its articulation in the as-structure, which is to say, Being is nothing apart from its referral to beings.

Alterity, however, does not belong to the as-structure of Being precisely because it is not of the order of Being. Alterity cannot be figured *as* the other, as the *as such* of the other. The *as* figures an accord between Being and beings: what is designated *as* something is understood *as* that *as* according to which we are to understand the thing. In other words, the as-structure is not predicable, something we add to a thing, but belongs to the thing. Responsibility to the other must, therefore, resist thinking's perennial attempt to think the other in opposition to identity and, instead, make place for the other, that is, affirm the outside, the incalculable, as the only possible invention, what is possible only as impossible. Derrida's deconstruction of responsibility turns upon the point that alterity cannot be represented. The aporia he locates in responsibility and is figured with unsurpassed power in the *Akedah* belongs to "the strange economy of the secret as economy *of* sacrifice" (*GD*, 101). Abraham's decision, like all decisions, is secret; it cannot be deduced from knowledge that would explain it by general or universal laws, but "structurally breaches knowledge and is thus destined to non-manifestation" (*GD*, 77). As soon as he decides (to be responsible to God and sacrifice his son), he fails to be responsible to any other one. This is the structure of all decisions.

We must understand that Derrida is not referring to the paradox that whenever we act responsibly to someone, we invariably lose the chance of acting responsibly to another. Prior to any ethical dilemma concerning responsibility is the secret, which signs or marks off irreducible singularity. Derrida says Abraham's decision is absolutely singular and is "inscribed in the structure of our existence" (*GD*, 85). A certain originary repetition must govern the singular. To be what it is, singular, the decision must be freed from its attachment to a date, a here and now, by an act, a decision, that carries it off, detaches it from itself in order for it to remain itself. This structure of repetition makes a decision both responsible and irresponsible. When Derrida says the decision obscures the boundaries between the religious and the ethical, he indicates that the singular decision must be marked by a certain universality or else its singularity could not be acknowledged. If the singularity of Abraham's decision is a universality (the sacrifice of the other is the sacrifice of every other), then Abraham's secret, what marks his irreducible singularity, runs the risk of being lost. And this risk must be run or else the singularity of Abraham's decision would be lost in the idiomaticity of the act. What makes the decision singular is his secrecy. By keeping his secret, Abraham, according to Kierkegaard, betrays ethics, which requires speaking in order to justify oneself in the generality (see *GD*, 59–60). The secret, however, is not Abraham's alone but is shared with God.

The strange economy of the secret is that it must be shared if it is to be secret. The secret requires an interiority, a subjective space, consciousness, that allows a secret to be formed within it, yet "the *as such* of the secret . . . denies itself because it appears to itself in order to be what it is" (*HAS*, 25). According to this testamentary structure, a certain repetition assures that the secret be "readable" even in the absence of a witness, of someone who might share it. The secret shows that something is not shown. It is a shibboleth, a "ciphered singularity," a "private name" (*SPC*, 35; *Aporias*, 74). Even when the secret appears, it begins to dissimulate itself, as secret. "There is no secret *as such*," but Derrida asks, "does something like the secret *itself*, properly speaking, ever exist? The name of God (I do not say God, but how to avoid saying God here, from the moment when I say the name of God?) can only be *said* in the modality of this secret denial" (*HAS*, 26). The modality of the secret is "a negation that denies itself." The ability to speak of the secret proceeds from the secret because it must appear to itself in order to be what it is. The secret has the character of the *retrait*; it holds in reserve. "There is a secret of denial and a denial of the secret" (*HAS*, 25). The inaccessible law before which and prior to which Abraham stands "appears infinitely transcendent and thus theological to the extent that, so near him, it depends only on him, on the performative act by which he institutes it" (*FL*, 993). Abraham suffers the ordeal of the undecidable: in order for his gift to be a sacrifice, all communication with God must be suspended. He "is in a position of nonexchange with respect to God, he is in secret since he doesn't speak to God and expects neither response nor reward from him" (*GD*, 96). Yet God gives back to him what he would renounce in the instant of his act of renunciation. By virtue of the secret, Abraham's act of faith that confirms the transcendence of God is without justification. The Kantian would say he acts without knowing whether God speaks to him or if the voice comes from within.[52] It is impossible to decide when Abraham acts whether his sacrifice is seen by God or by no one. This, as Derrida says, is "the secret of secrecy, namely, that it is not a matter of knowing and that it is there for no-one. A secret doesn't belong, it can never said to be at home or in its place [*chez soi*]" (*GD*, 92). Whenever there is something secret, we are faced with this possibility of not knowing or, as in the case of Abraham, of knowing not to know. This is what we share with Abraham, a secret we know nothing about, "nothing that can be determined," a passion that cannot be transmitted but which dictates to us we must start over (see *GD*, 80). Consequently, this consummate act of faith, this gift of death, takes place in secret as secret *and* in a narrative. What it transmits is nothing in itself but an example, of faith, of the secret. It is the example of the secret, what permits anything, even the sacrifice of what one loves most, without any expectation of reward. It gives us the law in an act that is without law, which is to say it cannot account for itself except in exemplifying the secrecy of the law, the law of secrecy: one cannot have a relation with the law but one must interrupt the relation, as when God's messengers come to stay Abraham's hand in the instant he would sacrifice his son.[53]

This responsibility to a prior singularization, an other that precedes any ideality or identity, allows Derrida to say without contradiction that any ontico-theological discourse preserves a trace of an event older than it and still to come. The call of the other always precedes the speech to which it is never present and "announces itself *in advance* as a recall," a repetition still to come (*HAS*, 28). If we are to think of God without being idolatrous, we can say:

> God is the name of the possibility I have of keeping a secret that is visible from the interior but not from the exterior. Once such a structure of conscience exists, of being-with-one-self . . . I have within me . . . a witness others cannot see, and who is therefore *at the same time other than me and more intimate with me than myself*, once I can have a secret relationship with myself and not tell everything, once there is secrecy and secret witnessing within me, then what I call God exists, (there is) what I call God in me, (it happens that) I call myself God—a phrase that is difficult to distinguish from "God calls me," for it is on that condition that I can call myself or that I am called in secret (*GD*, 108–109).

God is not identical with a structure of conscience but is the name for the testamentary structure of interiority; there is a witness (*témoigne*) to the nonmanifestation, the secret place, of the secret. The difficulty of distinguishing between "I call myself God" and "God calls me," between a voice within and a voice without, is the transcendental condition of all discourse. As long as there is no assured destination nor self-presentation of the call then we can say that the possibility exists for the self-presentation of God as the trace of the other (in) me.

The problem addressed in negative theology, the subject of "How to Avoid Speaking," is how to speak of God without making Him an object. We can speak of God, even if we say He cannot be an object of thought. What commits us or makes it possible to speak of Him "*has taken place*. The possible absence of a referent still beckons, if not toward the thing of which one speaks (such is God, who is nothing because He takes place, *without place, beyond Being*), at least toward the other (other than Being) who calls or to whom this speech is addressed [*à qui se destine cette parole*]." What theology calls "God" is what makes speech possible: the other that always already preceded the speech to which it can never be present. To speak of God is to speak of what has already taken place, a trace of an event older than ontico-ontological difference, which Heidegger said can never appear as such (*HAS*, 28 / *Psyché*, 559).

In *Of Grammatology*, Derrida writes, "entity and being, ontic and ontological, 'ontico-ontological,' are, in an original style, *derivative* with regard to difference; and with respect to what I shall later call *différance*" (*OG*, 23). God, the name for what is Being *and* an existent, is the addressee of the thought of difference. Derrida's *différance*, which is older than difference and is not a ground, can be thought only on the condition "that one begins by determining it as the ontico-ontological difference before erasing that determination" (*OG*, 24). In other words, *différance*, along with the other quasi-transcendentals, is neither a name nor a concept—it carries its own erasure within it—but the condition of possibility *and* impossibility for what has been determined by metaphysics. The warning that one must pass through or determine the quasi-transcendentals according to the language of metaphysics not only reminds us that the *"unheard"* of sense of Being as trace *"is not to be thought at one go"* but *is older*, more silent, than Heidegger's voice of Being *and* is *still to come*. It is not that these structural laws cannot be described but that they are marked in advance by an other, which is why "the enterprise of deconstruction always in a certain way falls prey to its own work" (*OG*, 23, 24). By this, Derrida means that deconstruction must borrow the economic resources of the old structures it inhabits, but it cannot totalize or control these elements because of their dependence upon alterity. This radical notion of alterity, the singularization of every other, means that the concepts of metaphysics—ideality, identity, difference, etc.—refer and defer in order to be themselves. This is originary repetition.

The secret is the name of the difference in presence; the secret is not phenomenalizable nor is it something noumenal, but *"there is something secret"* (*ON*, 25). And no experience can assure us of the secret, but there is something secret. Neither public nor private, but on the border between the two, it keeps us without our keeping it. The secret is "older" than speech and is not kept in keeping silent, which would subject it to representation. The secret of the secret is that it is without place. It does not belong to the orders of representation and Being. The invisible interiority that keeps the secret is always a matter of example.

This is why Derrida likes literature, or rather something about it; "this would be *in place of the secret*." There, in place of the secret, is the non-place which allows us to think of the other.[54] It is where "what remains is nothing—but the remainder, not even of literature." The remainder is what shelters the other, that which is never presentable. Literature is such a reserve. "There is in literature, in the *exemplary* secret of literature, a chance of saying everything without touching upon the secret" (*ON*, 28, 29). What is the example that allows one to say everything? What is the secret that is there (or should we say, what is there *in place of the secret*)? This place is not a hidden interiority, a place where I hear myself speak in keeping silent. It has something to do with decision, Abraham's decision that sacrificed ethics "*in the name of* absolute duty. And this name which must always be singular is here none other than the name of God as completely other, the nameless name of God, the unpronounceable name of God as other . . . [which] must remain transcendent, hidden, secret. . . . Secrecy is essential to the exercise of this absolute responsibility as sacrificial responsibility" (*GD*, 67). Abraham's decision, like every decision, "remains secret in the very instant of its performance" (*GD*, 77). The decision breaches knowledge and is destined to nonmanifestation—that is, to be secret, the decision is unthinkable; it has no *as such*. It occurs in the instant, the dehiscence or gap in time that belongs to an order other than Being. This is why "the concept of decision [cannot] be dissociated from this figure of the instant[.]" A decision, then, is secret but it is neither opaque nor ineffable. What Derrida calls "the stigma of its punctuality" is its structural character as singular and repeatable. He writes,

Abraham's decision is absolutely responsible because it answers for itself before the absolute other. Paradoxically it is also irresponsible because it is guided neither by reason nor by an ethics justifiable before men or before the law of some universal tribunal. Everything points to the fact that one is unable to be responsible at the same time before the other and before others, before the others of the other. If God is completely other, the figure or name of the wholly other, then every other (one) is every (bit) other. . . . It implies that God, as the wholly other, is to be found everywhere there is something of the wholly other. And since each of us, everyone else, each other is infinitely other in its absolute singularity, inaccessible, solitary, transcendent, nonmanifest, originarily nonpresent to my *ego* (as Husserl would say of the *alter ego* that can never be originarily present to my consciousness and that I can apprehend only through what he calls *appresentation* and analogy), then what can be said about Abraham's relation to God can be said about my relation without relation to *every other (one) as every (bit) other [tout autre comme tout autre] (GD, 77–78)*.

To respond to the other obliges me to sacrifice ethics, the duty to respond in the same way to another. I can only make sacrifices to the other of the other. The parenthetical remark recalls that, for Husserl, God no more depends upon me than does the alter ego. Because all experience is an experience for an ego, God as infinite other cannot be an intentional object for my ego, yet insofar as he exists for me, he is by "'my own conscious production'"; that is, "he has *meaning* only for an ego in general" (*WD*, 132). Thus, the only thing I can share with God is what cannot be shared, a secret we know nothing about except that there is a secret, the inaccessibility of the other, something I share with every other. In the parenthetical remark, we return to the analogical structure of Being. The possibility of another ego appearing to consciousness rests on analogy; there can be no immediate idea of the other, whether it be another ego, as in Husserl, or myself as other, except by analogy. The exemplarity of Abraham's sacrifice is the exemplarity of the instant, its taking place and not taking place. As exemplary it is singular and universal, which is to say it is inimitable; it is the ananalogical analogy for every sacrifice. There is no other like it; every sacrifice is like no other. This is what we share with Abraham, a secret we know nothing about, the secret of faith as absolute responsibility and absolute passion (see *GD*, 80). The secret is an absolute passion because it does not receive its determination from itself but suffers from being what it is not, a nonplace: that is, something that exceeds the oppositions of interior/exterior, manifest/nonmanifest, phenomenal/noumenal, known/not known, being/not being.

Abraham's decision has the structure of the trace, the minimal condition of relation without which there can be no responsibility to the other. At the same time, it is irresponsible because as trace it cannot be rendered present or even sensible. It is secret. It is incommensurable with knowledge and objectivity. This secret of secrecy is figured in the secret between God and Abraham, where Abraham does not simply share a secret with God but does not know what He knows. This concept of interiority, wherein God alone can penetrate the secret, introduces "the paradox of the secret as irreducible in its interiority" (*GD*, 100). Without God, there can be no secret, for there is no secret without an invisible interiority, but there can be no such interiority without the penetrating gaze of God. As soon as there is this space, this interiority, it is no longer certain who speaks when I hear myself speak. The secret anachronizes being; there is something like the secret, but what is there in the place of the secret is neither sensible nor intelligible. It is "mute, impassive as the *khôra*," and like it, the secret is an-analogical (*ON*, 27). There is only one secret, and so the "secret" is a name for what is without properties (the properties attributed to it—consciousness, interiority, self-presence—are transferred a posteriori: "God is the name of the possibility I have of keeping a secret that is visible from the interior but not from the exterior" [*GD*, 108]). Once there is this structure of conscience, then God, as absolute subjectivity, exists, and "he manifests his nonmanifestations when, in the structures of the living or the entity, there appears in the course of phylo- and ontogenetic history, the possibility of secrecy" (*GD*, 109). Such a history of God and of the name of God as the history of secrecy is the aporia of the secret. It can only be said to come into being once there is the interiority that renders absolutely invisible that which constitutes subjectivity as secret witnessing. There is neither God nor subjectivity without this impossible possibility of keeping a secret that is visible for a witness who is other than me and more me than me.

The secret is a name for something that is not: it is not visible, passive, active, noumenal, or phenomenal (see *ON*, 24–27). But we do not stop speaking about it and thereby denying it. This negation of the secret belongs to it originarily. This is the testamentary character of the secret. It must bear witness to itself because it must appear to itself to be what it is, "the secret shared *within itself*, its partition 'proper,' which divides the essence of a secret that cannot even appear to one alone except in starting to be lost, to divulge itself, hence to dissimulate itself, as secret, in showing itself" (*HAS*, 25). There is no secret *as such*, but there is something like the secret. This formula confirms what Gasché says about the self-presentation of the trace: "the trace, in the same way as Being, does not *relate,* does not stand in *relation,* to God. In the same way as Being is the Being of beings and of God, the trace is the trace *of* God." The trace is the structure of referral and of deferral presupposed by self-identity; it is nothing in itself, and hence it is an-analogical.[55] Like God, the secret is an-analogical, which makes it an analogy of the trace. The verification of the quasi-transcendental structure of the trace, as the trace of God or as the secret, always involves some sacrificial offering, what we might say is an attestation, a testimony (*témoigne,* which also means bearing witness), that is never reducible to knowledge (see *ON,* 23). The testamentary structure of sacrifice is that it bears witness to the self-presentation and, hence, oblivion, of transcendental structures, such as God, the secret, the moral law.

This is why alterity "is" the disjointure of time; it is inhuman, which does not make deconstruction inhumane or nihilistic. What allows for the thought of God is the aporetic condition that He is— that is, no matter what one says He is, whether love, charity, justice, He is prejudged to exist, which is to think him as an existent—and He is nothing apart from his relation to beings. How then can God be the ultimate cause if Being is nothing but the Being of beings? There would be nothing outside the difference between Being and beings, and we cannot speak of a relation between them. Our aporia, then, is God *is* (and therefore, He stands in relation to what He grounds), and He is without relation to Being (there can be no relation between Being and beings). God is an effect of the trace. To say God exists is to say He is merely an entity among other entities; to say He is beyond Being is to say He is without relation to what is. God can only be God as the example of exemplarity; the example of what is cannot be an example of itself. What makes it possible to think God if God is the example of the unthought? The trace, the minimal structure for any difference (between Being and beings, Self and Other). We cannot think God except as existing, and to think Him as existing is to deny what He is, without difference. The aporia, the coimplication of God and Being—God is and God is not, or God is the exemplary example of what is unthought (which is not the same as unknowable)—is irreducible.

And yet we think God, as example, which is not to think Him as such, insofar as the *as* is the vehicle of phenomenologization.

This is why exemplarity never allows us to know what we are speaking of when we speak of an example because examples are oblivious of difference, the condition of knowing, presence, God. This is also why Derrida's infrastructural terms, such as trace, iterability, *différance*, supplementarity, are "older" than Being because they articulate what makes possible the difference between essence and appearance. They do not obey the conventional logic of time because as "older" than Being, they do not constitute thought or concepts—this is one of the meanings of being "older" than Being—but they account for the possibility of difference, appearance, presence, God. They are the possible conditions of impossibility—of identity, presence, God. As "older" than Being, the trace makes possible the relation to alterity that, within metaphysics, has been determined from the point of view of identity.[56] As the wholly Other, God is an effect of the trace.

It could be said that my differences with Caputo are a matter of tonality, not so much as it concerns his messianism, but tonality as a quasi-transcendental that suspends relation to the other— before every other is the *relation* to alterity. An other haunts every other. Without repetition and the risk of irresponsibility, there can be no responsibility, no single *yes* to the other. I therefore need to come back to Caputo's statement, "Literature is the name of the trace and the text, which for Derrida implies 'the unlimited right to ask questions.'" If the trace is what keeps open the relation to the impossible, God as other, then literature, for Caputo, is the experience of God. As the exemplary revelation of the secret that is no secret, literature is another name for apocalypse. Derrida has, in fact, asked, "wouldn't the apocalyptic be a transcendental condition of all discourse, of all experience even, of every mark or every trace? And the genre of writings called 'apocalyptic' in the strict sense, then, would be only an example, an *exemplary* revelation of this transcendental structure" (*AT*, 156–57). If God is the exemplary revelation of the trace, then he is dependent upon the "*divisible* envoi *for which there is no self-presentation nor assured destination*" (*AT*, 157). Apocalypse would then be the occultation of the trace of God. That is, if God were not carried off by the trace, which is what it means to think him *as* example, then He would be the wholly Other, which would place Him beyond time.

If God is the exemplary revelation of the trace, and apocalyptic writing the revelation of the transcendental structure of the trace, how are we to know when we speak of examples we are speaking of God or giving an example of God? How do we know when we listen to conscience, we are listening to ourselves or God? Whenever it is impossible to decide between the "thought of Being . . . [which] permits us to say, without naiveté, reduction, or blasphemy, 'God, for example'" (*WD*, 318, n. 78), and the being that is thought, that is, as soon as the ontico-ontological difference opens itself to an older difference, the trace of difference, then something like literature will have begun.

This undecidability is what Derrida likes about literature. Without liking it "for its own sake," he likes something about it; "this would be *in place of the secret*" (*ON*, 28). Literature, as Caputo conceives it, would be the revelation of that which has no name, God, or what he calls the "secret without truth." Derrida's passion for literature is a passion for the name (of the trace, of God, of the absolute secret)—to wit, literature "maintains the absolute secret." Thanks to this *maintenance*, literature, for Caputo, is what compels us to have faith—there is no secret, no divine revelation to put an end to not knowing, and we are infinitely responsible to the Other who is every other.[57] This is another version of the Spirit that endures and maintains itself in death[58]— responsibility, faith, love maintain themselves in the impossible, the secret. Revelation is the death of faith. If we return to Derrida's suggestion that the apocalyptic is "a transcendental condition of all discourse, of all experience even, of every mark or every trace[,]" we find that this is so "as soon as one no longer knows who speaks or who writes" (*AT*, 156–57). Derrida employs a similar expression in "Passions," which I quoted earlier and do so once more: "Something of literature will have begun when it is not possible to decide whether, when I speak of something, I am indeed speaking of something (of the thing itself, this one, for itself) or if I am giving an example, an example of something or an example of the fact that I can speak of something" (*ON*, 142–43, n. 14). It is a matter of the an-analogical structure of the secret. Literature is always a matter of something else. "There is in literature, in the *exemplary* secret of literature, a chance of saying everything without touching upon the secret" (*ON*, 29). I would almost like to say that Derrida's secret, his passion for literature, is that it allows him to say everything without touching upon the secret (of literature), which is precisely that, there is no secret except as one can speak about it. Therefore, to speak about literature is, inevitably, to speak about something else, secrets for example, or philosophy. I say this not to suggest that literature is a universalizing discourse, or that all discourse is literature, or that literature is the other of philosophy, nor even that literature is the name of the trace of the text (there are other names for the trace, God, for example), but that literature is without identity, without essence or substance, but there is literature/literature is there only where it receives its determination from something else. Literature is always *in place of.* It can never assure us of the "there is." This is the passion of literature and why Derrida has a passion for it. This is why in this book I will speak only of literature and never, or almost never, about "literature," that is, novels or poetry. I will speak instead of law, justice, the Jewish unhappy consciousness, apocalypse, nuclear destruction, and the gift. When I speak of literature, I am speaking in place of ethics.

Abraham's sacrifice is an example of the possible impossibility of justice in Derrida: a decision is called forth by an aporia, the impossibility of passage to the source or origin of justice, an anterior moment that would, in advance, validate every decision performed in its name. The responsibility demanded of us in the name of the secret engages us before we turn to it. If Derrida has shown that it is impossible to step outside metaphysics because the desire to control metaphysics by what is external to it introduces a new master term and a new, which would not be so new, metaphysics, and on the other hand, if he has demonstrated the limits of metaphysics to determine the facticity or empiricity of non-metaphysical discourse, he leaves one thing that is neither in metaphysics nor outside it, one thing that cannot be deconstructed—justice. The call for justice, the absolute responsibility to the other, is what demands deconstruction, but it is the aporia which it cannot traverse.[59] To hear the infinite demand of justice is to understand that "justice always addresses itself to singularity, to the singularity of the other, despite or even because it pretends to universality" (*FL,* 955). Acts of judgment can only remark this aporia of the singular and the universal; every just act is singular and therefore impossible but necessary all the same. For as singular, it must be done in the name of all who command our respect, our responsibility, and at the same time the decisive act is meant for that one instance in violation of all who demand justice. If there is no access to justice, if justice is what cannot be experienced, then justice is still possible, which is to say as an infinite demand, justice is not subject to knowledge or reducible to a rule; it cannot, as Derrida says, be deconstructed.

Justice is the impossible "name" for the originary repetition that makes acts and institutions possible precisely because it is impossible; that is, it cannot be reduced to a presence or erected into an absolute. When Derrida says justice is an experience of the aporia, he points out that an experience is a traversal, a passage toward a destination, but an aporia is a non-passage (that is its literal meaning). Justice exceeds the opposition of present and absent, empirical and transcendental. It is neither the code of law nor the institutions that apply the code, for these are subject to change, nor is it transcendental, an eternal or absolute law, for then it would be a principle of universality, which is incompatible with judgment if it is to be responsible to singularity. Whereas Kant proposed that the question of what is right can be settled by determining its universality, Derrida's deconstruction answers that any just decision must cut and divide; it can be neither purely singular nor purely universal. The institution of law, which is as much an act as an institution, is violent insofar as it depends upon the decision that at once conserves the law and puts it in place. Justice, therefore, is situated where the relation between the transcendental and the empirical, the universal and the singular, cannot be controlled or determined. Justice is neither arbitrary nor uniform, neither absolutely singular nor general, but iterable. It is a promise that puts in place what ought to be conserved; "it inscribes the possibility of repetition at the heart of the originary." There is no pure opposition between the positing and conserving, the singular act and the universal rule, but a "*différantielle* contamination" (*FL,* 997). Deconstruction concerns or is the thinking of this very contamination between the singular and the universal. Derrida calls it iterability, which requires "the origin to repeat itself originarily, to alter itself so as to have the value of origin, that is, to conserve itself" (*FL,* 1009). This impossible logic of originary repetition is the very possibility of any experience. What constitutes the singularity of the event is the possibility of iteration; indeed, once anything is admitted as possible, such as the repeatability of a message in the absence of a sender, then this possibility is a necessary part of its structure and cannot be controlled or

excluded. As the minimal possibility of identity, iterability constitutes the singularity of the event, dividing it and setting it aside
from the start. As an institution that produces discursive forms
that contest institutional foundations, literature is the site of
juridico-political production—it sets itself up by marking its relation to the other, which we acknowledge insofar as literature is
still thought within metaphysics. Having no essence, literature
institutes itself in dividing itself from what it is not, or in marking
its otherness from other discursive forms. In re-marking its non-
identity, literature is the arena where the relation to the other is
staged, and it is on this basis that we can recognize the relation
between literature and ethics.

1

"Aporetic Conclusion": The Law of the Name

An archive is growing about Derrida and deconstruction. If we consult the bibliographies of both his own writings and of works on him, it would appear that the institutionalization of this thought, this invention, is well under way, if not already established.[1] With any institutionalization comes the law—how to read/not read this text signed "J. Derrida." Of course, this already is a discourse made familiar to us by Derrida, anticipated by him in text after text. To speak of an institution is to speak of that which is governed by laws, which are not to be confused with rules. Instead, law must be understood in conjunction with judgments, both apodictic and legal. When we decide what is "deconstruction," we must not only appeal to the texts signed "Derrida" but to something held in advance, a law, to which our judgment must conform. Such a judgment fails, however, to the extent that it obeys a law and does not reinstitute or reinvent the law in a new judgment.[2] It is a matter of doing justice to what is to come, the other, to singularity, to the singularity of the coming of the other, an impossible but necessary task, for the "other" is a name for what can bear no name, not even (and least of all) "Being." It is to come precisely because it does not have the status of a present being, nor is it an object of knowledge. The other is what calls for a response.

Derrida's writings on judgment and institution are hardly an exercise in paradoxism, although they do examine the aporias in which deconstruction finds itself. One such aporia, the problem of institution and justice, involves a certain experience of the future or what he calls in several texts an *à-venir*, a "to come." If a judgment is to be just, it has to have this future, this *à-venir*, or else it would be the application of a rule. If there is a future for justice, then deconstruction is not reducible to the status of an institution; on the other hand, it does not do away with institution altogether.[3]

31

The event of deconstruction, the deconstructive event, is unique, an act, and the making of an institution, an archive, at the same time. The event, to be worthy of its name, must be both unanticipated and remarkable, that is, capable of being remarked and identified or distinguished from other events. The event, then, is a monstrosity—marked by this (com)promise, it gives itself as singular or unique and it betrays itself by instituting a system of marks, a law or an injunction that demands a response.[4] We cannot, therefore, speak of the event or the *à-venir* in terms of an absolute future, as that which is still outstanding, or as the "horizon of intelligibility."[5] The event takes place or falls within the destining of dispatches— at the very instant it takes place, it destines itself. It is a question of arrivals, not departure, of repetition, not inauguration.[6]

In addition to being a "new" work in "philosophy" and, therefore, the subject of commentary, analysis, etc., deconstruction can also be situated in histories of literature, as well as of philosophy, placed in conjunction with Mallarmé, Joyce, Ponge, and Blanchot, as well as with Plato, Aristotle, Husserl, Heidegger, et al. This event called "deconstruction" could be said to countersign these signatures: "There is as it were a duel of singularities, a duel of writing and reading, in the course of which a countersignature comes both to confirm, repeat and respect the signature of the other, of the 'original' work, and to *lead it off* elsewhere, so running the risk of *betraying* it, having to betray it in a certain way so as to respect it, through the invention of another signature just as singular" (*SIL*, 69).

The "singularity" of deconstruction, its invention of another signature, means, above all, it is not a method, act, entity, or thing. Indeed, we are on the wrong track to speak of what "deconstruction is" or "is not"; it does not, in other words, lend itself to normative or predicative forms because such forms are themselves deconstructible. To avoid the ontological categories or concepts implied by the predicative form "deconstruction is," Derrida says, "Deconstruction takes place [*a lieu*], it is an event that does not await the deliberation, consciousness, or organization of a subject, or even of modernity. *It deconstructs it-self. It can be deconstructed* [*Ça se deconstruit*]." Deconstruction has no site because it cannot be assimilated to something like a definable subject or act, but it can be said to take place as a writing about/in the general text, that is, in "a chain of possible substitutions, in what is too blithely called a 'context.'"[7] As the system of infrastructures, deconstruction both produces itself as a writing about the general text, which functions as a general mode of inscription, as the system of the "law" of generality that accounts for referentiality and ideality and, at the same time, for the founding power of writing, producing "rules—other conventions—for new performatives and never installs itself in the theoretical assurance of a single opposition between performative and constative" (*PIO*, 42).[8] According to J. L. Austin, a performative is an utterance that is an action, and a constative is a statement or an utterance "with a historical reference."[9] Deconstruction is both performative and constative, or act and archive. In other words, as event it is marked in advance by a divisibility that permits it to be read but not translated; that is, it gives itself over to countersignatures—it affirms the singularity of the other that precedes it and signs in a new way, confirming its own signature (see *SIL*, 66–67).

In the singular relation between invention and institution, act and archive, the unique and its repetition—in its iterability—deconstruction shares with literature the impropriety, the impurity, of chance. It's not only a throw of the dice that doesn't abolish chance; there is always the chance event as soon as *there is* something rather than nothing—the singular event, the signature (of the other). That is, the singular is the impossible event that demands, delegates, a response (it is impossible because it is not attributable to ontological categories of identity or act). Chance involves a certain direction, a destiny, fall, or cast of events that is both unforeseeable and predictable insofar as chance always presumes a system or code that regulates and a deviation from or violation of this system. We might even say that the aleatory destiny of the event, its coming about as unique and repeatable, promises a future that is something like an invention *and* an apocalypse, a first and last event, unique and repeatable at the same time.

It is possible that deconstruction's "singular" contribution may be that it prepares for the coming of the countersignature, the aleatory signature that exceeds or opens the world/event to another experience. The event comes about by the necessary transgression or contamination that leaves no event in the purity of its singularity. This problem of the singular rests upon the basic proposition that the absolutely singular, that which is, properly speaking, unique, would never be accessible to the understanding or even presentable at all if it were not subject to repetition from the beginning. It is on these grounds rather than on some notion of style that deconstruction resembles a literary practice. This does not mean that deconstruction is more literary than philosophical, but it could be said, as Derrida suggests in an interview, that a performative text like *The Post Card* seeks to create, let us say "invent," itself as unique, as an "inaugural performance" that simultaneously must invent a reader capable of countersigning— that is, in confirming the signature of the other, a countersigning reading answers to the text's iterability.[10] "The work then becomes an institution forming its own readers, giving them a competence which they did not possess before: a university, a seminar, a collo-quium, a curriculum, a *course*" (*SIL*, 74). The countersignature "is held under the law of the first, of its absolute pastness. But this absolute pastness was already the demand for the countersigning reading. The first only inaugurates from after, and as the expecta-tion of, the second countersignature." This "incalculable scene," Derrida concludes, programs the history of literary criticism (*SIL*, 70). The countersignature is neither dialectical nor chronological. Nor can we call it metaleptic, if we understand this to mean trans-ference or reversal. If the first inaugurates *from after* the second, it does not merely follow the second but could be said to await a second that precedes it.

Deconstruction situates itself to the side of literature and philosophy; however, it cannot be reduced to the simple opposition between singular event and institution, act and archive. To sustain its status as act or invention, the literary work must come back toward the past, toward a set of conventions and laws that allow us to recognize it as unique. Therefore, act and archive meet in the literary work because it links the advent of the new with its rein-scription in a system, in generality. This makes the literary work a first time and a last time, "an event that seems to produce itself by speaking about itself, *by the act of speaking of itself*" (*PIO*, 29). Invention and destruction meet in the singular event that signs itself as unique and fails to coincide with itself; that is, it states its uniqueness in a discourse that projects forward the possibility of its repetition. It is not that literature only transgresses the institu-tions that stand in place, it reveals the precariousness of the same institutions that would define it. There is no natural essence of lit-erature; literature is "inscribed on the side of the intentional

object, in its noematic structure" (*SIL*, 44). Having no internal criterion, no identity, literature would, at the same time, seem to be
an exemplary institution because its existence is tied to a historically specific origin (in approximately the seventeenth century)
and an institutional bulwark, the law (that is, copyright, licensing
and printing laws, censorship, etc.).[11] On the one hand, the literary
work exemplifies invention—it comes as a surprise, as a unique or
singular event, the invention of a new institution. On the other
hand, this event is destined to betray its being as a new institution
because it reveals itself as such: "it appears in an institutional
field designed so that it cuts itself up and abducts itself there"
(*SIL*, 74). The new work, in other words, never arrives alone; it
inscribes itself in a context and a genealogy. The new work, if it is
to be read, institutes the conditions of its unique being and the
possibility of response. It is better, therefore, to speak of the literary "experience" than the literary thing or object on the grounds
that literarity is "the correlative of an intentional relation to the
text" (*SIL*, 44). The literary event is not natural because it suspends the thetic or naive belief in the referent. At the same time,
when we look for the essence of literature, that which the reduction is to lead to, we find no internal criterion to govern it.

If the new work must, as has often been said, instruct its
audience on how to read, then the reader is invited, as Derrida
says, to countersign. This recalls us to the notion that the possibility of the signature, its effect as a singular and reproducible event,
is its iterability.[12] The signature is the operation of the text as a
whole, "the whole of the active interpretation which has left a
trace or a remainder" (*EO*, 52). The new work, the invention,
appears already marked *de jure* by a time and place that opens the
present of the signature, its assertion of a here and now, to a
countersignature. Consequently, the literary event, like juridico-
political acts, consists in producing a law that transgresses the law
or institution that it comes after and makes this law possible and
impossible by virtue of its status as event. The literary event is a
dividing/divisive act.

Watching over the literary event is the fabulous referent, the
absolutely unique name or signature. Such a unique name would
be a pure invention on the basis of an event that has never
happened, that is still to come. This is what makes invention an
anthrocentric principle: "Man himself, and the human world, is

defined by the human subject's aptitude for invention, in the double sense of narrative fiction or historical fabulation and of technical or technoepistemic innovation" (*PIO*, 44). The double senses of "invention"—it means *fabula* and *technê*, *historia* and *epistémè*—cannot be opposed; they are the statutory conditions for the encounter with the wholly other, that which appears for the first and last time, the absolute invention, the entirely other, "a still unanticipatable alterity and for which no horizon of waiting as yet seems ready, in place, available" (*PIO*, 55). Watching over this alterity is literature. If, as Derrida has argued, "there is nothing outside the text"—that is, "every referent, all reality has the structure of a differential trace" (*LI* 148), then literature poses the problem of the event to the extent that as idiomatic or unique, as other, it affords itself to be "read," using this term in the broadest sense as interpretation, even "recognition," by inviting the countersignature.[13]

The event is a double signing, a countersigned signature or contract without exchange (see *SS*, 48). In other words, the event/invention irrupts within an already constituted field where, as something surprising and unanticipated, it "inscribes itself as act (action and archive)" (*SS*, 54). The event is not outside the field—if it were, it would be an infinite other[14]—but designates, inscribes or signs itself, by giving itself to be read or countersigned. As something new, the literary event institutes itself in a chain of conventions (but not without altering these conventions), thereby ensuring its repeatability or legitimating it for the future. The literary event has the force of law: it is the injunction of the entirely other that I be responsible to that which is singular and different. It is, therefore, an impossible debt.[15] Literature is what gives us to think the entirely other, the unanticipatable other, that which "is not inventable, and . . . is then the only invention in the world, the only invention of the world, our invention, the invention that invents us. For the other is always another origin of the world and we are (always) (still) to be invented. And the being of the we, and being itself. Beyond being" (*PIO*, 61). The event that watches over the future, an event that invents us, invents or affirms the coming of the other, would be the arrival of the other in a performative that unsettles its status or condition as a performative—unique and repeatable. In the pages that follow, I hope to demonstrate that literature's status as such an event rests upon its capacity to say anything. The ethical claim for literature rests, therefore, not in its capacity for representation, something it shares with other texts, but in its exemplifying the infinite referral of the trace.

In his essay on Kafka's parable "Before the Law," Derrida raises the questions, what do "we understand under the name of literature? And who decides? Who judges?" He proceeds to confess

> that I cannot give nor am I withholding an answer to such a question. Perhaps you will think that I am leading you toward a purely aporetic conclusion . . . that there is no such thing as a literary essence or a specifically literary domain strictly identifiable as such; or, indeed, that this name of literature perhaps is destined to remain improper, with no criteria, or assured concept or reference, so that 'literature' has something to do with the drama of naming, the law of the name and the name of the law. You would doubtless not be wrong (*BL*, 187).

I begin with Derrida's "aporetic conclusion" that literature has something to do with law and the name. In asking who "decides, who judges" what belongs to literature, he not only suggests that literature belongs to judgment in the purely conventional sense that in naming certain writings "literature," we are engaged in an act of adjudication with all its attendant social and political ramifications, but more importantly, he implies that literature shares with law a common status, one that belongs to the aporia of judgment, the encounter between the universal essence of law and singularity of decision.

"Aporia" simply means an impossible or barred passage and should be distinguished from a double bind in which we are caught between two incompatible or conflicting choices precisely because an aporia demands a decision, even if this decision cannot cut a passageway through the aporia, which is impossible insofar as an aporia is necessary and irreducible. In what may be his most famous example, Derrida locates an aporia in Saussure's exclusion of writing as derivative of speech in his theory of the sign. If the unity of the signifier and signified is arbitrary and conventional, then the condition of the phoneme, the "natural" sound-image of speech, is already an institution, a system of differences, and is nothing natural; it is an "originary" repetition. Saussure's theory that neither the signifier nor the signified exists outside the linguistic system and both are constituted by conceptual and phonic differences effects both language (as system) and speech. Moreover, "these differences are themselves *effects*" (*M*, 11). They cannot be reduced to a form of presence but are constituted by a minimal structure of difference and repetition that Derrida calls "arche-writing" or "arche-trace." The ideality of the phoneme, and any ideality for that matter, is dependent upon the aporetic structure of repetition that puts into question the ideality it makes possible. For instance, for an "I" to be an "I," it must *always already* be subject to repetition and difference. It cannot be discernible as an "I" if it were not recognizable in different contexts; hence, there is no absolute repetition, only alterity of repetition or iterability. The suppression of the difference that makes identity possible and impossible in any absolute sense is originary violence, a violence necessary to the constitution, or institution, of any transcendental or natural category.

Aporia, being both necessary and irreducible, belongs to singularity. A literary work has a radical singularity, much like a person, but the possibility of interpretation, or even the recognition of the work as singular or idiomatic, implies a law or ideality, a structure of repetition that marks the text in advance.[16] Traditionally, we might think of the literary text in terms of particularity; it would be an individual governed by a general law, such as the law of genre. This presupposes that the law is general enough to govern all particulars without doing violence to what it determines, and, indeed, much literary theory is devoted to a search for such a general law, such as dialogism and the novel, or the structural ritual of sacrifice, or the political unconscious. As we will see in a moment, no law can be general enough to avoid doing violence to singularity, and the singular, in distinction from particularity, always exceeds the borders of the law. The literary work is singular but insofar as it is readable, it must divide itself, differ from itself, in order to be repeated in its singularity. It must be subject to what Derrida calls "the law of iterability," the principle of alteration in repetition. Iterability is what anchors the work in a historical context as something that takes place just once and *at the same time* opens the work to recontextualization (see *SIL*, 63–68). This aporia of singularity and generality should not be confused with indeterminacy or equivocation; the aporia is not accidental to the work but constitutes it and deconstitutes it. And when we say that Derrida deconstructs the specificity of the literary work, for example, we should understand this to mean that deconstruction affirms singularity by demonstrating that it is constituted by the possibility of repetition. Literature is, possibly, just one example of the general law of writing, the limitless play of *différance*, trace, supplement, etc.

The structure of generalized writing (which has nothing to do with notation or scriptive signs of phonetic values) is what accounts for idealities and their necessary contamination. Writing in this sense links together singularity and its limit, repetition, iterability. The singular work comes about only by affecting itself, or compromising itself, by iterability, whereby it opens itself to others. This repeatable singularity produces "'effects of generality'" (*SIL*, 62). The aporetic condition of singularity—the work cannot be singular unless it is always already repeatable and, hence, general—also means that the work must stand in relation to generality but never be comprehended or covered by it. It exceeds itself as singular in order to be singular: the uniqueness of the work, the singularity that demands our response, is never absolute or else there could be no response; it must, as I have said, divide itself and be repeated in its singularity to be what it is. What cannot be deconstructed is the aporia itself, the event that comes about by the crossing of singularity and generality. One does not seek a way out of an aporia but recognizes that it is necessary for judgment (and for a future).

The aporia of singularity and generality—it must be general enough to be recognizable but always exceeds generality insofar as it is singular—is undecidable: the former is not reducible to the latter nor possible without it. What counts in undecidability is not, Derrida says, some semantic richness that prevents any final decision but "the formal or syntactical *praxis* that composes and decomposes it [i.e., the undecidable]" (*D*, 220). Undecidability does not produce an impasse but demands decision. The aporia opens the space that exceeds the calculable order; without it, there can be no ethical decision. A calculable order would preclude deciding because the "decision" would be programmed in advance (see *LI*, 116).

Any effort to think the unique within a system is the effect of arche-writing, the originary violence that severs the proper from itself. This is the drama of the name and the law of the name. The proper name, as "the unique appellation reserved for the presence of a human being" (*OG*, 109), comes into being only with its erasure, its articulation within a system, familial or linguistic. Once we admit that the proper name functions within a system of classification and requires articulation, then it must be recognized as being already improper, a function of difference and writing. The name is already subject to the law of repetition, as the law itself must be (see *D*, 123). The distinction between law and transgression upon which civil society rests is possible only on the basis of arche-writing, which is not the common act of writing but the originary structural unity of difference and repetition that accounts for all idealities, empirico-transcendental differences, and all instituted or disciplinary spaces (this last, we might say, comprehends all that depends upon the opposition of nature and culture: community, law, the human sciences, or anything we might call "system" or "institution").

Richard Beardsworth argues in convincing fashion "that the ethico-political dimension of deconstruction resides in this relation between aporia and judgment." He rightly stresses that "[t]he institution of law is necessarily violent as an effect of the 'originary violence' which exposes a being to the world and to others prior to any particular relation (ethical, political, social) which this being then entertains with them."[17] As we have seen, the necessity of repetition and the impossibility of the proper name or self-identity opens up singularity to contamination, which does not fall upon the proper from outside but originarily displaces it, and insofar as some minimal equivocacy or difference is necessary for decision, this contamination is the possibility of invention or of fresh judgment. In his analysis of Claude Levi-Strauss's account in *Tristes Tropiques* of how he coaxed Nambikwara children to violate custom and reveal each other's and then the adults' proper names, Derrida distinguishes three levels of violence. Arche-violence appears in the prohibition against pronouncing the proper name: "To think the unique *within* the system, to inscribe it there, such is the gesture of the arche-writing: arche-violence, loss of the proper, of absolute proximity, of self-presence" (as soon as the so-called proper name is subject to law, it belongs to a system of difference and repetition, which Derrida calls "writing"); there is next "a second violence that is reparatory, protective," instituting the law that attempts to put an end to or conceal the originary violence; and a third violence, "which can *possibly* emerge or not . . . within what is commonly called evil, war, indiscretion, rape; which consists of revealing by effraction the so-called proper name." This last violence, Derrida says, can be called reflective because it reveals "the native non-identity, classification as denaturation of the proper, and identity as the abstract moment of the concept" (*OG*, 112). Beardsworth remarks that the economy of law—the more the law attempts to control violence, the more violent it is— undermines the oppositional thinking that posits an other outside the metaphysical system. This law of law—the law must repeat itself in order to maintain itself as the law—"reveals its necessary illegality" and the "repetition of the originary violence which has 'always already' accompanied the foundation and guarding of the law." These three forms of violence do not occur in chronological succession but arise together and reveal the essential inability of law to be the law, that is to legislate in a pure present.[18]

We should not conclude from Derrida's deconstruction of the law that what follows is either anarchy or decisionism[19] but, as he says in "Before the Law," the contradictory prohibition against entering into relation with the law itself "allows man the freedom of self-determination [if the law were present, there would be no freedom as measured by the necessity of judgment; one would be bound to follow the absolute law], even though this freedom cancels itself through the self-prohibition of entering the law" (the man from the country in Kafka's tale remains "*outside the law* (an outlaw)" because he is *before* the law, which is to say, he remains subject to the law) (*BL*, 204). The prohibition against entering the law is the prohibition against approaching "the origin of *différance*. . . . That is the law of the law, the process of a law of whose subject we can never say, 'There it is,' it is here or there. It is neither natural nor institutional" (*BL*, 205). This law of law implies that there can be no essence of law, no presence, and hence, no end to the responsibility that the law entails because the non-identity of the law makes judging an interminable process.

The law, like literature, is always an idiom, a singularity, but not an absolute singularity. The law, and the name of the law, must repeat itself in order to be available; this is the law of the law, repetition as institution and transgression, at the same time.

This is the "aporetic conclusion" with which any response to singularity (of law, of literature) must begin: the non-originary status of the law means it cannot be "a universal generality" but must always remain an "idiom" (*BL*, 210). Deciding or judging (in the name of the law, the law of the name) always involves this impossible relation between the singular and the general, as the man from the country in Kafka's tale discovers: the law is meant for everyone and is always singular or unique. This aporetic relation wherein "the categorical engages the idiomatic" is common to both literature and law (*BL*, 213). Kafka's tale, in Derrida's reading, reveals that there can be a relation with law precisely because there can be no access to it; the law is "a prohibited place," an aporia: "one cannot reach the law, and in order to have a *rapport* of respect with it, *one must not* [*il faut ne pas, il ne faut pas*] have a rapport with the law, *one must interrupt the relation*. One must *enter into relation* only with the law's representatives, its examples, its guardians" (*BL*, 203–204). In order to have a relation with the law, one must not know who or what the law is. In Kafka's tale, the doorkeeper does not know the law because, as he confesses, he is afraid to look upon the third of who knows how many other guardians. Entrance into the law would mean the end of (respect for) the law; the force of law consists in its inaccessibility. The law is not the privileged site for the disclosure of justice but is the suspension, the interruption, by which justice emerges. Therefore, judgment is not a calculable act but something to be endured, an undergoing of the aporetic experience that leaves us before the law, prejudged as having to judge. Every act of judgment, if it is to be ethical, must respond to the idiomatic or singular, and at the same time, this act pronounces the law that makes it possible and with which it cannot coincide. It is this non-coincidence, non-identity, of the idiomatic with the general—and, thus, the inaccessibility of their origins—that is common to literature and the law.

We can only enter into relation with the law's guardians or examples, which, as in the case of Kafka's tale, bar access to what they stand for. The law prohibits narrative accounts that would make the law present, allow one to enter into it. "To be invested with its categorical authority, the law must be without history, genesis, or any possible derivation. That would be *the law of the law*. Pure morality has no history: as Kant seems at first to remind us, no intrinsic history" *(BL,* 191). As Derrida's reading of Freud's account of the origin of the law in *Totem and Taboo* reveals, any account of the origin of moral law runs into the aporia of originary repetition: the sons who kill their father in order to take possession of what he possesses feel remorse for their act and consequently prohibit its repetition. In writing a narrative of the origin of law, Freud must place the law before the law—why else should the sons feel remorse if prior to their deed no moral law existed to cause them pain? He is, after all, offering a narrative that begins before the origin of moral law. They would have no concept of a crime unless morality, in contradiction to Freud's story, preceded the law. Furthermore, once the father is killed, he exerts more power than ever; the sons are not able to take his place, and he is deified in the ritual of the totemic meal. The father is murdered only to become more alive than when he was alive. This event, Derrida concludes, is a "non-event, an event of nothing or a quasi-event which both calls for and annuls a narrative account. For this 'deed' or 'misdeed' to b44e effective, it must be somehow spun from fiction. Everything happens *as if*" *(BL,* 198). Freud's event without event, this "pure event where nothing happens . . . both demands and annuls the relation in its fiction. Nothing new happens and yet this nothing new would instate the law," the fundamental prohibitions against murder and incest. The origin, the pure event, is without a proper place, and in this manner resembles a fiction or a simulacrum. It is an event that compels neither belief nor disbelief. This event, which is at once "fiction *of* narration as well as fiction as narration . . . is the origin of literature at the same time as the origin of law" *(BL,* 199). Both literature and law originate in this quasi-event that fissures the question of the reality of the referent (did the murder really take place? did Freud believe his story?) or of history and fiction. The story of the origin of prohibition "is a prohibited story" *(BL,* 200). What demands the story and denies the story is the prohibition against entering the origin of *différance.* An originary event, which must always be at once a first time and a repetition—that is, a singularity (and thus a last time)—does not take place as such. The law of the law, the violence of originary repetition that haunts the event, is a rupture or dislocation of time where *différance* remains irreducible and renders possible, calls forth, a response. "The event comes about, or promises itself initially, only by thus compromising itself by the singular contamination of the singular and what shares it. It comes about as impurity—and impurity here is chance" (*SIL*, 68–69). Because singularity comes about by repetition, there is always a ghost of a chance, which is precisely that, a ghost or spectral haunting that is the non-origin of the law.[20]

Freud's simulacrum of a fiction works because it fails: it accounts for the law precisely because it fails to account for the law, assign it a place and proper name, an origin. The law requires a fiction; Freud tells a story to account for what has no origin in nature. Even when we speak of legal codes and legitimation of the law, we ordinarily assume some fiction dependent upon the opposition between *nomos* and *physis*, convention and nature. This quasi-event of the "origin" is the minimal condition that there be something; it is *différance*, a differing-deferring force. This event, in other words, cannot be reduced to presence, an occurrence in a here and now. The law arrives only in narrative, a simulacrum, that cancels itself as narrative the very moment it posits, by means of narrative, an origin of moral law. If Freud's tale reveals an irreducible unaccountability for the origin of moral law, its failure to present as an event the very thing that forbids such a narrative accountability, the law, is its success. The law as law must be disinterested, unmotivated,—it serves nothing other than the law—and, therefore, it is characterized by unconditionality. The performative structure of law interrupts time and rents or fissures the historical referent. As in Freud's fiction, this rupture produces the law, but it is not prior to the law. This is what Derrida calls the "*[v]iolence* of the law before the law and before meaning, that interrupts time, disarticulates it" (*SM*, 31). As event, the force of rupture that produces the law carries repetition in itself, so we can say there is no law before its repetition. The aporia of law/literature is that of an event that begins by returning: "It is all a question of time, and it is the time of the story" (*BL*, 202).

It is also a matter of ghosts, what "*begins by coming back*" (*SM*, 11). We cannot pass through this crossing of singularity and generality, this iterability of the law/law of iterability. Literature re-marks the aporia of law: in order to be the law, that is singular and universal, the (origin of) law must be prohibited. The law never shows itself but must divide itself, differ from itself, in order to be repeated in its singularity. Kafka's story tells us that the presence of the law is the death of law. "The aporia of law appears as the radical impossibility of relating the story of the origin of the law. If this appearance takes form as the 'literary,' it also forms the prescription to interrupt our relation to the law because we must not relate to the appearance."[21] The law is kept only by suspending the law. This impossible relation is the possibility of law: the prohibition that bars access to the law in Kafka's tale also establishes the man from the country's relation to the law as singular and universal. There can be no work (of law or of literature) that does not at once engage the singular and its repetition because the work comes about by its iterability; it always promises to lead off elsewhere, to a new reading, to a fresh judgment. Therefore, the suspension of the law does not block judgment but makes judgment necessary (I will return to this). This is law/literature's pledge to the future.

Derrida's claim that in order to have a relation to the law, one must interrupt the relation, refers to Kant's demand for infinite respect for the moral law. The moral law is an idea of reason, which means it cannot be derived from examples but is an idea of perfection which reason formulates a priori. According to the principle of the sovereignty of reason, imitation and examples have no place in moral matters because they would make visible the practicability of obeying the law and, in so doing, deny that the original for the idea of moral perfection lies in reason. Derrida finds what we might call a necessary irony in Kant's quoting "*against the example*, the very example of *passion*," Christ's sacrifice, which stands as the example of what one must not do, "offer oneself as an example." Because the pure law conforms to no example, Kant would exclude iterability from the concept of moral duty. There can be no experience that "can assure us of the 'there is'" of the moral imperative. To be assured there is a moral duty is to rob the individual of free will; therefore, the passion of Christ serves as exemplary example of what one must not do: offer oneself as an example because God alone is good. The Kantian concept of God as the highest good is an idea of reason. The passion "demonstrates *in an exemplary way*, singularly, par excellence, the inadequacy of the example, the secret of divine invisibility and the sovereignty of reason. . . . The example is the only visibility of the invisible" (*ON*, 140–41, n. 10). Kant would derive moral law without any recourse to history. Even God, whom we do not see, must be compared to the idea of moral perfection provided by reason. In demonstrating the inadequacy of the example, Christ makes the law "present" as invisible. He announces that the law presents itself by withholding itself, remaining secret or invisible. This invisibility constitutes the "phenomenality" of law without imparting any content of the law, which remains secret. The structure of exemplarity is something other than the visible representation of a transcendental ideality. We could say it belongs neither to appearance nor essence. The example sets aside, makes secret, what it would present. "The example itself, as such, overflows its singularity as much as its identity. This is why there are no examples, while at the same time there are only examples" (*ON*, 17).

We are approaching literature. Just as it is impossible to decide between (Freud's belief in) the reality or fictitiousness of Freud's narrative of the origin of moral law, so we are at the point where it is undecidable whether the example of the passion is an example of something (the moral law) or of the example that I can speak of something (the invisibility or secret of the law): "Something of literature will have begun when it is not possible to decide whether, when I speak of something, I am indeed speaking of something (of the thing itself, this one, for itself) or if I am giving an example, an example of something or an example of the fact that I can speak of something" (*ON*, 142–43, n. 14). Derrida offers the example of saying "I" and writing a text in the first person; we would not be able to contradict him if he said that rather than writing his autobiography he was writing about autobiography or that he was writing not about himself but on the "I" in general. More importantly, this undecidability does not require any discursive statement at all; it begins as soon as there is a trace, that is something, even a mute gesture. We are approaching literature wherever there is an event without an internal criteria that allows us to decide between the singular and the general, the idiomatic and the universal, the example and what it is an example of. This is exemplified in the example of the passion of Christ, which demonstrates the inadequacy of the example: in presenting itself as singular and inimitable, it is repeatable. To be recognized as unique, exemplary, it must be structurally iterable to offer itself as an example. Kant insists that respect for the law is "never addressed to things, [but] is nevertheless aimed at persons only insofar as they offer an *example* of the moral law: this respect is due only to the moral law, which never shows itself but is only the cause of that respect" (*BL*,

190). As we have seen, the passion of Christ exemplifies the invisible secret of the moral law precisely because he fails to be an example of the moral law, and this is the secret of his success. As the exemplary example, he demonstrates the inadequacy of the example to present the moral law and thereby preserves the law as universal and singular. As the visible presentation of the "divine invisibility and the sovereignty of reason," Christ presents no determinable "content"; that is, no revelation of a hidden truth but gives himself as secret, the moral law that commands respect precisely because it is without a proper sense. Respect for the law is possible on the basis of its being subject to "iterative identification which contaminates the pure singularity and untranslatability of the idiomatic secret" (*ON*, 140, n. 10).

The secret is what preserves the law and contaminates it. To accede to the law, in the form of a person or example, means the end of the law. We are enjoined to respect the law, but respect for the law requires that the law must remain an idiom, unique, and never be an object of the understanding; it cannot be known. The law is without history, genesis, or derivation, and narrative accounts, like Kafka's, that would attempt to enter into it, says Derrida, remain extrinsic to it (*BL*, 191). What remains secret in the law is "the law itself, that which makes laws of these laws. . . . The law yields by withholding itself, without imparting its provenance and its site. This silence and discontinuity constitute the phenomenon of the law" (*BL*, 192). I want to emphasize that the connection between literature and law does not rest in some notion that literature, as mimetic or symbolic representation, makes visible the hidden law or even tells in thematic fashion of the inaccessibility of the law (that literature can do this is not disputed, which is one point Derrida makes about "Before the Law"). The secret is a matter of the trace, both in the sense of writing and of literature (see *ON*, 132, n. 1). We have seen this in our discussion of the prohibition of the law/the prohibited law: the law announces itself without revealing itself. It says *there is* (something) (secret). I resort to the bracketing of the object in order to emphasize that what Derrida calls "law," "secret," "example" concern the trace, which is neither a place or a thing but is there wherever the real crosses the fictive, the singular crosses the general, or wherever something happens that we would like to keep alive. It is the minimal structure that "begins" or carries within itself repetition. It does not produce identity or self-presence but promises or pledges itself as the writing of the other. This structure of unity and alterity in repetition constitutes the "eventiality"—if I may be allowed such a term—of the event; beyond it we cannot go, but it is what promises a future.

The secret, Derrida says, is a matter of the trace both in the manner of writing, the general system of referral and iterability, and the writing of literature, in the sense that literature as narrative fiction and as fiction of narrative (the double genitive encompasses fictive narration and the narrativity of fiction) is the very "place" where we experience the aporia of meaning, essence, or truth. In its character as being-suspended, its bracketing or *epochê* of reference, literature never dissociates itself from reference but never allows us to forget *différance*, the unaccountable. When Derrida says that the quasi-event of the origin of moral law "bears the mark of fictive narrativity," he points not only to the recourse to narrative to explain what cannot be explained but to the origin of literature and law in the quasi-event (we can say "aporia") that demands and denies the story. That fictive narrativity exceeds our conventional notion of literature is born out by the similar point made by Derrida's analysis of the example in Kant. Literature is exemplary of what happens everywhere and every time there is something that cannot be controlled or legislated or made accountable in an economy of presence and re-presentation. What literature tells us is that in order for something to be, there must already have been instituted a system of marks, traces, etc.—that is, writing—that can make what is go astray. The aporetic condition of the eventiality of the event, of which law/secret is an example, necessitates that in order for there to be something rather than nothing, *différance* remains irreducible. As non-phenomenalizable, the non-presentation of the secret/law precipitates singularity by opening the future, the to-come or *à-venir*, because the possibility of responding to the secret or the law depends upon its structure as inaccessible or unreadable. Were it accessible or present, fulfilled by an intentional consciousness, there would be no possibility of response. Iterability contaminates the pure singularity of the law and the idiomatic secret, and this ensures the possibility of respect for the law. Without iterability, repetition, and simulacrum (such as Freud's simulacrum of narrative), there can be no possibility of law and responsibility, "that is, of their recurrence. Impurity is principally inherent in the purity of duty, that is, its iterability. Flouting all possible oppositions: *there* would be the secret [*là serait le secret*]. The secret of passion, the passion of the secret" (*ON*, 142, n. 12). The secret is there is no secret, nothing the secret would confide. No experience can assure us of the *there is* and no author can assure us of the truth hidden behind the text. Even if the author intended a meaning, the possibility of truth is held in non-truth. Consequently, the possibility of "truth" depends upon the pure phenomenality of the text, the possibility of the simulacrum and of repetition. Literature does not tell us what is hidden in the secret but that the secret hides nothing: "There is in literature, in the *exemplary* secret of literature, a chance of saying everything without touching upon the secret" (*ON*, 29).

Something like literature begins whenever it is impossible to decide between the example and what it is an example of. "And passion is always a matter of example" (*ON*, 141, n. 10). We cannot know absolutely if the passion of Christ exemplifies the moral law or is a visible substitute for the invisible moral law. This is the exemplarity of the passion: it demonstrates the inadequacy of the example; the secret of divine invisibility remains (secret). This aporia is not a dead-end; it impassions. For Kant the moral law is always idiomatic and morality precludes imitation; the example can serve only as encouragement. The exemplarity of the passion of Christ lies in its being at once idiomatic and iterable: this is the secret of the passion; it keeps the secret intact. The passion bears witness to the possibility of exceeding what it would represent. It neither answers to itself nor does it correspond to or answer for anything else. What then is revealed in the passion? It is the exemplary revelation of referral and difference, the conditions of all self-reference. Were the passion a matter of revelation in the conventional sense, it would be an absolute event, an apocalypse without remainder. To be what it is, exemplary, it must be without self-presentation. "The secret gives rise to no *process* [*procès*, which also means "lawsuit" and "trial"]. It may appear to give rise to one (indeed it always does so), it may lend itself to it, but it never surrenders to it" (*ON*, 27). Consequently, the secret can never be reduced to some judicial, legislative, philosophical, or theological program. If it always gives rise to one, it does so by virtue of its muteness, its nonrelation to phenomenality and history. The possibility of ethics lies in this non-responsibility, this non-response. We can always not respect the law. By this Derrida does not mean a Kantian or Christian notion of freedom, for non-response is more original and more secret than the modalities of responsibility. He locates in this non-responsibility the condition for justice. Justice requires a certain dissymmetry between the general and the singular, a suspension of axioms or rules that would guide a decision. This is to be distinguished from an empirical suspension of positive law in the name of a higher law and from notions that would untie judgment from the law. The responsibility invoked in non-responsibility is a temporalizing of judgment, not an abandonment of law. To be just, a decision must suspend the law, bracket it, so that an interval or space opens in which the demand for justice will be felt.

In "Force of Law," Derrida writes that the decision is structurally finite since it marks the interruption of the juridico-cognitive "deliberation that precedes it." A decision must be precipitative, "acting in the night of non-knowledge and non-rule," which does not entail the absence of rule but is a reinstitution of rules that cannot precede any knowledge as such (*FL*, 967). This notion that decision is not the application of a rule but the *re*institution of what follows upon the act leads Derrida to conclude that acts of justice have the performative structure of speech acts, as opposed to constatives, which are defined as statements. "A constative can be *juste* (right), in the sense of *justesse*, never in the sense of justice." To be just, a decision must not be the consequence or the effect of historical or theoretical knowledge but must be an irruptive repetition, an act that institutes what it cites. Because a performative can be just only "by founding itself on conventions and so on other anterior performatives, buried or not, it always maintains within itself some irruptive violence." The performative utterance at once invents, transforms, and cites the very event it enacts. It designates in the sense that a decision at once cuts or divides and founds itself on some anterior performative (such as instituted law). The just decision, even when it takes the form of a constative statement that points to a law, is somehow reflexive. When I announce a judgment, I implicitly do so in a fashion that is performative. "'I speak to you, I address myself to you to tell you that this is true, that things are like this, I promise you.'" This reflexivity is at once the making of the law, its institution, and its irruption, to the extent that it produces a dissymmetry (*FL*, 969).

The undecidable relation between justice and law is not an impasse where one is caught between respect for singularity and the imperative of guiding or determinate rules but is the experience of the anxiety that comes in the performativity of decision, where one gives oneself up to "the impossible decision" and assumes the law at the same time. Ordinarily, one appeals to the law as the guiding principle of a decision, and in the name of justice, one disavows the harsh legalism that would mandate the content of a decision. Even this notion, familiar to us in debates centered upon automatic sentencing for certain crimes, bases itself on the notion that justice constitutes a horizon, "the opening and the limit that defines an infinite progress or a period of waiting" (as in the opening words of William Gaddis's *A Frolic of His Own*, "You get justice in the next world, in this world you have the law"[22]). Justice, says Derrida, does not wait. A decision is always structurally finite; it rends time (*FL*, 967). Therefore, it is impossible to say "*in the present* that a decision *is* just (that is, free and responsible), or that someone *is* a just man— even less, '*I am* just'" (*FL*, 961–63). In other words, justice cannot be an object of knowledge, nor is it something determined in a present, no more than it can be said to rest in an infinite horizon of expectation. Justice is to come, *à venir*; it has the dimension of an event that, "as event, exceeds calculation, rules, programs, anticipations and so forth. Justice as the experience of absolute alterity is unpresentable, but it is the chance of the event and the condition of history" (*FL*, 971). Literature, in its character as incalculable event, in its suspension or bracketing of its relation to meaning and reference, makes law.

I began by quoting Derrida's "aporetic conclusion" that literature, which is "destined to remain improper," without essence, has something to do with "the law of the name, the name of the law." In Kafka's text, the man learns at the moment of his death that the door is unique and meant only for him. He "comes to his end without reaching his end" (*BL*, 210). In leaving the man (and the reader) before the law, the text presents nothing but its own unreadability, "if one understands by this the impossibility of acceding to its proper significance. . . . The text guards itself, maintains itself—like the law, speaking only of itself, that is to say, of its non-identity with itself. It neither arrives nor lets anyone arrive. It is the law, makes the law and leaves the reader before the law." In its non-identity with itself, this text lays down the law (of its singularity); it performs the very law that keeps or maintains it as secret: "its 'form' presents or performs itself as a kind of personal identity entitled to absolute respect" (*BL*, 211). This denial of any hidden essence or proper meaning rests upon the principle of singularity, which must be distinguished from a concept of unity. Being without essence, the text is different from itself; "only then does the possibility of relation exist." Derrida says Kafka's text is unreadable—we are left "Before the Law" unable to gain entry to its proper significance. Yet it must be understood that "proper significance," like pure presence or absolute unity, is equivalent to or synonymous with death.

Without this gap or dissociation there would be no possibility of a relation to a reader, to the other, which is the condition of ethics and justice. We can extend this to what he says about readability—without the radical otherness of the text that prevents any full access to a proper significance, there could be no reading, no relation to the singularity of the text. We can only read the text in its difference from us, in its unreadability, and we know this in a mundane sense when we return to texts that leave us unsettled, those which provoke us by a certain difficulty or secretness that we cannot resolve; these are texts that leave us before the law. The lure of absolute understanding is a fantasy of identity (we can recognize here that this applies as much to the author as to the reader), a dream of knowing the text from the inside. When Derrida endorses Blanchot's and Levinas's notion of the "*rapport sans rapport*," the relation without relation, as the condition of responsibility and ethics, he says, "It is a relation in which the other remains absolutely transcendent. I cannot reach the other" (*VR*, 14). This absolute transcendence makes relation possible; it demands our response.

The inaccessible law/text announces or reveals the structure of referentiality upon which literature and law depend. The text declares itself at once as belonging to a tradition or heritage we call "literary," which itself is constituted by positive law of copyright, authorship, etc. Watched over by the law whose guardians include literary critics and philosophers, literature is determined by what is external to it, positive law, and at the same time, it has the right to say anything, which means "literature" exceeds the boundaries that define literature as literature. "It would no longer be itself if it were itself" (*BL*, 215). "Literature" is not some essence belonging to literature, but once we situate literature within textuality in general, then we can begin to recognize that "it is an institution which consists in transgressing and transforming, thus in producing its constitutional law; or, to put it better, in producing discursive forms, 'works' and 'events' in which the very possibility of a fundamental constitution is at least 'fictionally' contested, threatened, deconstructed, presented in its very precariousness" (*SIL*, 72).

At this point, Derrida is very close to aligning literature with deconstruction. The "juridical subversity" of literature lies in its being constituted, its being as constituted, which is to say literature is neither purely natural nor purely conventional or instituted. Once we admit that it belongs to the structure of textuality, as do other texts and institutions, particularly that of the law, then we must acknowledge that being without essence, literature bears in itself a temporal equivocation—literature's present, its now, is not now but to come. This "inadequation between the now and now" designates the possibility or, rather, the demand, of literature's (un)readability, its demand for a countersignature (*VR*, 24). The literary text is not one, a transparent univocity, but already repeats itself and dissociates itself from itself.

"Before the Law" is a twice-told tale: it re-marks the law of law in its content (there can be no entrance to the origin of law) and performs it as event (as idiomatic or singular, it re-marks its own inaccessibility, even comments on it in the dialogue between the priest and Joseph K). When we ask, what is literature and who judges, we appeal to the conventions and laws that Kafka's parable tells us cannot be interior to literature. His story tells of the being-before-the-law of literature, if I can use such a phrase to describe how literature remarks in performative fashion the impossibility of accounting for its own origin, its own law. This reflexive re–marking of the law of law means that "literature itself makes law, emerging in that place where the law is made" (*BL*, 216). This place is the non-place, *atopos*, of the aporia. In order to have a relation to the law, one must interrupt the relation, as "Before the Law" tells us. Thus, Derrida remarks that literature in its equivocity "can *play the law* [*jouer la loi*], repeating it while diverting or circumventing it. . . . In the fleeting moment when it plays the law, a literature passes literature." It "splits the being-before-the-law," being at once both prior to it and before it (*BL*, 216). In its performative capacity to remark its own institutionality (that is, its equivocacy as a legal fiction), literature plays at being the law and deceives the law (both meanings are implied by the French "*jouer la loi*"). We can say it parasites the law in the sense that it is not only dependent on positive law for its identity, but also, insofar as it shares with law the revealing power of language, the power to testify to and affirm truth, it also exposes the proximity of this truth-making power to fiction. There can be no law without repetition—and this is true whether we speak of positive law or natural law—and, consequently, law is structurally linked to the simulacrum and impurity (cf. *ON*, 142, n. 12). Literature, however, splits being-before-the-law because as it is an institution that produces discursive forms that contest its own constitution, its being-before-the-law. Literature remarks, in other words, the failure of the law to be present, which is the experience of the aporia as told to us in the story of the man from the country. He does not cross the threshold but remains outside the law. The law is meant for him alone, and he is forbidden entrance to it.

The law cannot be made present, which is another way of saying that a just decision cannot be an object of knowledge. The eventness of the event of deciding consists in its non-knowledge, its moment of suspense or *epochê*. This non-knowledge, I hasten to add, is not ignorance or indifference but is structural. For a decision to be just, it must submit to the heterogeneity of not-knowing, to "a more ancient, more originary experience, if you will, of the secret" (*Points*, 201). This *epochê* of the decision is something that never takes place in a present. Literature shares with law this anxiety of the decision, which is made clearer in the later essay "Force of Law," where Derrida says that law, as institution, is deconstructible, but justice is not. What gives us the passion for justice is its undeconstructibility. As non-identical with itself, non-calculable, justice is "infinite transcendence" and can never be fully answered (*VR*, 16). Only when one is not responsible to the calculable order of absolute reason, can one begin to be responsible for the singularity of the other. A response that would be just must assume for itself the law of this singularity and enact it in another singular event.[23] We touch the transcendence of the law only when we accept its ineradicable otherness, its non-identity with itself. No response would be possible if the singular did not carry within itself the possibility of repetition and parasitism; this is the condition of its intelligibility and its ruin. Accordingly, respect for the law demands this acceptance of the iterability that contaminates the pure singularity of the idiomatic secret (see *ON*, 140, n. 10). "Abolish the possibility of the simulacrum and of external repetition, and you abolish the possibility both of the law and of duty themselves, that is, of their recurrence" (*ON*, 142, n. 12). Impurity is inherent in responsibility inasmuch as the possibility of response begins in the irreducible otherness that announces itself as such, as what it is not, as that which is not recuperable in a present.

The exemplarity of literature lies in its capacity to play with all the marks and non-marks of the other. We are familiar since, at least, *Of Grammatology* that the mark or trace is the visible sign of the absent other, but the substitution of trace for other depends upon the arche-trace, the absolutely other that is not the absence of a presence. The arche-trace is the possibility of all signification, both graphic and phonic. It is, he says, unmotivated, in the sense that it is not intentionally or naturally linked to the signified, and as instituted, it exceeds the metaphysical opposition between nature and culture. The arche-trace is not something created or installed, instituted in a conventional sense, and cannot be thought outside "a structure of reference where difference appears *as such*" (*OG*, 46–47). The appearance of difference *as such* means the appearance of difference, the other, as "self-occultation. When the other announces itself as such, it presents itself in the dissimulation of itself . . . that is to say the dissimulation of its 'as such', [which] has always already begun and no structure of the entity escapes it" (*OG*, 47). The appearance of the other, the dissimulation of its *as such*, is constitutive of presence. The arche-trace is an absolute past, the always already there of difference, and thus the "origin" of sense, time, and space (*OG*, 65–66).

Consequently, when Derrida writes of the contamination or inseparability of duty and nonduty, responsibility and nonresponsibility, he reminds us that their relation does not conform to some empirical or phenomenal limit that circumscribes an ideal but that the very possibility of responsibility or duty is structurally linked to the occultation of difference, the dissemination of the other that has always already begun. Abolish the parasitical simulacrum and you abolish the possibility of duty and responsibility.

Thus, nonduty and nonresponsibility are not accidents that befall duty but are necessary for its possibility, its repetition or appearance. In "Passions," Derrida refers to Kant, who said it is "'absolutely impossible to establish by experience with complete certainty a single case' in the world" whether an act of moral sacrifice is performed out of pure duty or in conformity with duty (a distinction based upon that between spirit and the letter of the law) (*ON*, 142, n. 12). Kant's distinction between pure and impure duty turns upon the belief that a responsible act must be singular; it should testify to its uniqueness and irreplaceability. Yet a responsible act that would testify to itself as pure would at once declare that it be repeatable and universal, even that repeatability be a postulate of the pure act. It would be exemplary and a matter of passion. The structure of exemplarity makes morality possible because it keeps secret, occults, the law that would destroy morality and turn pure duty into conformity with duty. The responsible act that stands in relation to what it would act in the name of—duty, moral law—must always already be repeatable. The example would have already begun.

I quoted Derrida above on the inadequacy of the example; it cannot be both singular and representative, at once singular and regulative. This is why Kant must treat Christ's passion as an example against the example; as delimited by sensibility, it cannot serve as the idea of the moral law, which would be reserved for God. Exemplarity begins with the instituted trace, which means it cannot be thought without thinking the possibility of imitation and repetition. What Derrida calls the "economy of exemplarity" is the formalizing power whereby what is singular affirms itself as singular in splitting itself, dividing itself; it is the becoming-iterable as the constitution of the singular. Iterability is the minimal structure that makes history comprehensible and is the condition for translatability as well. Once we have marks and non-marks, we have exemplarity and something like literature will have begun. The logic of the example is that a finite being, a particular, can stand in place of the universal, but no finite being can "provide an economy . . . of anything that iterability contaminates" (*ON*, 141, n. 10). A certain heteronomy already contaminates the example, which must efface itself if it is to serve as example, as the instantiation of something that transcends or lies outside it. For example, the passion of Christ must efface itself in order to serve as an example of moral reason. A self-contained or self-determined example would be an idol. The example must not only efface itself, but it also must be determined by what lies outside it. Once we admit this, then we acknowledge that not only may the example be passed over but we can never decide what the example exemplifies.

It is this disjunction or heteronomy of the example that permits exemplarism: "Each thing, each being, you, me, the other, each X, each name, and each name of God can become the example of other substitutable X's. A process of absolute formalization. Any other is totally other [*Tout autre est tout autre*]" (*ON*, 76). Exemplarism is a matter of testimony: it is the formalizing process whereby every idiom or singularity bears witness to what it is and what it is not, without its being determined by what is inside it (*ON*, 77). Exemplarism can be contrasted with Hegelian dialectic, in which negation joins self and other in an undivided whole. In Hegel's dialectic of self and other, man as knowing subject is separated from what is known, and the task of philosophy is to show how this and other oppositions, such as infinite and finite, are identical in their opposition. Identity and difference are linked through negation; neither one can stand on its own but is mediated by its other. The substitutability of one thing for the other is the work of contradiction whereby something passes over into its opposite as a result of the identity of identity and difference in the Absolute.

Whereas difference is maintained in the identity of identity and difference, exemplarism always carries with it a remainder, difference *as such*, that permits the liberty of an other substituting for any other. This constituting alterity of the same defeats all dialectic. The irreducible retention of difference within identity, the trace, which maintains itself in its difference from its other, is "older" than self and other and explains the possibility of identity as resting upon a minimal reference to an other. The trace as arche-trace marks the spacing or interval within presence that constitutes and divides it.

The non-phenomenality of the trace, its character as *différance*, means that we know it only by its effects. There is no trace *as such*. It cannot be derived "from a presence or from an originary nontrace . . . which would make of it an empirical mark" (*OG*, 61). It precedes any primitive identity or absolute simplicity; "it permits the articulation of signs among themselves within the same abstract order—a phonic or graphic text for example" (*OG*, 62–63). The pure trace or *différance* founds the oppositions between sensible and intelligible, signifier and signified, but is "not more sensible than intelligible" (*OG*, 62). It is in this sense of arche-trace that language must already be writing and history a text. The misunderstanding that Rodolphe Gasché has been most insistent upon correcting is this belief that arche-writing is a kind of literary writing. Arche-writing is, he says, without worldly value and essence but is "the quasitranscendental synthesis that accounts for the necessary corruption of the idealities, or transcendentals of all sorts, by what they are defined against, and at the very moment of their constitution." Arche-writing has no extratextual referent; nothing is outside the general system of writing and difference. It does not fulfill itself in any referent, empirical or transcendental, that might halt the play of referral.[24] As I have indicated in my discussion of aporia, this notion of writing does not point to some abyss or ontological absence, which would only be thinkable in conjunction with presence, but expresses the nonphenomenal character of the general text. Because Gasché's argument against assimilating Derrida's thought on writing and textuality to literary writing has been so authoritative, I take the time to sum up his analysis of the notion of the text. At this point, I have said enough about writing to allow us to conclude that writing in general or the generality of writing is something "older," more "originary," than writing as material notation or the production of visible signs. When we speak of general writing, we refer to the infrastructures (trace, *différance*, iterability) that account for the possibility of such idealities as identity, meaning, presence, etc. *Différance* does not depend on any sensible plenitude, whether spoken or written, nor does it exist, but there is no plenitude, no sameness or identity, without *différance*.

I wish to emphasize that just as general writing should not be confused with writing in the colloquial sense, literariness should not be confused with our traditional concept of literature. The misunderstanding that grew up around Derrida's introduction of "writing" and "textuality" were only partially corrected by assertions that he uses these terms metaphorically because such defenses ignored his argument in "White Mythology" that metaphor is thought within metaphysics. It would be more accurate to say that writing and text in the colloquial sense are metaphors of a general writing and a general textuality, the system of infrastructures that are revealed by deconstruction.

Gasché wishes to counter those critics who take Derrida's statement "there is no extra-text" to mean that the text is without any external referent and is purely self-reflexive. Besides reminding us that Derrida does not deny referentiality and the referent, Gasché indicates that this phrase points to the structural impossibility of the text fulfilling itself either in some extra-textual referent or in some internal identity with which it could coincide (*TM*, 281). This is a structural, not an empirical or ontological concept of the text, and it accounts for why we can say a conventional literary text, a poem or a novel, may have an inexhaustible meaning— there is no extratextual referent or signified that would serve as the fulfilling object of the work, which is not to deny a relation to otherness but is to insist that this relation remains unfulfilled. Even if we assumed there could be a totalizing referent for the poem or novel with which it could coincide, we would still have to demonstrate that the meaning of the referent itself could be exhausted. Because of the dependence of the bounded text on the text in general, there can be no empirical or intelligible endpoint to the process of reference (cf. *TM*, 282).

What is perhaps more troubling than this denial of the fulfilling function to the text is Derrida's statement that the text does not exist: "If the text does not, to the letter, exist, then *there is* [*il y a*] perhaps a text" (*D*, 270). The *il y a* translates Heidegger's thinking of the gift of Being: Being is not, but there is (*es gibt*) Being. In the late work *Time and Being*, Heidegger writes that to think Being one has to disregard Being insofar as it is thought within metaphysics and interpreted in terms of beings or entities: "Being *is* not. There is, It gives Being as the unconcealing of presencing."[25] We recognize here Heidegger's attempt to step outside metaphysics and the thinking of Being as present. Beginning with *Being and Time*, he asserted that the ontico-ontological difference, the difference between Being and beings, has been forgotten in the history of metaphysics. In *Identity and Difference*, he writes, "we think of Being rigorously only when we think of it in its difference with beings, and of beings in their difference with Being."[26] Thinking is bringing the difference between Being and beings into view. Being is not above or beyond beings, or entities of this world, nor is it to be thought in distinction from beings as if it had some representational or constitutive relation to beings, which would make it another being. Being is nothing but this difference, but this difference is also non-phenomenalizable (Derrida will say that this makes it impossible to speak of Being except in ontic metaphor [*WD*, 138]). Whenever we employ a verbal formula on the order of "Being is . . ." we obscure Being. We can only say, "Being is not, but there is (*es gibt*) Being."

What has this to do with Derrida's "text" and the literary text? Taking up the latter, we can say that the text is not its material embodiment. Husserl pointed out that the text is an ideality; were I to destroy a copy of Goethe's *Faust*, I would not have destroyed his *Faust*.[27] I will return to this in some detail in a later chapter, but I simply wish to emphasize this point, because even a manuscript cannot be considered the full instantiation of the text, which is something editors acknowledge when they construct an ideal text that may not correspond to either the author's manuscript or any single edition. Something more, however, is at stake in Derrida's claim that "If the text does not, to the letter, exist, then *there is* [*il y a*] perhaps a text." *There is*, Gasché writes, does not mean the same thing as "to exist," but is an ideality, such as the principles of geometry or, in our example from Husserl, Goethe's *Faust*. *There is* "characterizes the mode of givenness of phenomena in general, and of Being in particular, as the phenomenon par excellence." Being, according to Heidegger, does not exist; it is not a being because as such it would not be able to ground or account for what it is supposed to explain. Being "only has the mode of *being there*" (*TM*, 284–85).

Derrida's "text" is not simply a translation of Heidegger's "Being," just as his *différance* is not difference. The general text does not belong to metaphysics because it has no being that can be determined: it does not exist. But there is/*Il y a*, perhaps, a text. *Il y a*, like the German *es gibt*, means "it gives," as well as "there is," which is the more common translation. The "text is said *to be there* only if it *is not*, if it is not endowed with being, if it lacks presence" (*TM*, 284). This is not to say the text is an absence but that the general text is not a phenomenon, which means it is neither absent nor present because it does not belong to Being but to the margin of Being. As the nonphenomenolizable, the general text accounts for the appearance, the phenomenality, of texts without presuming the order that grounds appearance—that is, the opposition between appearance and essence that this order presupposes; "this also means that Being itself, in order to be the gift of Being, must already be within the text" (*TM*, 288).

Gasché's argument corrects those who think textuality means there is nothing outside language or that literature refers only to itself. The notion of general text is something other than Being and the opposition between appearance and essence, text and textuality. The determinations of being as present (or absent) and of the oppositions between appearance and essence belong to the text of metaphysics but not to the general text, which accounts for them *and* makes them impossible. Yet if Derrida's textuality is not literature and even means that there is no literature *as such*, he confesses to a secret passion for literature. In a note to "Passions," he writes, "literature is only exemplary of what happens everywhere, each time that there is some trace (or grace, i.e., each time that there is something rather than nothing, each time that *there is* (*es gibt*) and each time that it gives [*ça donne*] without return, without reason, freely, and *if there is* what there is then, i.e., *testimony, bearing witness*) and even before every *speech act* [English in original—Tr.] in the strict sense" (*ON*, 143–44, n. 14). Keeping in mind that for Heidegger, Being is not some ultimate signified but is "rooted in a system of languages and an historically determined 'significance'" (*OG*, 23), we should remark that the thinking of literature must take the form of the thinking of difference, between literature and literariness, example and essence. But to say what literature properly is we must erase this difference. In other words, any effort to determine the essence of some thing, to determine it *as such*, requires both the thinking of difference and the forgetting or effacing of the difference between Being and beings. To think something in its essence is a thinking oblivious to difference, to the other that determines it *as such*. This thinking is the dream of pure plenitude or full presence, which is impossible without the thinking of the trace, of *différance*, and this defeats such dreams even if it makes them possible.

At the conclusion of "Ousia and Grammê," Derrida argues that Heidegger's thinking of Being as difference (between Being and beings) is itself a metaphysical determination because, as the quotation above reveals, it is rooted in an onto-theological language and history, a system that, in Heidegger's own account, effaces difference. "In order to exceed metaphysics it is necessary that a trace be inscribed within the text of metaphysics, a trace that continues to signal not in the direction of another presence, or another form of presence, but in the direction of an entirely other text" (*M*, 65). Derrida's point, which, as we will see, embraces our discussion of law and literature, is that if difference (between Being and beings) cannot be named, cannot be thought—Being is nothing but the difference between Being and beings—then what has been forgotten in the history of metaphysics and the determination of Being as presence and of presence as present is not difference, which is always determined by the metaphysical order, but the *trace* of difference, which "is neither perceptible nor imperceptible." It is neither an essence nor something phenomenolizable. It is nothing present nor absent but produces its own erasure. "If one recalls that difference (is) itself other than absence and presence, (is) (itself) trace, it is indeed the trace of the trace that has disappeared in the forgetting of the difference between Being and beings" (*M*, 65–66). The ontico-ontological difference is not originary but is derivative of the trace of *différance* (*OG*, 23). The notions of trace and *différance* belong to the self-deferral that compromises all idealities or essences. Derrida exposes an aporia in Heidegger's claim that the ontico-ontological difference is not thinkable as such. The claim that the difference cannot appear is contradicted by Heidegger's naming the "ontico-ontological difference." This difference must be derivative of something more originary, something that erases itself in the metaphysical text—the trace.

What does it mean, we might ask, to say that literature is exemplary of what happens each time there is some trace? If the trace is "older" than difference, there is always already some trace. There is some trace each time that there is something rather than nothing, each time *there is*; that is, there is some trace each time there is/it gives (*il y a*). Literature is exemplary of what happens everywhere there is some trace, the infinite referral to the other. Erasure belongs to the trace as part of its structure—the trace is not an entity—and the trace, which cannot be thought apart from difference, never appears as such but "produces itself as self-occultation" (*OG*, 47). The trace of the other presents itself as self-dissimulation. Literature, which is inseparable from the possibility of saying everything, is exemplary of what happens everywhere there is some trace, everywhere "difference appears *as such* and thus permits a certain liberty of variations among the full terms. The absence of *another* here-and-now, another transcendental present, of *another* origin of the world appearing as such, presenting itself as irreducible absence within the presence of the trace, is not a metaphysical formula substituted for a scientific concept of writing." It not only questions metaphysics itself but "describes the structure implied by the 'arbitrariness of the sign,'" once one thinks its possibility without resorting to derived oppositions between presence and absence, nature and culture (*OG*, 46–47).

It would seem, then, that "literature" names what happens when the ceaseless referral to the other begins, which is to say literature is exemplary of what happens, that is, of the announcement of the completely other within what it is not. "Literature" is a strange event that invents an other "capable of countersigning and saying 'yes'" and thus confirming, testifying, to the uniqueness of this event, this signature (*SIL*, 74). This "yes" or countersignature invented by the work does not follow it in chronological fashion but is instituted by it as its own possibility. The singularity of the work is guaranteed by the trait of referral that betrays the new work by revealing it. "The trace, where the relationship with the other is marked, articulates its possibility in the entire field of the entity [*étant*], which metaphysics has defined as the being-present starting from the occulted movement of the trace" (*OG*, 47). This passage is important because the notion that the instituted trace precedes the entity disrupts the opposition between nature and convention, *physis* and *nomos*, which lies at the heart of Saussure's theory of the sign and most, if not all, theories of literature. What the instituted trace puts in question is "the idea of naturalism rather than that of attachment" (*OG*, 46). We should see in the appearance of difference *as such* within the structure of reference the possibility of literature saying anything. This is not a matter of the capriciousness of language, the inventiveness of the author, the arbitrariness of the sign, or even of freedom from censorship as an enlightenment ideal, but of the instituted trace, which marks the possibility of the other in the field of entities or beings that metaphysics defines as presence. The occulted movement of the trace has already begun and nothing escapes it. Literature begins not with the pure invention of language—it is no more cultural than natural—but with the "movement of 'unmotivatedness' [that] passes from one structure to the other when the 'sign' [arbitrary and conventional] crosses the stage of the 'symbol' [motivated and natural (and excluded by Saussure from linguistics)]" (*OG*, 47).

Literature is the event (itself) or, as he says in an interview, more an event than any other because less natural and, therefore, impossible to verify, not having any criteria, any essence (see *SIL*, 73). The instituted trace introduces the possibility of saying anything because it disrupts the ontological difference and the appearance of beings *as such*; it is the possibility of the appearance of difference *as such*, the retention of the other in the same and the dislocation of presence, the present, Being. It is the (structural) possibility of a wholly other identity.

Literature's capacity to say anything is not capriciousness but is a possibility inherent in the movement of the trace wherein the other announces itself as other. It is the appearing of what metaphysics has defined as "non-living," that is, the non-natural or instituted. This "event" is impossible to verify because it is referral to the other and neither essence nor existence. I appear to be on the verge of saying literature is the infinite play of *différance* and, consequently, equating it with writing. But "literature," as I use it here, is not literature in its colloquial sense, which might better be thought of as a metaphor for "literature." When Derrida speaks of literature as event, he refers to literature both in its special sense and in its conventional sense. "Literature" is not the ground or being of literature, but in its mode of exemplifying what happens everywhere there is some trace, "literature" breaches the order by which literature can be said to take place or institute itself. "Literature" as event is not some entity nor is it the general text but is the eventiality of event, even, I would like to say, experience (itself). And there is nothing "natural" about it.

When asked why literature constitutes such an important object for him, Derrida replies that what counts for him "is the act of writing or rather, since it is perhaps not altogether an act, *the experience of writing: to leave a trace that dispenses with, that is even destined to dispense with the present of its originary inscription*, of its 'author' as one might say in an insufficient way" (*Points*, 346; my emphasis). Literature, or rather the experience of writing, he says, "gives one a way that is better than ever for thinking the present and the origin, death, life, or survival." Although the trace cannot be confined to what is called literature, the experience of writing gives one a way to experience the event as trace, the constituting possibility of self and other, which means that it is an experience "older" than difference because the "trace is never present without dividing itself by referring to another present" (*Points*, 346). It accounts for difference but is not itself the difference between self (Derrida's dispensable author) and other; it is the minimal structure by which reference to self takes place through reference to an other, which is why erasure belongs to its structure. Since the trace is "the simulacrum of a presence that dislocates itself, displaces itself, refers itself," it maintains itself by setting aside, erasing its mark. The structure of the trace inverts the metaphysical concept of the present and "becomes a function in a structure of generalized reference [*renvoi*]," that is, of return (*M*, 24).

Derrida's characterization of the experience of writing implies literature is the experience of the *renvoi*, of what begins by coming back. This is its gift, its better way of thinking the present, origin, life, death, survival. Although the trace cannot be limited to what is called literature, literature remains privileged for Derrida because "of what it thematizes about the event of writing, and in part because of what, in its political history, links literature to that principal authorization to 'say everything' whereby it is related in such a unique fashion to what is called truth, fiction, simulacrum, science, philosophy, law, right, democracy" (*Points*, 346). Literature, as the experience of the trace, thematizes the economy of institution or formalization, the possibility of thinking structure and its limits. It is, therefore, as much counter-institution as institution. It is both one and the other. This is the "origin" literature shares with the law: constituted by alterity, the detour through the other, they are without essence; simulacrum belongs to their very possibility.

Literature is not the text in general, nor is it arche-writing, but Derrida says literature may be an example of some general textuality. In the same context, he remarks that *différance*, arche-trace, supplement and other quasi-transcendentals "are implicated in every literary text, but not all texts are literary—Gasché is right to remind us of this. Once you have situated the structure of textuality in general, you have to determine its becoming-literature, if I can put it like that, and then distinguish between fiction in general (not all fiction is literature, all literature is not strictly of the order of fiction), poetry and belles-lettres, the literature which has been called that for only a few centuries, etc." (*SIL*, 71). The "becoming-literature" of textuality would be something like phenomenological thematization, although this designation is inaccurate to the extent that it involves raising the givenness of evidence in ordinary experience to a level of reflection. We can say, however, that becoming-literature does not follow upon the givenness of textuality but arises with it in the spacing or interval that makes thematization possible (and ruins it) (see *IOG*, 140–41). This explains why the literary text can have no fulfilling object of referral, or why meaning cannot be exhausted. The becoming-literature of textuality describes the manner in which the quasi-transcendentals fold back upon themselves to re-mark the general structure of textuality without reaching any reflexive totality. This interval or "fold is not a form of reflexivity. If by reflexivity one means the motion of consciousness or self-presence that plays such a determining role in the Hegel's speculative logic and dialectic . . . then reflexivity is but an effect of the fold as text" (*D*, 270). Becoming-literature is not a totalizing movement of self-reflection but is the movement of dissemination or what happens when there is some trace. In other words, literature as it is conventionally understood has been dependent on what lies outside it, particularly in mimetic theories, but writing of Mallarmé, Derrida says, "Literature is at once reassured and threatened by the fact of depending only on itself, standing in the air, all alone, aside from Being" (*D*, 280). This self-dependence cannot possibly comprehend self-reflexive totality, as the phrase "aside from Being" tells us, but signals that literature is without ontological status.

   Literature begins, or rather, there is literature, which is to say literature in Derrida's sense of the term is more an event than a thing or entity—it is not contained by its phenomenolization, but is characterized by its exemplarity. Then what is it exemplary of if it is not the presentation of an essence? Literature has/is the structure of exemplarity; it is owing to literature "one can say: I can speak of myself without further ado [*sans façon*], the secret remains intact, my politeness unblemished, my reserve unbreached . . . I am responding without responding" (*ON*, 144, n. 14). In other words, it is owing to the structure of exemplarity that one can say something other than itself. Thus, we must distinguish the structure of exemplarity from paradox, in which I say something that is merely contrary to or beside logic, from contradiction, in which I say something that the act of saying or what is said denies, and from irony in its conventional sense as saying the opposite of what I mean. Exemplarity permits something to be, say, do something other that itself, which is exactly that, other than itself, that is, the self-differing, self-occulting movement of the trace. Literature is only exemplary of what happens everywhere there is this possibility, and this possibility is everywhere.

This is why he likes literature, or rather, "something *about it* [I take this to mean its being without essence or any self-determination], which above all cannot be reduced to some aesthetic quality, to some source of formal pleasure, this would be *in place of the secret*. In place of an absolute secret. There would be passion. . . . *In place of the secret*: there where nevertheless everything is said and where what remains is nothing—but the remainder, not even of literature" (*ON*, 28). The literariness of literature consists in its suspension or *epochê* of the essence, its remarking of its own impossibility of achieving an identity in a present. Being neither natural nor instituted, literature plays at the law, plays at being/giving the law insofar is it reveals the founding violence of iterability: in order to be what it is, a work, it must be singular, a performance that takes place just once, and *at the same time*, to be identified as such, as a work and, therefore, idiomatic, it must be iterable (for any responsible reading of a literary work, or any responsible judgment, begins by recognizing the singularity of what is read/judged). For the work to be singular, iterability demands that the work repeat itself singularly, to alter itself in order to preserve or conserve itself as singular. "Iterability inscribes conservation in the essential structure of foundation" (*FL*, 1009). In all rigor, iterability precludes the possibility of a pure founding, a pure judgment in the sense of one free from suspense. Any founded "thing" is a ruin, but ruin, Derrida says, is not "a negative thing. . . What else is there to love, anyway? One cannot love a monument, a work of architecture, an institution as such except in an experience itself precarious in its fragility: it hasn't always been there, it will not always be there, it is finite" (*FL*, 1009). To love it as mortal is to love it through its birth/death because iterability makes of the thing or text a ghost, something that begins by returning (which is what is meant by beginning as iterability).

Iterability exposes the originary violence of foundations and the conserving violence that perpetuates the thing as originary. I have discussed above the three levels of violence—arche-writing, the law, reflection—that Derrida locates in Levi-Strauss. Here I wish to propose that this third level, which we can now call "literary" but cannot confine to what is conventionally known as literature, exposes the iterability that severs the proper from its self-sameness. This third violence, Derrida writes, not only "reveals the first nomination, which was already an expropriation, but it exposes also that which since then functioned as the proper, the so-called proper, substitute of the deferred proper, *perceived* by the *social* and *moral consciousness* as the proper, the reassuring seal of self-identity, the secret" (*OG*, 112; trans. modified). The third violence of reflection exposes the arche-violence of the proper, its being already improper, and simultaneously with this, it exposes the second violence, the law, as that which supplements and conserves nature, the so-called proper. The law functions in place of the proper; it functions as the secret of the name. This makes it necessary, but insofar as the proper itself is already improper, the law is also necessarily violent. Literature shares with law the revealing power that there is something secret, an event that takes place just once and renews itself by conserving itself and dispropriating itself. This event is without a proper content but is the stratification and temporization of writing; we cannot say of it "it is there" but only "it exists." It is the possibility of non-response, the possibility of not being drawn into the process, be it legal, literary, philosophical, that would regulate and account for the violence but opens the possibility of something new. "The secret gives rise to no *process*" (*ON*, 27), that is, to no trial but perhaps it is the possibility of *The Trial (Der Prozess)* and other singular events.

2

Edmond Jabès and the Question of the Jewish Unhappy Consciousness: Reflections on Deconstruction

> The Jewish consciousness is indeed the unhappy conscious-
> ness, and *Le Livre des questions* is its poem; inscribed in the
> margins of the phenomenology of the spirit.
> —Jacques Derrida

In the previous chapter I advanced the thesis that literature's capacity to say everything derives from its exemplary status as the experience of writing as trace. The passion Derrida confesses for literature, "and passion is always a matter of example," may be said to derive from literature's endless referral to the other; "it always is, says, does something other, something other than itself, an itself which moreover is only that, something other than itself. For example or par excellence: philosophy" (*ON*, 141, n. 10; 144, n. 14). As the experience of the trace of the other, literature cannot be separated from alterity and negation but does not belong to the absolutely Other, absolute negation, but is possible on the basis of the arche-trace as the movement of the completely other. The completely other announces itself as such in what it is not; this self-occultation of the other opens up the possibility of reference and relation to an other. Literature, therefore, is not the arche-trace but is exemplary of what the arche-trace makes possible, the possibility of saying everything. Because literature is exemplary of the self-dissimulation of the other, it would contain as a part of its structure an undecidable destination, an endpoint, that is always to come, and as a discourse that announces what can never be verified—a destination to come—literature is apocalyptic, not because it announces this or that apocalypse but because the text becomes apocalyptic "as soon as one no longer knows who speaks or writes" (*AT*, 156).

Literature begins as soon as we recognize that no experience can assure us of the "there is," what is given (see *ON*, 141, n. 10). Literature is an apocalypse without apocalypse, example without example, which is to say it is derivable from the other. This makes literature a matter of testimony, a bearing witness to secrets, that can never be reduced to knowledge. Kant feared that such a promise of supernatural communication would be the death of philosophy.[1] Derrida's response is that this secret, which "exceeds the play of veiling/unveiling," is irreducible to the truth (*ON*, 26): as what refers without ever being in relation to an other, it makes relation possible without itself ever being answerable to anything (*ON*, 30).

Derrida's secret may seem to move in the direction of mystification, but, in fact, it concerns the limit of demystification, not in the name of the secret as incommunicable knowledge but as what traverses apocalyptic and revelatory discourses, the trace as the possibility of reference to the other. The revelation of a secret as promised by apocalypse would be the effacement of difference, hence his love of literature, which can speak of everything without touching upon the secret. If the secret is what makes relation to the other possible without ever belonging or being gathered in that relation, if it makes possible relation to the other without answering to the other, then it retains within its structure of reference a remainder, a difference, that cannot be reduced. The secret is an effect, but not the only one, of the trace. It can be contrasted with the desire for a total or proper meaning, which would require the absolute erasure of the trace. But any such dream of absolute presence, full meaning, plenitude, etc. is impossible without the trace.

In "Passions," Derrida writes that "literature is only exemplary of what happens everywhere, each time that there is some trace" (*ON*, 143, n. 14), which is tantamount to saying literature is exemplary or the example (itself) because we can never be done with the trace, which is not a present thing, no more than there is an example itself. The example always exceeds its identity, which "is why there are no examples, while at the same time there are only examples" (*ON*, 17). Literature is the exemplary example of the example, of the experience of the trace, which allows us to take examples or not. I have cited Derrida on the trace as the "retention of difference within a structure of reference" (*OG*, 46), which is the condition for any reference to self and other, and have indicated that the notion of the self-occultation of the trace constitutes literature's capacity to say everything—the trace permits interminable referral. The possibility of an absolute reference is the dream of absolute presence, of an uneraseable trace, "a son of God, a sign of parousia" (*WD*, 230). This is the dream of an end to referral, of positive infinity. But if the trace is the minimal structure necessary for reference to an other, then absolute presence, let us say "God," is "the effect of the trace, of a structure that retains the Other as Other in the full plenitude of a self-present entity." Yet because the trace contains erasure as its possibility, it also contains as its structural possibility its "occultation and oblivion by the idea of God. . . . Without the possibility of its effacement in the name of God, the trace could not be more 'originary' than God."[2] Rodolphe Gasché, from whom I have been quoting, remarks how the idea of God, like the apocalyptic tone, can always get around demystification. It is always possible, in the manner of Meister Eckhart, to renounce God in the name of God, or in the desire for the true presence of God.[3] I wish to set beside Derrida's statement that literature begins everywhere there is some trace his statement that God is an effect of the trace (*WD*, 108). Gasché writes that as the absolute Other, God is exemplary of the "structurally infinite network of referrals that comes to only an illusion of a halt when it represents itself, reveals itself, in exemplary fashion, as the One example."[4] If exemplarism involves thinking something as what it is without making it an object, as when we think of God as an example of the infinite (see *WD*, 318, n. 78), then the trace itself can never be an example because it has no *as such* but is the occultation of its *as such*. God and literature are two examples of what are announced when the trace of the other announces itself as such. But God and literature are not the same: for one is the absolute Other and the other is the experience of the other (I will confine my use of the capital *O* when referring to the absolute *O*ther). I do not wish to set the two in opposition nor to suggest that literature is the demystification of God; quite the contrary, if God is dependent upon the trace as the structure of referral, then as the example of the trace, "*of the divisible* envoi *for which there is no self-presentation nor assured destination*" (*AT*, 157), then the thought of God as trace, as Gasché suggests, means He "is the self-presentation as *primum exemplum* of the non-exemplifiable structure that constitutes the structure of the example."⁵ Literature will begin when it is impossible to decide when I speak of something, whether I am giving an example of something or an example that I can speak of something. Literature is what there is when I give testimony to the example of the unexemplifiable; it is what happens when there is some trace (of God, for example).

Nietzsche famously wrote, "I fear we are not getting rid of God because we still believe in grammar."⁶ Derrida might be taken to say, we cannot get rid of God because we still believe in writing, and what is it to write but "to confuse ontology and grammar" (*WD*, 78)? We cannot get rid of God, because we cannot help but forget the trace of the other, which we always do in our desire for a presence, for reappropriation and representation. This is what Derrida calls the "theological trap" inscribed in the occultation of the movement of the trace, when the other announces itself as such and the trace turns back into a presence or a sign (*D*, 258). An absolute interrogation of the Other would be the end of writing. I am proposing that if God is the prime example of what makes the structure of referral and substitution or analogization possible, then literature would be a discourse distinguished by, exemplifying, the capacity to be always saying, doing, being something other, such as theology or philosophy. The dream of a pure literature that awakens to itself as the absolute erasure of the other, of the end to representation and the simulacrum, would be the death of literature, and God as well. I begin with this apocalyptic tone (Derrida writes, "wouldn't the apocalyptic be a transcendental condition of all discourse, of all experience even?" [*AT*, 156]) because the question of deconstruction has been enfolded within the question of literature, which contains its own "theological trap." Literature can no more be purely "Literature" than the trace of the other can be the pure Other. I take Edmond Jabès for my example.

When Derrida invokes Hegel and identifies the unhappy consciousness as Jewish, he appears to endorse the dialectic wherein Judaism would be incorporated in and by the Hegelian discourse of a postmodernism that essentializes the Other as the negative image of logocentrism. I wish to investigate this "Hegelian" reading of Jabès because it turns upon the question of the representation of God as Other and is, thus, a question of Being and the

Book. We should keep in mind that Derrida's Hegel is not only the philosopher of the Absolute Idea, "the last philosopher of the book," but he is also "the first thinker of writing" (*OG*, 26).[7] This both/and status of Hegel is, I will argue, applicable to Jabès's *Book of Questions*: it is both metaphysical and non-metaphysical, a text that constitutes itself as a self-reflexive totality and a writing that opens this closed totality, this Book, to question. Most readings of *The Book of Questions*, particularly those that interpret it as an example of postmodernist deconstruction, are primarily critical accounts of its self-reflexivity. Insofar as Jabès would constitute the world within the Book—"The world exists because the book does"[8]—he treats the book as the model of meaning, even the meaning of Being itself. His work appears to exemplify the theological trap. But, Derrida asks, what "if Being lost itself in books" (*WD*, 77)? Derrida goes on to say that to condemn Jabès for not asking this and similar questions "would be ludicrous. . . . They can only sleep within the literary act which needs both their life and their lethargy. Writing would die of the pure vigilance of the question, as it would of the simple erasure of the question. Is not to write, once more, to confuse ontology and grammar" (*WD*, 78)? I wish to explore this question of literature, which is a question of ontology and writing, a question of the divided being of literature as belonging to the "*epoch* of Being" and, as an "illegible writing," belonging to "an age other than the age of the book" (*WD*, 77). It is a question, then, of the "Jewish" unhappy consciousness.

Because of the all too familiar saying that Jews are the people of the book, Derrida's particular emphasis on writing has led to a much too easy association of Jewish writing with what has come to be called deconstruction—and Edmond Jabès's *Le Livre des questions* is its poem.[9] There are modern precedents for this identification of the Jew and writing, such as Marina Tsvetaeva's pronouncement, "All poets are Jews," which Paul Celan cited as the epigraph to "Und mit dem Buch aus Tarussa" in *Die Niemandsrose*, but this association culminates in Jabès, who writes, "*First I thought I was a writer. Then I realized I was a Jew. Then I no longer distinguished the writer in me from the Jew because one and the other are only torments of an ancient word*'" (*RB*, 195 / *RL*, 60).[10] In this allegorical discourse, the Jew is marginalized, represented, as metaphor. We might say the "Jew" is the figure of difference, of the Other. Exiled from history, the Jewish people bear witness to the death of God: "So, with God dead, I found my Jewishness confirmed in the book" (*YEA*, 143 / *E*, 40).

In explicitly linking writing to the death of God, Jabès affirms the bond between the word and silence that implicates the book in the margins of a metaphysical tradition wherein writing is the material trace of a lost presence. Reading would be the effacement of the signifier, a recovery of this origin, but insofar as reality has its being in the book, Jabès resists this transcendent reading. If, as Derrida says, "literary writing has, almost always and almost everywhere . . . lent itself to . . . [a] *transcendent* reading," then literature has always been logocentric and metaphysical (*OG*, 160). Here I follow Derrida's argument that literature is a concept located within metaphysics—it is governed by mimesis and reflection—and insofar as literature is Platonic or metaphysical, it is non-Jewish, which is to say that literature is an idealist concept governed by the notion of the symbol or the Word made flesh. To open the discourse of literature to the margin is not simply to invert or negate such binary opposites as speech and writing or presence and absence, let alone Christianity and Judaism (as if their relationship could be reduced to a binary opposition), but to situate the text within an order other than Being. And if *The Book of Questions* is the postmodernist and exemplary Jewish text that its readers claim it is, then its relation to mimesis, arguably the central concept supporting the Western theory of literature from Aristotle to Auerbach, lies in its status as the writing of annihilation, a writing that displaces representation and, therefore, ontology.

The question that I am raising is not has Derrida misread Jabès and made this "Jewish" writing—a problematic notion to say the least—metaphysical, but whether there is such a thing as deconstructive criticism.[11] Samuel Weber has said that Derrida's "early readings of Jabès, Mallarmé, and Sollers were not, by any stretch of the imagination, 'deconstructions.'"[12] This has not lessened the tendency to identify deconstruction with literary writing. Rodolphe Gasché has been even more emphatic in challenging the claims of deconstructive criticism to be, in fact, deconstruction. In "Deconstruction as Criticism" and again in *The Tain of the Mirror*, Gasché has argued that such criticism represents a diacritical analysis wherein "[m]eaning . . . spring[s] forth from the self-canceling of the text's constituting oppositions."[13] Such criticism remains dependent on the idea of the self-reflexivity and autonomy of the literary text and has not begun to question the mimetologism that subjects mimesis to truth.

Derrida has argued that mimesis rests upon the precedence of the imitated over the imitation and that literature is determined by the *"ontological* interpretation of mimesis"—that is, as the movement of *physis,* mimesis signifies the presentation of nature or the process of appearing—*alêtheia*—wherein *"physis,* having no outside, no other, must be doubled in order to make its appearance, to appear (to itself), to produce (itself), to unveil (itself)" (*D,* 193). Literary criticism thematizes this unveiling of the truth of Being—reading assists the text in making Being manifest itself. In saying Derrida does not deconstruct Jabès, I do not mean to suggest that he misreads Jabès or is himself logocentric. (I am not trying to deconstruct the deconstructer.) On the contrary, when he situates Jabès's poetry within the margins of Hegel's phenomenology of Spirit, he indicates how literature occupies a certain space between metaphysics and an order other than Being. This "betweenness" is not localizable within a homogeneous whole but is a "space" that is recognizable by its "economic" function—its *praxis* that articulates the relation between philosophy and literature. Jabès's *Book of Questions* transforms the world of history into the infinite speculum of reading/writing or commentary: Being has its being in the Book. Herein lies Derrida's binding of *The Book of Questions* to the *Phenomenology of Spirit*: he identifies Jabès's idea of the Book with the Hegelian dream of the totalizing Idea, or as Alexandre Kojève defined it, with the Hegelian Book that coincides with the concept and the totality of Being.[14]

We are only a step away from Derrida's famous declaration, *"Il n'y a pas de hors-texte"* (*OG,* 158). This statement has been taken to mean that all reference and meaning is enclosed in a book, whereas in fact, Derrida is saying that reading cannot transgress the text by turning to an outside, whether it be historical or metaphysical, or, for that matter, an inside, a pure concept or essence, because the referral functions of the text are infinite by virtue of "every referent, all reality . . . [having] the structure of a differential trace" (*LI,* 148). When Derrida reads Jabès or Mallarmé, he raises the question of the Being of literature, for if he does not deconstruct the literary text itself, he does, in a manner of speaking, deconstruct Literature as idealist concept. In doing so, he does not deny the reflexive and mimetic functions of the text but affirms that the literary text belongs to metaphysics and simultaneously puts its being as metaphysics at risk.

Hence, if *The Book of Questions* is the "deconstructed" text that many of its critics, but not Derrida, say it is, then rather than represent itself as something other than a Christian or logocentric text—that is, as the cancellation of a kind of idealism stretching from Plato to Hegel—it must mark nonbeing; it must put literature in parentheses by opening itself to a radical otherness or illegibility. In other words, it must be shown to resist the transcendentalizing movement of reading. To do so requires that we read it in conjunction with the marginal positionality of the Jew in Hegel. Our reading turns not upon the opposition of philosophy and literature, Hegel and Derrida, or even reflection and writing, but in their convergence in *The Book of Questions* as a fold or between that resists the totalizing movement of reflection. Reading Jabès will not mean proving that he is Hegelian but that the marginality of *The Book of Questions* marks it as both aside from Being and dependent upon it. To be brief, Derrida's readings of Jabès and Mallarmé raise the question of the ontological status of literature. Therefore, we must read the literary text in conjunction with philosophy—read the *convergence* of literature and philosophy. In our reading of *The Book of Questions*, this means a convergence of reflection with writing, the differential/supplementary condition of "meaning" or "history." And this means reading Jabès in conjunction with Hegel, and our reading must, perforce, situate itself between philosophy and literature or in the margin of the phenomenology of Spirit.

But few texts lend themselves more readily to a metaphysical and transcendentalizing reading of the Other than does *The Book of Questions*. And there is no greater testimony to this than that of critics who read it as a deconstructed text. In the deconstructive readings of Jabès so well represented in the collection *The Sin of the Book*, the discontinuities of Jabès's writings come to essentialize God as the absent Other, thus signaling the forgetting of the ontological difference and the thinking of God as the infinite Being and people as finite beings.[15] Absence is here thought only within the confines of presence. If God has withdrawn Himself from the world, He still remains present in and as a silent inscription in the text and, thus, He is subject to phenomenalization or, simply, representation.

It is necessary, therefore, to distinguish Derrida's reading of Jabès from so-called deconstructive readings. When Derrida writes, "for Jabès, the book is not in the world, but the world is in the book" (*WD*, 76), he situates *The Book of Questions* within the epoch of metaphysics of which Hegel is the last philosopher. If Derrida's essay does not represent a deconstruction of Jabès, is it then an exercise in thematic criticism? Perhaps, but perhaps not. Perhaps, insofar as Jabès's texts are literary and Derrida's reading treats the theme of writing as the metaphysical play of absence and presence. Perhaps not, insofar as his reading of *The Book of Questions* turns to the conditions of the (im)possibility of literality and metaphoricity. Writing on the opposition of origin and exile, Derrida follows Jabès's thematics of writing as commentary on a lost text: "The necessity of commentary, like poetic necessity, is the very form of exiled speech. In the beginning is hermeneutics. But the *shared* necessity of exegesis, the interpretive imperative, is interpreted differently by the rabbi and the poet. . . . The original opening of interpretation essentially signifies that there will always be rabbis and poets. And two interpretations of interpretation" (*WD*, 67). One interpretation is that of the rabbi, who "dreams of deciphering a truth or an origin which escapes play and the order of the sign, and which lives the necessity of interpretation as an exile"; the other is that of the poet, "which is no longer turned toward the origin, affirms play and tries to pass beyond man and humanism" (*WD*, 292). It would be too easy to make Jabès, and even Derrida, interpreters who affirm exile, for Derrida is also a rabbi—after all, he "signs" the essay "Reb Rida." But just as Derrida's "plus R" signifies the textual difference in the proper name, he also is the other reader. He does not, however, unify these two readings: the "two interpretations of interpretation . . . are absolutely irreconcilable even if we live them simultaneously and reconcile them in an obscure economy" (*WD*, 293). Derrida's reading of Jabès, then, is not deconstructive insofar as it critically analyzes the thematics of exile, writing, and absence. He finds that commentary must conceptualize Being in order to remark the exile from it: "The original exile from the kingdom of Being, signifies exile as the conceptualization of Being" (*WD*, 74). Reb Rida reads *The Book of Questions* as the thematizing of exile as writing, and to this degree he cannot be said to deconstruct the text, as Derrida does the works of Hegel, Husserl, and Heidegger. Only at the conclusion of the essay, when he turns to the nonquestion of "the unpenetrated [*inentamée*] certainty that Being is a Grammar" (*WD*, 76) that we can say he addresses the question of logocentrism, if we cannot precisely say he deconstructs the text. The Jewish anxiety that informs the poetry of the unhappy consciousness is an anxiety that is history itself, poetry itself; it shows itself in a certain *image* of God, an image that figures everywhere and nowhere in *The Book of Questions*, for this image has no face: "'*All faces are His. Hence, He has no face*'" (*BQ*, 70 / *LQ*, 75). This anxiety is the threat of non-Being that emerges with the rupture with God; this is why the Jewish consciousness is the unhappy consciousness, the divided consciousness of master and slave lodged in a single being. Derrida writes, "The Jew is split, and split first of all between the two dimensions of the letter: allegory and literality" or between an "algebra of an abstract universalism" and an "empirical history among others if he established or nationalized himself within difference and literality" (*WD*, 75).

Caught between the literal and the figural or history and the abstract, "the poet is thus indeed the *subject* of the book, its substance and its master, its servant and its theme. And the book is indeed the subject of the poet, the speaking and knowing being who *in* the book writes *on* the book" (*WD*, 65). Derrida's reading confirms the reflexive structure of the book, but it remains to be seen what engenders reflexivity. At this stage we can say it is difference, spacing as writing and exile, that allows for it, as the following dialogue suggests:

My exile is anticipated in the exile of God.

My exile has led me, syllable by syllable, to God, the most exiled of words. And in Him I had a glimpse of the unity of Babel.

God will speak to us in the language we happen to speak. (*BY*, 86 / *LY*, 92)

In such passages, commentary seems superfluous. Exile designates not only a place but also a language that the Jew shares with God, whose "face" is that of the words addressed to him. It is not enough to say exile makes writing possible, for writing is exile. God exists because the Book does. The reflexivity that marks this passage makes commentary a mere paraphrase or translation, another marker of the reader's distance from God and the Book. Reading Jabès's book is like looking into a *mise en abyme*. So consistent, and insistent, are the themes of the wound, absence, exile and writing that any reading of *The Book of Questions* appears to mirror the very condition of the text's self-(re)presentation.

The question then remains whether *The Book of Questions* is a self-reflexive totality. Even the interminability of writing does not preclude closure since it is thematized as the withdrawal of God:

> *("God was the first to break the silence," he said. "It is this breakage we try to translate into human languages."*
>
> *"Vowels make us see, make us hear. Vowels are image and song. In our ancestors' script, vowels are points.*
> *"God refused image and language in order to be Himself the point. He is image in the absence of images, language in the absence of language, point in the absence of points," he said.) (LB, 15 / EL, 19)*

If writing begins in God's withdrawal, a nonpresence that the poet translates into human language, then writing posits God as absence, which is to say all writing bears witness to this (non)event, the death of God in creating ("God died in creating" [*YEA*, 35 / *Y*, 49]). The nonevent of the death of God—a nonevent insofar as it is known by its signs and traces and, as infinitely repeated in/as writing, without singularity—indicates the link between reflexivity and representation. The death of God is what never appears in *The Book of Questions* and is its only subject; it is figured as the refusal of His image. Jabès reminds us that Hebrew is written without vowels; points or dots are used instead of letters, and in ancient texts, as in Torah scrolls today, the points are left out. As the *point*, He is not only the erased vowel but the stop and the negative (*le point* means "period"), the not, as well: "Point of space unmarked by any letter" [*Point d'un espace qu'aucune lettre ne désigne*] (*LB*, 16 / *EL*, 20). To say God is the point—He is an image without face, the absence of image and the image of absence—is to invoke the prohibition against writing or speaking his name (the vowels are omitted by custom: YHWH). We can only write His name, but insofar as the points are left out, this, too, is impossible. As the "point in the absence of points," God makes language possible but is its impossibility as well; He is the non-foundational ground, the impossible condition, of language. We are as close to the objectification or representation of the unthematizable as we are likely to get.

A deconstruction of *The Book of Questions* would have to show how a non-phenomenal structure "opens a breach in the ideological closure of self-reflection." As Gasché points out, the limit to the text's reflexivity is neither an "empirical outside" nor an "ideal immanence" but lies "in the non-reflexive margins of the text."[16] Derrida indicates this limit in writing that *The Book of Questions* is inscribed in the margins of the phenomenology of Spirit, situating Jabès's text between philosophy and literature, or between text and writing. For if there is such a thing as deconstructive criticism, it will invariably involve a tracing of the threads that bind the literary text to the philosophical one. And as Derrida's signature suggests, the reader of the literary text must be both rabbi and poet and engage in two interpretations. I can only sketch the preliminary of such a reading of *The Book of Questions*, and to do so requires an inquiry into the relation between ontology and mimesis and between the philosophy of reflection and writing.

The convergence of the thematization of writing, the book, and the Other in the figure of the Jew leads us back to Hegel, "the last philosopher of the book and the first thinker of writing." If Hegelian negation encompasses all thought within the self-certainty of reflection, Hegel "is *also* the thinker of irreducible difference . . . [who] rehabilitated thought as the *memory productive* of signs" (*OG*, 26). Derrida's reading of Hegel's semiology uncovers not only the contradictions within his thought upon language but also his reintroduction of the necessity of writing in philosophical discourse. Thus, deconstruction is not an inversion of Hegel's privileging of phonetic writing over the hieroglyph but a displacement of the opposition and a locating in the dyssemetry of Hegel the non-dialectical condition for metaphysical thinking. Following upon this reading of how the grounding possibilities of metaphysics include an irreducible difference, I suggest that Hegel's consignment of Judaism to the past cannot simply be dismissed as anti-Semitism or as his misplaced faith in the Absolute Spirit. It is, I argue, a part of the system, but one that appears in mysterious places, usually converging on the problem of the sign—places which open to question the movement toward Absolute Knowing.

As the people of the book, Jews are, for Hegel, no longer *in* history but merely *of* history, and their continued presence in the world bears witness to the historical truth of the man-God of Christianity. Derrida succinctly characterizes the relation between the Christian God and history in Hegel's thought: the God of Hegel is "he who leaves himself, determines himself in his finitude and thus produces history" (*TB*, 167). History originates with the externalization of Spirit and ends with the return of Spirit into itself. History can be defined as "meaning" or as self-differing sameness by which subject has become substance or the unity of Thought and Being. But for Hegel, the God who remains Other, the Jewish God, rigorously maintains the separation of divine from human. The Jewish God introduces universal self-consciousness into history, but this is an abstract self-consciousness and is thus superseded in the mediating presence of the man-God who makes the Other actual, unlike the abstract negativity of the Jewish God.[17]

Every reading of *The Book of Questions* as the inscription of the Otherness within writing or of the absence of God remains within metaphysics. This is not to say that these critics are wrong; they are, in fact, quite accurate in describing the mimetic function of Jabès's writing, but then his texts cannot be said to fulfill the demands of deconstruction. They would simply be another variant of the *deus abscondus*. If the Hegelian God dies in producing history, the Jabèsian God dies in order to become the Book: "God warrants the disappearance of God as the word warrants man's complicity with death. Thus God and man join the streamlined furrows of the immaculate page" (*YEA*, 233 / *A*, 41). Otherness remains an intentional Other phenomenolized by Jabès's fragmentary texts. The name for the Other is "God," whose absence is memorialized by the book. In writing "*God gives death the dimensions of His absence*" (*YEA*, 153 / *E*, 55), Jabès implies that the book itself is the measure and sign of His death because "The letters of the alphabet are contemporaries of death" (*YEA*, 33 / *Y*, 47). At issue here, as Derrida points out in several contexts, is the being of the Other, a problem that certainly preoccupied Hegel.

Hegel's claim to think the Other as Other takes the form of the self-knowing spirit that inscribes the Other at the limits or margins of the phenomenology of Spirit. In Hegel's words, "the self-knowing Spirit knows not only itself but also the negative of itself, or its limit: to know one's limit is to know how to sacrifice oneself."[18] The Other is thought on the order of *kenosis*: the self-othering of God who becomes man in order to become the God of revealed religion. The sacrifice of the sovereignty of Spirit ensures the triumph of Absolute Knowing. The claim of the Science of Knowledge is that it thinks the negative as Absolute Other. There can be nothing that is not both meaningful and representable for self-knowing Spirit, including death: the life of Spirit "endures it [death] and maintains itself in it. It wins its truth only when, in utter dismemberment, it finds itself" (*PS*, 19). The absolute negativity of death is saved from meaninglessness by the divine comedy of the death of God. Georges Bataille is Hegelian when he writes death has "to become (self) consciousness at the very moment when it annihilates conscious being." This is possible for the individual only through the "subterfuge" of sacrifice whereby death is revealed to man in the death of the Other: "For man finally to be revealed to himself he would have to die, but he would have to do so while living—while watching himself cease to be."[19] Man can only watch himself cease to be in the death of another.

Derrida has identified the logic of sacrifice as the restricted economy that subordinates difference to presence and meaning. Perhaps the most remarkable claim made by the Hegelian system is to the conservation of nonmeaning within the discourse of Absolute Knowledge. Bataille's notion of general economy introduces a silence that transgresses "the limit of discursive difference" (*WD*, 263). But as Derrida goes on to show, this difference must be limited to Hegelian difference, just as Bataille's general economy is limited to Hegel's restricted economy. To define something as the negative of Hegel would be to maintain the Hegelian system. Therefore, "major writing" will exceed "the *logos* (of meaning, lordship, presence, etc.)" (*WD*, 267). In other words, the Hegelian system can account for what lies outside philosophy but not for what lies within it as the originary structure that both makes discourse possible and transgresses it.

Those critics who speak of the Otherness of the Jew or the Otherness of the Jewish God are perfectly Hegelian and confirm the meaning of the sacrifice of the Christian God. But can there be a death that transgresses the logic of the sacrifice of Spirit? A death that does not represent for the Other the externalization of Spirit? And if there were such an unthinkable thing, how would it be written? To write of Auschwitz—to use a synecdoche of the *shoah*—is to write of that which exceeds representation; it is the excess that denies representation.

This excess is controlled by the economy of sacrifice, an expenditure that guarantees a return upon its investment: Spirit leaves itself only to return by way of sacrifice with a greater value than was originally invested. Any transgression of the discourse of Absolute Knowledge, even death, is controlled by the economy of sacrifice: the life of Spirit endures death and maintains itself in it. But the death that is not sacrifice but annihilation—a death that neither maintains life nor reveals one's own impending death to consciousness—is the negative that inhabits the Hegelian system and marks its limitations from within; it is, in other words, that which escapes the merger of *Aufheben* and *Erinnerung*. It could be a silent reading of that slip of paper on which Hegel writes "Now is the Night" and dissolves the Night rather than maintain it as the universal. It is a reading that is the death of writing/the writing of death, what Maurice Blanchot calls the "Writing of the Disaster" and Jabès simply calls writing: "One cannot tell Auschwitz. Every word tells us it" [*On ne raconte pas Auschwitz. Chaque mot nous le raconte*] (*BM*, 173 / *LM*, 182; translation modified). If each word tells us of Auschwitz, then each word names absence, and to write gives being to the author and deprives him of being.[20]

Jabès presents an alternative notion of the Book, one that, unlike Hegel, is not "indifferent to the comedy of the *Aufhebung*" and does not blind itself "to the experience of the sacred, to the heedless sacrifice of presence and meaning" (*WD*, 257). Derrida has identified death and sacrifice as the "blind spot of Hegelianism." They constitute a negativity so radical as to be an expenditure "*without* reserve": "they can no longer be determined as negativity in a process or a system" (*WD*, 259). If Hegel is blind to what he lay bare, then our reading of Hegel must make the blind spot visible. As sacrifice, a sacrifice without supersession, this blind spot is a kind of writing—"Jewish" writing—that lies in the margins of the phenomenology of the Spirit—that is, it makes necessary and impossible the representation of that which the name "sacrifice" is blind to, annihilation.

The margin is what separates the Jew from God, and writing measures the distance between humanity and the absent God, a distance never to be overcome but always renewed in and as writing: "'In the book,' he said, 'writing means absence, and the empty page, presence. Thus God, who is absence, is present in the book'" (*YEA*, 213 / *A*, 19). If God is present in the book, he is present not as the blank page, the possible space of writing—God is absence, not presence—nor simply as writing but as the point, the nonsignifying mark of punctuation and the effaced vowel, the erasure that exiles the Jew to silence and writing: "A man of writing is a man of the four letters which form the unpronounceable Name. God is absent through His Name. Writing means taking on God's absence through each of the four" (*YEA*, 250 / *A*, 60–61). Whereas in the Jewish tradition, exile presupposes the invisible God is present in prayer and in reading the Torah, for Jabès, exile signifies God's originary separation or difference from Himself: "The book is for the exile what the universe is for God. So any book of exile is God's place" (*YEA*, 129 / *E*, 19). As Derrida notes, exile from the kingdom of Being always presupposes Being "and signifies that Being never is, never shows *itself*, is never *present*, is never *now*, outside difference" (*WD*, 74). Jabès's first volume of *The Book of Questions* treats absence as an absent presence, but in the later volumes, absence is understood only within the idea of the book: "Could God be the book? But in the book, God is without God as, in the word, man is without man" (*YEA*, 265 / *A*, 80). Were God the book, He would be self-same presence. This most absolute Book would be the apocalyptic presence of God and a most definite end of writing; hence, the Book ends and writing begins with the erasure of His Name:

> Abolishing His Name, God broke all His ties because He knew that every name is an indestructible knot.
> There is a law which governs the absence of the book. It is the law which the book announces and to which it refers in order to be a book.
> Law within the revealed Law. We read it in the margins. (*YEA*, 291 / *A*, 115)

The Law governing the absence of the book finds one form in the prohibition against the Name of God—the unpronounceable name, the writing that defers presence as something other than Being or the totalizing Book.

At this point, we can offer a translation of Derrida's characterization of Jabès: Jewish consciousness is the prosaic discourse of a radical illegibility, and to be inscribed "in the margins of the phenomenology of spirit" is to be inscribed in the margin of the Book. The Otherness of God is revealed in His unutterable name, which, as Jabès remarks in an interview, means He is beyond representation:

> God is perhaps a word without words. A word without meaning. And the extraordinary thing is that in the Jewish tradition God is invisible, and as a way of underscoring this invisibility, he has an unpronounceable name. What I find truly fantastic is that when you call something "invisible," you are naming something, which means that you are almost giving a representation of the invisible. In other words, when you say "invisible," you are pointing to the boundary between the visible and the invisible; there are words for that. But when you can't say the word, you are standing before nothing. And for me this is even more powerful because, finally, there is a visible in the invisible, just as there is an invisible in the visible. And this, this abolishes everything. . . .[21]

With the unsayable name we reach the limits of representation and the limits of dialectics.

Derrida's "Hegelian" reading of Jabès must be distinguished from those by critics who find in Jabès the heterological discourse of the pure Otherness of God. For these critics, Jabès's writing bears witness to "the painful feeling of the Unhappy Consciousness that *God Himself is dead*" (*PS*, 476). But whereas Hegel thought this death to be sublated by self-knowing Spirit, Jabès, in these Hegelian readings, testifies that this death is borne as "an interruption that is in some way absolute and absolutely neutral."[22] I quote Blanchot, who, more than any other critic, is responsible for the understanding of Jabès as the poet of the Jewish unhappy consciousness. The persuasiveness of this Hegelian formulation of the

Other lies in the pathos it lends not only to Jabès's texts but also to the encounter between Christianity and Judaism. Judaism comes to mark the difference between self and Other and to restore to Christianity the discourse of the Other within the logic of the Same.

This formulation of the Jewish God as the absent Other signals the forgetting of the ontological difference and thinks God as the infinite Being and people as finite beings. Absence is here thought only within the confines of presence. The discontinuities of Jabès's texts bear witness to the irreducible otherness of the Jewish God. This characterization of the Jewish God as the Other and Jabès's texts as the naming of the Other operates within the conceptual schema of reflection that Hegel criticized. The word and the void exist in a primordial unity and this unity is mimetically represented in the fragmentariness of *The Book of Questions*. In other words, Jabès's texts function as the self-reflexive thematization of God as the infinite Other. But as Derrida demonstrates in a reading of Emmanuel Levinas, "The other cannot be what it is, infinitely other, except in finitude and mortality (mine *and* its). It is such as soon as it comes into language, of course, and only then, and only if the word *other* has a meaning" (*WD*, 114–15). The other is infinite only by virtue of its finitude and mortality, for if it were a positive infinity it would not be other but simply unknown or unsayable, nothing. It comes into being in language and thus as finite and mortal. Consequently, the infinite Other or the Absence that is God can only be thought within ontic metaphor.[23] In such readings of Jabès, metaphor would be the unveiling of Being, which Derrida calls "the nonmetaphor" (*WD*, 112).

The question of Jewish writing concerns neither theology nor religion but a claim for literature itself to be other than metaphysical. Blanchot, in "Etre Juif," quotes Hegel on the Jewish God but modifies Hegel's portrait of the absolute Otherness of God: "When Hegel, interpreting Judaism, declares, 'The God of the Jews is the highest separation, he excludes all union' . . . he is merely neglecting the essential, which, for thousands of years, has been given expression in books, in teaching, and a living tradition: this is the notion that if, in fact, there is infinite separation, it falls to speech to make it the place of understanding; and if there is an insurmountable abyss, speech crosses this abyss." In Jewish thought, writes Blanchot, speech does not mediate but "inaugurates an original relation" wherein distance is at once instituted, traversed, and maintained.[24] This estrangement or separation is maintained by the Tables of the Law: "the first text (which is never the first), the written word, the scripture . . . is also at the same time a commented text that not only must be re-uttered in its identity, but learned in its inexhaustible difference."[25] Exile from the word is the loss of the unmediated language of God, a loss confirmed in the letter of the Law that must be learned in its identity, which is also the identity of God as "inexhaustible difference," that is, as the infinite Other.

But Blanchot turns from the infinite Other of the rupture to its interrogation, "a double movement": "In such a way that *The Book of Questions* is always written twice—the book that interrogates the movement of the rupture, by which the book is made, and the book in which 'the virile word of the renewed history of a people folded in on itself' is designated—a double movement that Edmond Jabès supports: supports, without unifying it, or even being able to reconcile it."[26] The "commented text" is always written twice; it refuses the *Aufheben* whereby reading reconciles consciousness with the world.

The other, for Blanchot, is finite, and the finitude of the other can be thought only as a writing that is foreign to the Book. As pure exteriority, writing exists on the order of the concept, that is, as the material representation of the Idea or the Law (see *WD*, 151). The book would be the ontic determination of the infinite beyond. When Jabès is read as the poet of the unhappy consciousness, his texts are taken as the sign of the absent infinite. The text is the site of the Otherness of God, a principle well within the realm of logocentrism. For Blanchot, however, absence is not exterior to or prior to the text but within it.

Writing realizes meaning, even as the deferred presence of meaning, that is to say, as the deferred presence of God. The errancy of Jabès's texts would be what Derrida calls "the passageway of deferred reciprocity between reading and writing" (*WD*, 11). As the poet of God's Otherness, Jabès presents his work as always having been read. "The book writes itself [*s'écrit*] by allowing itself to be read as it will be" (*BM*, 10 / *LM*, 16, trans. modified). He writes what has already been read—the absence of God *in* the world. *The Book of Questions* remains within the mimetic tradition insofar as the meaning of the text is determined by its appeal to the Other as a phenomenolizable being that, in turn, determines the being of the literary text. The inversion whereby the logocentric God of Christianity is replaced by the absent God of Judaism does not upset the mimetic and philosophical determination of literature. The citations of fictional rabbis, the fragmentary tale of Yukel and Sarah, and the commentaries scattered throughout the book do not break from the logocentric concept of the book as a unitary whole. In this scheme, Jabès's fragmentary text represents absence as the constitutive idea of the Book, and *The Book of Questions*, as the representation of an idea (*eidos*), remains fully within the confines of mimetic representation. The openness or refusal of closure that critics attribute to *The Book of Questions* is but a reflexive mode of being.[27] Insofar as Otherness is inscribed in *The Book of Questions*, all reference to the Other is self-reflexive.

If Jabès's text is something other than the negative image of the Christian and logocentric text, then it must put its own being as literature at stake; it must negate itself by declaring its limitless formalization of writing as the speculum of the Other. Derrida, in writing of Mallarmé's *Mimique*, argues that literature has been governed by the idea of mimesis, but a mere reversal of the hierarchy of the imitated over the imitation would in no way displace the metaphysical system wherein mimesis is "commanded by the process of truth," that is, by the movement of appearance (truth as *alêtheia*) or by its coincidence or agreement with the object of imitation (truth as *adequatio*) (*D*, 193). Moreover, to say that literature suspends the referential and/or representational dimension of language by virtue of its literariness, or its being as fiction, confirms its subservience to the Platonic determination of mimesis. When Derrida locates in Mallarmé's *Mimique* a miming of representation itself that puts literature in quotation marks, he finds a doubling of mimesis, a supplementary doubling of the simple wherein what is "added to the simple and the single, replaces and mimes them" (*D*, 191). The supervention of the image upon the simple constitutes the order, the metaphysical order, that anchors mimesis in ontology. But the logic of the supplement constitutes a doubling of the mark: "This double mark escapes the pertinence or authority of truth: it does not overturn it but rather inscribes it within its play as one of its functions or parts. This displacement does not take place, has not taken place once, as an *event*. It does not occupy a simple place. It does not take place *in* writing. This dis-location (is what) writes/is written" (*D*, 193). In Mallarmé, the graphics of supplementarity by which the ontological priority of the imitated is displaced or disrupted turn the imitated into an effect of writing: "this imitator having in the last instance no imitated, this signifier having in the last instance no signified, this sign having in the last instance no referent, their operation is no longer comprehended within the process of truth but on the contrary comprehends *it*" (*D*, 207). This multiplication of the mimetic, authorized "by the hymen that interposes itself between . . . *mimesis* and *mimesis*," renders the distinction between the imitated and the imitator undecidable; writing is no longer subordinated to a prior being or to truth (*D*, 219). The graphics of supplementarity account for the "original," whether it be Nature or the Idea.

Literature will displace metaphysics only when it negates itself as literature, that is, as a self-reflexive totality in which mimesis is judged in reference to truth. This would not mean mimesis, reference, or even self-reflexivity are to be denied; instead, they are to be accounted for by a non-phenomenal structure that displaces the concept of the signified and opens the text to an outside. Mallarmé's concept of the book is not too distant from either Hegel's or Jabès's, albeit the relation is highly complex; but whereas a text like *Mimique* performs itself as the internal theater of reading/writing, Jabès's texts thematize the redoubling of the written text as reading, thus restoring to literature an exteriority which will ground the text in a realizable Other. This is not a sign of Jabès's mystification, but is prescribed by the "theological trap": "the mark-supplement [*le suppléent de marque*] produced by the text's workings, in falling outside of the text like an independent object with no origin other than itself, a trace that turns back into a presence (or a sign), is inseparable from desire (the desire for reappropriation or representation)" (*D*, 258). As the pure speculative Other contemplating Himself, God withdraws from man, and in the space of this withdrawal writing begins. God's self-contemplation, however, does not exclude man, for it is within the reflection of God upon Himself that He comes to be read: "When a writer bends over his work he believes, or rather makes us believe, that his face is the one his words reflect. He is lying. He is lying as God would be if He claimed to have created men in His image; because which then would be His image" (*BY*, 57 / *LY*, 61)?

Resemblance depends upon alterity, a difference that opens a space in identity that makes reflection possible.

For Jabès, God is another name for the text or writing; He is the difference originative of all resemblance. He is without a face precisely because He is all faces or difference itself. Similarly, the writer who bends over his words does not, like Narcissus, find his image reflected therein; the words reflect the other's face, the reader's. The writer always returns to the text as reader and, therefore, as other. And if reading is what gives rise to writing, then there can be no text that is not originally a read text or one that bears the mark of its iterability. In Jabès, this means that the text consists of a double movement of self-reference and division that can never be resolved into a single image, for such an image would preclude the difference upon which any notion of the book and identity depends. This is why he refers to the creation as God's self-destruction; only in His death does He become visible: "Nobody has seen God, but the stages of His death are visible to all of us" (*YEA*, 224 / *A*, 33). This trope of the death of God stands for the materiality of the book, the letter of the Law: "God resembles His Name to the letter, and His Name is the Law" (*YEA*, 203 / *A*, 7). If, as this passage suggests, God is writing, the material letter, the read letter, reveals His mortal existence: "In death, the word [*voca-ble*] becomes visible. It is the Law read" (*RB*, 172/ *LY*, 36). Writing constitutes God as trace, or as that which maintains itself in its own oblivion. God is the name for ideality or infinitely repeatable self-relation, but the condition for iterability is death, material being as the read letter.

Unlike Jabès's God who dies in creating, the God of Christianity enters life in becoming another to itself: "abstract Spirit becomes an 'other' to itself, or enters into existence, and directly into *immediate* existence. Accordingly, it *creates* a world." In entering into existence, Spirit is "the individual Self which has consciousness and distinguishes itself as 'other,' or as world, from itself" (*PS*, 467). In becoming other to itself, Spirit enters immediate existence and is not yet universal self-consciousness. Only when the Notion as Notion rises above its representation (*Vorstellung*) does Spirit rise above natural existence to become universal self-consciousness. This moment is the death of the Man-God: "The death of the Mediator is the death not only of his *natural* aspect or of his particular being-for-self, not only of the already dead husk stripped of its essential Being, but also of the abstraction of the divine Being" (*PS*, 476). In the death of Christ, universal self-consciousness is actualized as Spirit that knows itself as Spirit. But in Jabès, the death of God is His becoming a material being, a text, the Tables of the Law: "Judaism is perhaps, outside any interpretation, the singular idea that absence has it out with death [*idée de l'absence en tant que explication avec la mort*] at the moment we approach God, moment of a striking erasure among the circumscribed words, providential breech opening a passage for the book" (*YEA*, 312 / *A*, 142). This breach is figured in Jabès's parable of the shattering of the Tables of the Law; reading is the violation of God:

> "We read the word in the sunburst of its limits, as we read the Law through Moses' angry gesture, through the breaking of the divine Tables," he said. . . . By turning their back on the Tables, the chosen people gave Moses a master-lesson in reading. From instinct—for is the Book not prior to man?—they raised the rape [viol] of God to the level of original death. And, rising up against the letter, their independence consecrated the fracture in which God writes Himself against God (*LB*, 39 / *EL*, 47–48).

In transforming the violation into a principle of reading, the elected posited God's death as the condition of legibility. At the origin, the Book is death, the visible body of God.

The destruction of the Tables of the Law serves as the master story, the parable, for most readings of Jabès, including Derrida's and Blanchot's.[28] It is a parable of writing as the exile from the Word of God and as the secondariness of the commented text. Hegel, however, in his mature writings turns to Genesis and the creation as his model for a Jewish notion of the word. In the creation through the positing power of God's word—"Let there be light"—we have Hegel's example of the sublime and Judaism as the religion of sublimity. Furthermore, the sublime is an instance of the symbol, and the symbol, we should recall, is characterized by the signifier's separation from or inadequacy to the referent. Moreover, the sublime is the discourse of the slave: "In the slave, prose begins" (*Aesthetics*, I, 387). If prose begins in the slave, we can conclude that for Hegel prose begins in the Jewish unhappy consciousness, for it is the consciousness of the slave. Prose, which should not be thought of in its conventional sense but as the diremption of the sacred and history, has its beginnings in the Law: "Thou shalt not make unto thee a graven image" (Exodus 20:4). This commandment may be termed the law of the sublime because the Hegelian sublime is distinguished by the incompatibility between nature and spirit. Consequently, Jewish writing is a discourse of trope and not of representation: "For visual art cannot appear here, where it is impossible to sketch any adequate picture of God; only the poetry of ideas, expressed in words, can" (*Aesthetics*, I, 373).

The separation of God from His creation destroys the unity of the symbol and leaves as the only "divine topic . . . the *relation* of God to the world created by him" (*Aesthetics*, I, 373). This relation, however, is not mediated but purely linguistic in the sense of being a result of pure predicative power. In this way, "natural things are not the presence of God but only powerless accidents which in themselves can only show [*Scheinen*] him, not make him appear [*Erscheinen*]" (*Aesthetics*, I, 374). As Hegel's pun indicates, posited in the verbal formula of creation, "Let there be Light," is the phenomenalization of God as sign—God is the object of his own predication, for if the natural world does not attest to God's presence but shows him as absent, the verbal formula shows (*scheint*) showing or light (*Schein*). It shows Him as a sign without any content; He is imageless.

In "Hegel on the Sublime," Paul de Man argues that Hegel's quotation from Genesis signifies that the creation is purely verbal: "The word speaks and the world is the transitive object of its utterance, but this implies that what is thus spoken, and which includes us, is not the subject of its speech act."[29] What is spoken is language itself, the positing power of words. It is an act of quotation—Hegel quotes Longinus quoting Scripture quoting God—in which language is itself both subject and predicate. Language is the object of its own utterance. There is no representation at work here—God cannot be represented in the sublime of Hebrew poetry. The creation is what Jabès calls "*commentaire*," commentary as quotation: "'*In the word* commentaire,' he repeated 'there are the words taire, se taire, faire taire, "to be silent, to fall silent, to silence" which quotation demands'" (*LB*, 11 / *EL*, 15). In the silence of God's absence, quotation is a pure positing without image making; the sublime does not infuse spirit into the world but leaves the world of things, Hegel writes, "as prosaic and bereft of God" (*Aesthetics*, I, 374).

Here we find that Hegel's resistance to Judaism lies not so much in its rejection of mediation but in what it has to say about language. It refuses to allow memory (*Er-Innerung*) to incorporate the gallery of images that constitutes the history of consciousness. Spirit, Hegel writes in the *Phenomenology*, is both Nature and History (which is precisely what Judaism denies):

> The other side of its [Spirit's] Becoming, *History*, is a conscious, self-*mediating* process—Spirit emptied out into Time; but this externalization, this kenosis, is equally an externalization of itself; the negative is the negative of itself. This Becoming presents a slow-moving succession of Spirits, a gallery of images [*eine Galerie von Bildern*], each of which, endowed with all the riches of Spirit, moves thus slowly just because the Self has to penetrate and digest this entire wealth of its substance. As its fulfilment consists in perfectly *knowing* what *it is*, in knowing its substance, this knowing is its *withdrawal into itself* in which it abandons its outer existence and gives its existential shape over to re-collection [*Er-innerung*; hyphenation in the German original] (*PS*, 492).

The re-collection or internalization of the forms of Spirit transforms the sign into an image. But the sign, Hegel writes in the *Encyclopedia*, "must be regarded as a great advance on the symbol." There is a complete divorce between the sensuous material and the idea in the sign: "Intelligence, in indicating something by a sign, has finished with the content of intuition, and the sensuous material receives for its soul a signification foreign to it" (*PM*, 212). In the *Phenomenology*, the foreign body of the shapes or forms of consciousness would be internalized or made over into recollection. But the indifferent link between signifier and signified makes the sign totally dependent upon memorization: "the significance of the sign must first be learned. This is especially true of language signs" (*PM*, 212). This kind of rote memorization implies that re-collection gives way to quotation—the forms of Spirit can only be repeated as signs devoid of content. We can receive the fullness of the past only as quotation.

The conflict between Hegel and Jewish thought is between language as image and a non-representational language that lacks the endurance of the image. The Jew, in saying "no" to the Messiah, turns away from an achieved redemption in the past and toward exile and silence. Jabès refuses the reconciliation of history with Spirit promised by re-collection but maintains a negative knowledge of the linguistic origin of the separation of divine and human: "In the face of absence, of emptiness, the symbols we keep copying—is not all writing the recorded sifting of a vast and poignant monologue?—reclaim traces of our origin" (*LB*, 83 / *EL*, 97). All writing is commentary, a doubling of the shattered tablets that measures the distance between the poet and his origins.

When Hegel equates Judaism with the divine/human difference, we find that the sublime is indistinguishable from the sign. If, as Hegel says, "memory [*Gedächtnis*] . . . has always to do with signs only" (*PM*, 213), then his ambivalence toward the sublime and Judaism can be seen as a larger ambivalence toward language as the diremption of history and Spirit. This ambivalence can best be seen when he once again cites Genesis in *The Philosophy of Religion*:

> God said, "Let there be light"; and there was light. This is one of the most sublime passages. "God said"—the text tells us how he works. But there is nothing that costs as little effort as a word; as soon as it is spoken, it is gone. Yet this breath [of God] is here light as well, the word of light, the infinite outpouring of light, so that light here becomes merely a word, something as transient as a mere word (*PR*, II, 433).

Hegel's complaint that "light here becomes merely a word" is as prosaic a commentary on Genesis as one can hope to find. The transitory word of creation, for Hegel, is the spoken word that does not endure. Hegel recognizes in the transitoriness of the word the instability of a world that receives its being from language. In the withdrawal or disappearance of the word comes the diremption of the divine from the human, and the disjunction that Hegel calls the sublime and Jabès exile: "People of the Book, we will never have a house. We shall die in words" (*YEA*, 146 / *E*, 44).

For Jabès, "The letters of the alphabet are contemporaries of death. They are stages of death turned into signs" (*YEA*, 33 / *Y*,

47). The strictures against representation include even the word; therefore, writing condemns the Jew to death: "The book is written at the expense of life, at the cost of flesh" (*YEA*, 192 / *E*, 113). Writing must, therefore, erase itself; it must mark itself as the limit of representation:

> Writing—being written—will be, then, without realizing it, to pass from the visible—the image, figure, representation whose duration is that of an approach—to the invisible, the non-representation against which struggles, stoically, the object; from the audible, whose duration is the time of listening, to silence where, obediently, our words come to drown; from sovereign thought to the sovereignty of the unthought, remorse and supreme torment of the word.
>
> The sacred remains unnoticed, concealed, protected, ineffable; that is why writing is also the suicidal attempt to take on the word down to its final effacement where it stops being a word and is no more than the raised trace [*trace relevée*]—the wound—we see of a fatal and common break: that of God with man, and that of man with the Creation.[30]

All writing is in violation of the Law, but this violation is necessary, for in giving being to God's absence, the Jew asserts the sovereignty of writing, and a sovereign writing represents itself as its own effacement.

In Hegelian readings of Jabès, the radical Otherness attributed to the Jew remains within the confines of a philosophy of reflection, but Hegel's theory of the sign moves him closer to Jabès and distances him from received readings of speculative philosophy. In Derrida's reading of Hegel, the Other that remains Other, the negative that refuses to be raised (*aufgehoben*), is signified by the Jew: "The Jew falls again; he signifies that which does not let itself be raised up [*élever*]—raised again [*relever*] perhaps but denied from that moment on as Jew—to the thought of the *Begriff*" (*G*, 66, left hand column). This negative that cannot be *relevé/aufgehoben*, that does not work "in the service of meaning," does not overturn or replace Hegelian thought, for the latter is always already implicated in "this structural incapacity to think without *relève*" (*M*, 107). The very capacity to make oneself understood within the system confirms this. This unassimilable negativity or otherness points us back to Derrida's readings of Mallarmé and Jabès, where we find that literature is determined by the non-phenomenolizable structure of the fold that limits the literary being of the text, that is, marks the non-being of the text: "If there were no fold, or if the fold had a limit somewhere—a limit other than itself as a mark, margin, or march (threshold, limit, or border)—there would be no text. But if the text does not, to the letter, exist, then *there is* perhaps a text" (*D*, 270). There is a text, perhaps, only on condition of the differential/supplementary structure of the fold, which is to say that there is a text by virtue of the absence of an absolute reference. The text, therefore, is there (*il y a/es gibt*; literally "it gives") but *is* not; that is, it is given on the basis of nothing. "If there were no text . . . there would no doubt be no literature"; and since there is no text without the fold, literature is determined by its non-essence (*D*, 270). We can say that Derrida's analysis of Mallarmé reveals both how literature is subsidiary to metaphysics and how the text, as a generalized writing deprived of being or essence, situates itself between philosophy and literature as a fold: "But the fold is not a form of reflexivity. . . . [R]eflexivity is but an effect of the fold as text" (*D*, 270).

In suspending the "being of literature," Derrida proposes a non-metaphysical textuality that does not do away with self-reflexivity and mimesis but determines them to be effects of an "anterior" doubleness or supplementary structure. As I have indicated above, this both/and status of the literary text indicates that the text does not undo metaphysics but situates itself between literature and philosophy. This also means that a reading must take into account the text as both self-reflexive totality and as writing. When Derrida reads Jabès, he accounts for the status of *The Book of Questions* as "a simulacrum through which literature puts itself simultaneously at stake and on stage" (*D*, 291). And once again, our reading converges on the topics of the Jew, the fold, and the book.

At the outset of "Edmond Jabès and the Question of the Book," Derrida distinguishes the reflection that belongs to history, which here is another name for Western metaphysics, from the fold that is a double writing, a writing that refers to itself and to another writing, a reflection that does not resolve itself into unity but is abysmal:

The only thing that begins by reflection is history. And this fold [*pli*], and this furrow [*ride*] is the Jew. . . . This movement through which the book, *articulated* by the voice of the poet, is folded and bound to itself, the movement through which the book becomes a subject in itself and for itself, is not critical or speculative reflection, but is, first of all, poetry and history. For in its representation of itself the subject is shattered and opened. Writing is itself written, but also ruined, made into an abyss, in its own representation. Thus, within this book, which infinitely reflects itself and which develops as a painful questioning of its own possibility, the form of the book represents itself (*WD*, 65; trans. modified).

Derrida distinguishes between two types of reflection, closed and open, Hegelian and non-Hegelian. I refrain from saying Jewish, for the Jew is situated between writing and empiricity, allegory and the literal. To speak of the Jew, in the manner of Jabès, is to speak of the founding exchange between writing and the written, an "originary" exchange that is death. Perhaps this is why Jabès writes, "'You are all Jews, even the anti-Semites, because you are all marked for martyrdom'" (*BQ*, 163 / *LQ*, 180).

The reflexive form Derrida attributes to *The Book of Questions* is a negative reflection wherein "[a]bsence attempts to produce itself in the book and is lost in being pronounced; it knows itself as disappearing and lost, and to this extent, it remains inaccessible and impenetrable" (*WD*, 69). Derrida's reading points to the reflexive relation between absence and writing. The necessity of absence—it liberates writing—means that the fragmentary text of Jabès is not necessarily a rupture with totality. On the contrary, absence is the diacritical difference constitutive of writing—"*All letters give form to absence*" (*BQ*, 47 / *LQ*, 47; and see *WD*, 72). The infinite reflection whereby the Jew is the name for the "non-coincidence of self with self" (*WD*, 75; translation modified) presupposes a notion of the book that embraces all contradiction, a notion of unity that construes the negative as the infinite moment of writing so that nonclosure is staged within the reflexive space of the book. The question then remains of the outside—which is not the world, or even an empirical outside but "that which limits its reflexive structure and cognitive functions."As Gasché argues in what remains the most significant critique of deconstructive criticism, "The outside of the text is precisely that which *in* the text makes self-reflexion possible and at the same time limits it."[31] Gasché argues that the idea of self-reflexivity limits the text as play. This limit is what accounts for the oppositional terms of presence and absence; it makes, he writes, for the "real, empirically apprehensible experience and the concept of its 'ideal' and phenomenal opposite . . . by means of an irreducible non-phenomenal structure," such as, we might add, the "between" or the "fold."[32] The suspension of the being of literature would not, therefore, be a marking of the abyssal structure of the text but of the transcendental reduction that puts Being into question. So Derrida writes, "But what if the Book was only, in all senses of the word, an *epoch* of Being? . . . If the form of the book was no longer to be the model of meaning? If Being was radically outside the book, outside its letter? If Being lost itself in books" (*WD*, 77)?

The non-question in *The Book of Questions* is the "certainty that Being is a Grammar" (*WD*, 76). But if Being were radically outside the book, and if books were the dissipation of Being, what then would be writing? The reflexive writing, the writing that doubles itself, would then refer to a radical illegibility, an other writing that is the possibility of the book and its impossibility as well: "The radical illegibility of which we are speaking is not irrationality, is not despair provoking non-sense, is not everything within the domains of the incomprehensible and the illogical that is anguishing. . . . Original illegibility is not simply a moment interior to the book, to reason or to logos; nor is it any more their opposite. . . . Prior to the book (in the nonchronological sense), original illegibility is therefore the very possibility of the book and, within it, of the ulterior and eventual opposition of 'rationalism' and 'irrationalism.' The Being that is announced within the illegible is beyond these categories, beyond, as it writes itself, its own name" (*WD*, 77). To write, Derrida suggests, is "to confuse ontology with grammar," and this is the ruse of life, to forget the dead space of writing, the otherness that makes pure reflection impossible and pure literature a dream of Being (*WD*, 78). For literature needs both "Being that is announced within the illegible" and the Being that is a grammar. To question the latter would mean the end of writing, pure literature as the death of literature.

The Jewish God, Jabès writes, does not exist outside the book nor in it. God is an effect of reading/writing. He is the non-reflective trace of language; hence, the Jewish people survive in and by a writing that is the common torment shared by Jews and God: "God dwells in eternity; man, in a life unremittingly dedicated to the death that thought probes. Immortal word opposed to the word of any finitude [Parole immortelle opposée a la parole de toute finitude]. The book bears witness to this conflict that no page can resolve. And yet, God resides only in the word of man whom it inspires and destroys. Shared torment" (*BM*, 174 / *LM*, 183; trans. modified). The common torment of God and the Jew is to be dependent upon a reading that recognizes that there is no pure literature, which would be "death itself," as Derrida says, the disappearance of life in Being. To exist as literature, the text must bear a certain "radical illegibility." To say there is no literature is to say *The Book of Questions* is a book of life, at once putting the being of literature in question only as it questions the grammar of Being and, thus, the possibility of reconstituting the shattered tablets that would reclaim for the Book the presence of the Other: *"Ah, my books . . . What can I say? You see, it is perhaps just there, where we are silent while talking, where nobody can read us while we write, that what I have called Judaism resides"* (*LB, 36 / EL, 42*; ellipsis in original).

3

Deconstruction and the Future of Literature (or, Writing in the Nuclear Age)

I

When Derrida addressed the Cerisy-la-Salle conference devoted to his works, he chose as his title "On a Newly Arisen Apocalyptic Tone in Philosophy," as if to mark the occasion as one belonging to the discourse of crisis. His title refers to Kant's polemic against the "mystagogues" who threaten to destroy philosophy in their exaltation of inner feeling at the expense of reason and morality. Kant objects to those who rest the principle of morality on the feeling of pleasure or displeasure aroused by phenomena. Such a belief "concludes that the legislation of reason requires not only a *form* but also *matter* (content, purpose) as a determining ground of the will."[1] Kant warns that such a doctrine erases all morality because it necessitates that any action must follow upon the feeling produced by an object, which would do away with the principle of reason acting in accordance with the ideal. This doctrine of feeling makes morality follow upon the experience of an object, whereas Kant argues that the basis of morality rests upon belief in the supersensible, not the empirical (*RTP*, 61).

The new German thinkers suffer from a "mistuning" [*Verstimmung*] of the head because they seek a "supernatural communication (mystical illumination)" rather than listen to the moral law (*RTP*, 62). Kant characterizes the moral law as an inner voice whose call comes from an unknown location. When we listen, he writes, "we are in doubt whether it comes from man, from the perfected power of his own reason, or whether it comes from an other, whose essence is unknown to us and speaks to man through this,

101

his own reason." Rather than pursue this voice, he says, we should devote ourselves to the properly philosophical task of turning the moral law into clear concepts. When the law is personified, reason "is made into a veiled Isis . . . [which] is an *aesthetic* mode of representing precisely the same object." One can, he says, "use this mode of representation backward" to "enliven those ideas by a sensible, albeit only analogical, presentation, and yet one always runs the danger of falling into an exalting vision, which is the death of all philosophy" (*RTP*, 71). Kant's anxiety over philosophy lies in his need to place the law beyond representation, beyond the voice that speaks in or to us. This law, which always remains the same, must be singular and repeatable, which means that if it is to be binding upon us, it must—this is what Kant resists—differ from itself in order to be what it is. There would be no law without this iterability (the principle that identity is conditioned by repetition and difference). Kant had difficulty grasping that the law is both singular and iterable, when it should be universal, which it is. Like Kafka's man before the law, "He had difficulty with literature" (*BL*, 213).

We can hear in Kant's warning of the death of philosophy an apocalyptic tone, a tone we seem to have grown accustomed to as the *fin de siecle* approaches. Today, we now hear not only of the death of philosophy but of the death of literature as well. Yet I would argue that there is still a future for philosophy and literature; in fact, we might say that the future depends upon them. The irony of Kant's assuming an apocalyptic tone in a warning against the very same should alert us to the fact that the language of crisis destabilizes the very principles of transcendental and ontological critique. In demanding that we rise above a search into the source of the voice of moral reason, Kant offers to make peace with his adversaries. Yet in denouncing those who proclaim the end of philosophy, he has, as Derrida comments, himself marked "a limit, indeed the end of a certain type of metaphysics, [and] freed another wave of eschatological discourses in philosophy" (*RTP*, 144). With all this talk of ends, we cannot help but ask if Derrida's apocalyptic tone is not a mark of the limits of deconstruction. Indeed, many critics have denounced deconstruction precisely as an eschatological discourse that offers no way out of the very limits it reveals in other philosophies. But Derrida does not come to pronounce an end (of metaphysics, of literature, of man), but rather he speaks of what is to come, the future, or what he calls the invention of the other, and it is on this basis that he makes his claim for the responsibility of deconstruction.

In two essays originally delivered as talks at Cornell University in 1984, "No Apocalypse, Not Now (full speed ahead, seven missiles, seven missives)" and "Psyché: Inventions of the Other," he gathers around the topic of the future the apparently opposing notions of absolute destruction and absolute invention, two events, we might say, that lie in the future. They are figures for the future, that is, of the unanticipatable, the surprising, the monstrous. If the future, *l'avenir*, is what is to come, *à-venir*, it is not a repetition of the same but is something surprising, an event for which we are not prepared. Like invention, this event is illegitimate; it disrupts a norm or the order of things. It is, in a word, monstrous, hence, a catachresis, "a violent production of meaning." Derrida speaks of his own work, and philosophy itself, as a catachresis, and it is this figure that makes philosophy literary, that is, a showing, monstration, of the other (*montre* means "to show" and is etymologically linked to *monstre*). Derrida says, " I am trying to produce new forms of catachresis, another kind of writing, a violent writing which stakes out the faults and deviations of language; so that the text produces a language of its own, in itself, which while continuing to work through tradition emerges at a given moment as a *monster*, a monstrous mutation without tradition or normative precedent."[2] Deconstruction shares with literature this status as an event marked not by an internal criterion but by its movement toward the other. Deconstruction and literature—and by "literature" I mean a particular kind of writing that does not necessarily coincide with *belles lettres* or the institution of "Literature"—produce monstrosities, a writing that grafts itself onto traditions (for a monster is, by definition, a kind of hybrid violating a norm) and beckons toward something new, something other.

The other is not to be thought on some anthropological basis—it is not other people, nor is the other precisely some thing—the other is to come, which is not to say it is out-standing, as Heidegger said of death, but the other is, Derrida says, the only possible invention, "an event through which the future (*l'avenir*) comes to us" (*PIO*, 46). Rather than speak of it as the "not yet" or what is "out-standing," we can say the other is impossible; it is "the invention of that which did not appear to be possible" (*PIO*, 60). It is the condition of the future. For a future that is already known could not be a future, and so it appears as a monstrosity, which is always something new. But at the same time, a monstrosity means that a norm has been violated, and because the future would have to take the form of a monstrosity, it is turned toward a past that it dislocates. We can say that the future, like literature, is recognizable by its tone, its coming to us as something idiomatic or singular, as an other that unsettles the conditions of its coming. This is why there is no internal criterion to the literary "event," to borrow Derrida's term, no essence of literature. There is no idiom, no event, that can be pure; a singular event or work would find no place in the world. It must open itself to iterability, that is, "produce 'effects of generality,'" if it is to be experienced or read (*SIL*, 62). Hence, "the literary event is perhaps more of an event (because less natural) than any other, but by the same token it becomes very 'improbable,' hard to verify" (*SIL*, 73). This can be called the "law" of experience: any experience as such must be singular, but to maintain this singularity the experience must permit itself to be effaced, carried away, or re-marked by generality. That is, singularity as singularity can only be experienced if it is open to the possibility of repetition. Without this level of ideality, the singular is not recognizable in a human world; it must be conditioned by an "original" doubling, fold, or re-mark that permits it to be what it is: singular and recognized as such. Therefore, the literary event is more an event than any other because it is the unnatural and necessary, the monstrous, event that promises itself as unique and as repetition. It institutes and transgresses. This is why we can say that the only absolute referent of literature is nuclear catastrophe because literature has always pointed to an ultimate referent, the absolutely singular that has no place in the world. This is the monstrosity of literature: it aspires to the condition of its own demise—pure invention is pure destruction. That literature should die of its own aims, fail to achieve the singularity of absolute presence, means that it has a future, a future dependent upon the other. Thus, Derrida will say "deconstruction is itself a form of literature," which means that like literature it always engages the idiomatic.

It is a great mistake to confuse deconstruction with nihilism, for deconstruction is saying anything but that we are imprisoned in language or cannot distinguish reality from its fictional representations.[3] Deconstruction, like a certain kind of literary writing, is concerned with the impossible, but necessary, task of designating the other. Deconstruction, then, is not just another kind of writing but produces "what in fact looks like a discursive monster so that the analysis will be a *practical* effect, so that people will be forced to become aware of the history of normality" (*Points*, 386). If the future must be a monster, deconstruction welcomes it rather than tries to normalize it. It says *yes* to the future, promises itself to be responsible (for the other).

In the exergue to *Of Grammatology*, Derrida writes, "The future can be anticipated only in the form of absolute danger. It is that which breaks absolutely with constituted normality and can thus announce itself, *present* itself, only under the species of monstrosity" (*OG*, 5; trans. modified). The future announces itself as a monstrosity, an event "for which there is no self-presentation nor assured destination." The monstrous is a name for what has no name, for what is to come. It is to come precisely because it does not have the status of a present being, nor is it an object of knowledge. It would be a first event and a last, a destruction that leaves no remains, something like a nuclear apocalypse. Derrida uncovers an affinity between the rhetoric of nuclear war and literature that lies not in scenarios of mass destruction but in the anticipation of the wholly other, which he says is the only possible invention. The invention of the other addresses the problem of singularity and of an event to come, the "monstrosity" of an absolute referent, that which is without precedent and can be figured as nuclear catastrophe.

The absolutely singular, that which is, properly speaking, unique, would never be accessible to the understanding or even presentable at all if it were not linked to iterability. On the basis of the formalizing power of iterability, the law that subjects singularity to generality, nuclear war, or absolute destruction, and literature, or absolute invention, are similar. What allows us to think the singularity of nuclear war, "its absolute inventiveness," or the possibility of a destruction that leaves no remainder, is the total destruction of the "juridico-literary archive," that is, of literature (*NA*, 26).

The other, according to Derrida, is not inventable but is the only invention of the world. It allows for the unanticipatable, an origin, still to be invented. We could call it an experience of the impossible, a first event that is also a last event, an absolute invention, an absolute *epoché*. It would not be the achievement of absolute knowledge, the Husserlian project of a "voice without *différance*" (*SP*, 102), or what Husserl calls "consciousness free of all worldly being,"[4] but the experience of the precariousness of the event that goes by the name "literature" and whose possibility consists in the archivizing act. As act, literature produces "its constitutional law" in the "discursive forms, 'works' and 'events' in which the very possibility of a fundamental constitution is at least 'fictionally' contested, threatened, deconstructed, presented in its very precariousness" (*SIL*, 72). In other words, literature belongs to the law or the juridico-political production of institutional foundations—there would be no literature without institution—and at the same time, literature, in its fictionality, contests these laws.

This makes the literary event, as we have seen, more an event than any other. Literature has this status by virtue of its having no identity, no essence. It consists in the act, the *epoché* of the referent. As that which produces and harbors its referent inside itself, literature allows us to think the absolute *epoché*, "the *epoché* of absolute knowledge" (*NA*, 27). By virtue of its absolute dependence on the archive and its performative relation to the referent, literature is susceptible to the threat of total destruction, to nuclear holocaust. As we will see, nuclear catastrophe is thinkable only on the basis of that which has no referent outside itself; otherwise the possibility of continued existence or the capacity to be reconstructed still exists (See *NA*, 26). I find it, therefore, a grave misunderstanding of Derrida to charge him with textualizing the threat of nuclear destruction. In asking us to recognize the link between nuclear catastrophe and the literary archive, he is not confusing the real and its simulacrum but is indicating that literary writing affords us the possibility of thinking that which is too commonly said to be unthinkable—absolute destruction of the world. In other words, the absolute end of meaning and truth, the "unthinkable" end of the world, is thinkable on the basis of fictionality, literature's "*being-suspended*," its suspension of *and* dependence upon meaning and reference. The error of someone who charges Derrida with denying us the resources of distinguishing reality from fiction, not only confuses fictionality with fantasy, but misses the point that fictionality does not do away with reference to something outside of language. Literature's neutrality, its being without essence, means it is the place, the resource, where it becomes possible to think presence and absence, meaning and reference. Under the name of literature we experience the possibility of nothing—which is what a totally self-referential literature would be, if such a thing were possible—and therefore everything. To say, then, that absolute destruction is thinkable only within literature is to remind us that when we set ourselves the task of speaking about what constitutes the possible end of the world, we are speaking about the threat to absolute knowledge, the "absolute *epochê*," which means we must recognize that any possibility of speaking about what is to come rests upon literature's condition as being at once an ideality (Derrida says that if literature were to resist a transcendental reading absolutely, it would destroy the necessary referral function of the text—there would be no trace of the text) and the possible suspension of meaning. This is what gives literature its power to interrogate the categories of transcendental authority and absolute suspension that constitute the discourse and reality of the nuclear age.

I am describing what Derrida calls literature's provision of "'phenomenological' access to what makes of a thesis a *thesis as such*" (*SIL*, 46). Derrida's career began with the acknowledgment of the necessary recourse to phenomenological language when speaking about literature, and in his first book, *Edmund Husserl's "Origin of Geometry": An Introduction*, he explicitly linked the question of invention to absolute destruction. Husserl had to introduce the concept of writing to ensure the ideality of meaning, and it was this need for an intraworldly existence of the idea that also led him to assert that the absolute annihilation of the world would modify but not touch the existence of consciousness.[5] Eidetic or transcendental description (that is, the ascertaining of essences rather than "facts") required the *epochê*, the bracketing or setting aside of the natural attitude (the spontaneous thinking, feeling, desiring that goes on as long as I face the world in my everyday attitude), but as Derrida notes in agreement with Eugen Fink, Husserl had to have recourse "to a language that could not itself be submitted to the *epochê*—without itself being simply in the world—thus to a language which remained naive, even though it was by virtue of this very language that all the phenomenological bracketings and parentheses were made possible."[6] That is to say, phenomenology itself is not susceptible to thematization, the process wherein noetic-noematic experience is laid hold of in the *epochê* or reduction.

Literary critics have come under attack for assuming that literary language does not fall victim to the "blindness" of metaphysical language, but Derrida, in his thesis defense, writes of being "fascinated by the literary ruse of the inscription and the whole ungraspable paradox of a trace which manages only to carry itself away, to erase itself in marking itself out afresh, itself and its own idiom, which in order to take actual form must erase itself and produce itself at the price of this self-erasure."[7] These remarks suggest not that literature challenges metaphysics—quite the contrary—but that literary writing, a whole other thing than "literature," is that aspect of every text that puts phenomenology in crisis. As Rodolphe Gasché has written, insofar as literature is "characterizable only by its structure of bracketing," it "puts the transcendental authority and dominant category of being into question."[8] Indeed, it is only in approaching the question of literature through the phenomenological language of intentionality that we can approach anything like "nuclear criticism," the subject of a 1984 *Diacritics* colloquium and the stage for Derrida's delivery of "No Apocalypse."

II

The nuclear age, like literature, raises the possibility of another experience, an experience of another world, or the end of this world, which would be much the same thing. If we recall that in Husserl, the theme of phenomenology is intentionality,[9] and that thematization takes up what is presented in the unthought or what he calls the natural attitude toward the world and makes it an object of consciousness, then Derrida's assertion that literature is what allows us "to think the uniqueness of nuclear war" must be taken up in phenomenological terms as the nonthematic condition for thought. In acknowledging that the Idea is never "the *theme* of a phenomenological description" but is determinable as the horizon of intuition, as the *Endstiftung* that is infinitely deferred, Derrida concludes that "phenomenology cannot be reflected in a phenomenology of phenomenology" (*IOG*, 137–38; 141). In as much as phenomenology aims at the thematization of the "unthematized structures of consciousness" (i.e., to rise to the condition of a purely eidetic science) and is unable to thematize itself, the claim that literature belongs to the nuclear epoch, "the *epochê* of absolute knowledge" (*NA*, 27) means that literature affirms the unthematizable as the condition for the anticipation of the future as apocalypse without truth.

Nuclear war is, perhaps, the possibility of what has always been the defining condition of literature as the aleatory and unique event. It is the infinite horizon of what we call "literature": "nuclear war is the only possible referent of any discourse and any experience that would share their condition with that of literature" (*NA*, 28). Nuclear criticism, therefore, comes into view as the finite consciousness of the infinite capacity for a remainderless self-destruction. "'Nuclear criticism,'" Derrida writes, "like Kantian criticism, is thought about the limits of experience as a thought of finitude." The prospect of nuclear war, of a remainderless destruction, would be "waged *in the name of . . .*" (ellipsis in original—Derrida suggests it can only be "the name of something whose name, in this logic of total destruction, can no longer be borne, transmitted, inherited by anything living," a "name of nothing," a "pure name") (*NA*, 30–31).

Derrida explains that both nuclear criticism and Kantian criticism are predicated upon the opposition between a "receptive (that is, perceiving) being, of which the human subject is only one example," and "an infinite intellect which creates its own objects rather than inventing them" (*NA*, 30). The presupposition by "finite rationality" of "the possibility of infinite progress" is the very basis of criticism and phenomenology: "The *Endstiftung* of phenomenology (phenomenology's ultimate critical legitimation: i.e., what its sense, value, and right tell us about it), then, never directly measures up to a phenomenology. At least this *Endstiftung* can give access to itself in a philosophy, insofar as it is *announced* in a . . . concrete *consciousness* which is made *responsible* for it despite the finitude of that consciousness. . . . Husserl's phenomenology starts from this *lived anticipation* as a radical responsibility" (*IOG*, 141).

This responsibility arises from the Idea "as an infinite [task] implying an unending progress and hence a history."[10] Implicit in Husserl's notion of the nonthematization of the Idea is the distinction between the nonhistorical Idea and the history of the concept. As the telos of an intentional history, the Idea is not susceptible to destruction because it is not *in* history. (The Idea is represented to consciousness by conceptual thought.)[11]

The prospect of absolute destruction institutes the possibility of absolute consciousness, consciousness free from the annihilation of physical things—as Husserl proposed. Survival, however, is predicated upon iterability, the condition of the functioning of all language: "Iterability supposes a minimal remainder (as well as a minimum idealization) in order that the identity of the *selfsame* be repeatable and identifiable *in, through*, and even *in view of* its alteration" (*LI*, 53). Iterability both constitutes the ideality of truth and divides it. It is the condition for something to be recognized in different times and places, *and* it deconstitutes the "thing" as *eidos* or essence (that is, as self-identical). Iterability is an impure "idea," "a differential structure escaping the logic of presence or the (simple and dialectical) opposition of presence and absence, upon which the idea of permanence depends" (*LI*, 53). As long as nuclear criticism is devoted to anticipating absolute or remainder-less self-destruction, it conforms to Husserl's concept of historicity as the passage of sense. Nuclear catastrophe presents itself, makes itself available to thought, on the basis of its self-destruction before the truth, the name. Nuclear criticism remains bound to the notion that the destruction of phenomenological sense will be a destruction of ideal sense. To the extent that nuclear criticism anticipates infinite destruction, it is guided by the Idea of Reason.

Derrida's comparison of nuclear criticism to Kantian criticism ought to give caution to anyone who wishes to take up "nuclear criticism" as a regional discipline of deconstruction.[12] Insofar as nuclear criticism is a thought of finitude, operating within the poles of receptive being and infinite intellect, it is an attempt (the last?) to account for the concept of subjectivity and the existence of absolute consciousness. That is, to the degree that nuclear criticism is directed toward the future, it postulates a consciousness that will survive nuclear destruction.[13] It would be a mode of self-reflection, a turning back to the conditions of the world insofar as the world is to be grasped as the absolute referent, as what is there or given for experience.

"Such a criticism," Derrida writes, "forecloses a finitude so radical that it would annul the basis of the opposition and would make it possible to think the very limit of criticism. This limit comes into view in the groundlessness of a remainderless self-destruction of the self, auto-destruction of the *autos* itself. Whereupon the kernel, the nucleus of criticism, itself bursts apart" (*NA*, 30). The opening of this kernel, this dehiscence, would bring into view the opposition between finite and infinite that sustains criticism as a discipline subordinate to philosophy. A "remainderless self-destruction," a destruction without iterability, one that would leave no trace (of itself), is thinkable on the basis of presence. It confirms the idea of the future as apocalypse, as revelation. Such a notion of absolute destruction belongs to the text of metaphysics and the epochality of Being. Erasure, however, belongs to the structure of the trace (*M*, 23). If the trace "exceeds the truth of Being," then the disappearance of the trace of the ontological difference, the difference between Being and beings, would be fulfilled in the nuclear epoch. Our thinking of nuclear catastrophe is metaphysical insofar as it maintains, indeed fulfills, the opposition between presence and absence. Nuclear radiation, however, is not simply a metaphor of the trace left after the effacement of beings, the effacement of difference, but the threat of nuclear holocaust has been with us as long as the concept of presence, which is thinkable only in its opposition to absence. The concept of nuclear holocaust belongs to a concept of ideality and, therefore, to iterability and the effacement of the trace.

If iterability supposes that a "one time," such as a nuclear catastrophe, is already divided, then it undermines the opposition between finite and infinite upon which nuclear criticism rests. Nuclear criticism would be the completion of metaphysics according to the text of metaphysics. A criticism that holds "the groundlessness (*le sans-fond*) of a remainderless self-destruction of the self" up to view would be one that shows the only subject of criticism to be the effacement of the absolute trace, "the trace of what is entirely other ([*trace du tout autre*]" (*NA*, 28). Derrida's deconstruction points to a dehiscence, an opening, that displaces the oppositions between finite and infinite, and *de facto* and *de jure* by reinscribing philosophical discourse in the general text, "an intentionality without an intentum"; that is, the text displaces phenomenological intentionality with an intentionality that "cannot be *fulfilled* by a corresponding extraintentional referent."[14] Because nothing can exist outside the general text—there can be no extratextual referent, or nothing is without a context—the threat of nuclear catastrophe is thinkable only in terms of the destruction of that which has no referent outside itself—that is, literature. Literature gives us to think the totality of absolute destruction because it is without essence: as the trace that erases itself, it is the unthematizable. Literature is unique, the singular event, precisely because it is structurally conditioned through its being as suspended, its being-suspended. The epochal character of literature makes it totally dependent on the archive and, at the same time, it gives us to think the total destruction of the archive, which is to say, it gives us to think the formalizing power of philosophical discourse—of first times and last times, of invention and destruction.

III

Derrida's shocking, at least for some, assertion that literature "doesn't exist" may be taken to mean it does not exist in and by itself as some transcendental entity; nevertheless, there is an experience that may be called "literary." As an experience without essence, literature may be said to have no identity, to have no (or hardly any) Being. In his most extensive interview on the subject, Derrida insists on the need for a "phenomenological-type language" to speak of literary writing and reading. "The literary character of the text is inscribed on the side of the intentional object, in its noematic structure, one could say, and not only on the subjective side of the noetic act." Nevertheless, there is something particular to "literary writing or reading" that "puts phenomenology in crisis" (*SIL*, 44–45). Being without essence, literature does not pass over into the indefinable nor can it be reduced to its function within the confines of an institution.

The literary event, divided into act and archive, is a first time and, if it is to be unique, a last time: "archaeology and eschatology acknowledge each other here in the irony of the *one and only* instant." The reflexive structure of literature "not only does not produce coincidence with or presence to itself but . . . instead projects forward the advent of the self of 'speaking' or 'writing' of itself as other, that is to say, what I call a trace" (*PIO*, 29). The literary event is marked by a delay, an inaugural capacity for recitation, that is to say, by the production of iterability. To be both act and archive, the event is marked by what Derrida calls "a sort of retroverted anticipation" (*PIO*, 51). We might say that the event is "inaugurated" by a delay, an act that is an archivization. Therefore, the event is determined not by the opposition of a present to a past or an act to a nonact but as a relationship wherein the event becomes what it is by its reference to a past, an institution of a past, that does not govern the act but succeeds it. The act is inseparable from the archive it engenders.

A "first" time, in other words, is structured like a trace. The "presentness" of an event is related to its other as past element or archive, which does not come into being *a posteriori* but traverses the event in its "origin." If we turn to "Différance," we find that by means of the trace, the present (and, by extension, we may add, the event) is constituted by what it is not: "An interval must separate the present from what it is not in order for the present to be itself, but this interval that constitutes it as present must, by the same token, divide the present in and of itself, thereby also dividing, along with the present, everything that is thought on the basis of the present" (*M*, 13). If literature, as archive, has its referent in itself, this does not mean it is a self-contained, self-reflexive entity, but is constituted by the *epochê* of the referent, a bracketing of the referent, a putting it out of commission, in order to get at the "absolute" referent or, we might say, the ideality of ideality. When it is said that "literature," insofar as it is characterized by its structure of bracketing or suspension, is without essence, it does not mean there is no more literature in its traditional sense but the grounds of "literature" cannot lie in truth or Being.

We are approaching the problem of the ideality of the literary object, the topic of Derrida's first thesis in 1957.[15] Traces of Derrida's interest are present in his first book, the translation and introduction to Edmund Husserl's "The Origin of Geometry," particularly in the passage where he proposes that James Joyce and Husserl present two endeavors to assume the memory of the past in the face of radical equivocity: one can follow Joyce and rather than reduce writing to univocity employ a language that equalizes synchrony with the greatest possibility for accumulated meaning "within each linguistic atom." Husserl represents the effort "to reduce or impoverish empirical language methodically to the point where its univocal and translatable elements are actually transparent" (*IOG*,

102–103). We should not too readily assume which of the two endeavors Derrida chooses; although he rejects the "hypothesis of a univocal and natural language" as absurd, he affirms that Husserl was fully cognizant of the irreducible equivocity in "pure historicity" and that his "project, as the transcendental 'parallel' to Joyce's, knows the same relativity" (*IOG*, 103). When he writes in "No Apocalypse, Not Now" that "literature is not reduced to this form of archivizing and this form of law [i.e., its constitution by virtue of an objective archive built upon oral tradition, and its protection by positive law—copyright, etc.], but it could not outlive them and still be called literature" (*NA*, 26), Derrida is acknowledging the material and historical basis for what we call "literature," and he is also pointing to the impossibility of reducing literature to this naive form of natural existence (no more than we can imagine a culture without equivocity), which would mean denying literature's ideality (Husserl calls it a "bound ideality"). If literature were merely embodied in the archive and law, it would not be subject to the threat of nuclear catastrophe. Yet Derrida says, after the destruction of the archive, more poems and fictional narratives may be written, but they would not be "literature"—just as Homer never wrote literature since he "wrote" prior to the archive and positive law.

Literature cannot "outlive" its material base and still be called "literature" insofar as it has no referent outside itself or its "own possibility" (*NA*, 26). If literature possessed a real referent external to the juridico-literary archive, it would be able to reconstitute itself on that basis. Yet Derrida implies that such an external referent would make what remains something other than literature. This is something we have already known insofar as literature belongs to or is subordinate to the order of Being. To the extent that literature, the being of literature, is determined by mimetologism, it is subordinate to an essence exterior to itself. The truth-being of literature, its being of/as truth, is determined by its subordination to the transcendental authority of Being. Thus, "there is no—or hardly any, ever so little—literature" (*D*, 223); which means, on the one hand, insofar as literature's truth is elsewhere, in Being, there is no literature, and on the other, that "literature" in parenthesis is on an order other than Being.

We can turn to Derrida's first book, *Edmund Husserl's "The Origin of Geometry": An Introduction,* to find that the destruction of the archive need not mean an "intrinsic destruction" of absolute ideality's "sense-of-being as truth" (*IOG*, 94). Paradoxically, it is writing that frees the being-sense of truth from the threat of catastrophe even if as factuality the archive were destroyed. Writing permits the objectification that liberates language from the "actual intentionality of a speaking subject or community of speaking subjects. By absolutely virtualizing dialogue, writing creates a kind of autonomous transcendental field from which any present subject can be absent" (*IOG*, 88).

This may well be Derrida's most famous argument: writing is understood in the West as the sign of the deferred presence of a once present subject. Otherwise, if communication were founded upon presence and the present, it could only occur in the presence of a speaking subject and would have no validity beyond that present moment. But if we allow that someone who "invents" an idea, such as geometry, must communicate the idea to him or herself in order to think or make the idea clear, then the present of communication occurs in an intrasubjective moment that admits a dialectical temporality and alterity into the Living Present. For Husserl, meaning *must* be embodied and repeatable to escape the limitations of a unique present. This understanding derives from an "intentional analysis" that preserves writing's relation to a pure consciousness and disregards writing's "factuality," its worldly existence. The possibility of communication depends upon an ideal Objectivity—that is, the object as it is for transcendental consciousness—that remains the same from one moment to the next. As absolute Objectivity, writing is able "to dispense with, *due to its sense*, every present reading in general" (*IOG*, 88). Were it not for writing, language would remain the captive of the actual intentionality of speaking subjects or a community of speaking subjects. Consequently, language would be tied to *de facto* intentionality, which would ensure the meaning of a communication only within the confines of the intentional act and give no guarantee of intelligibility beyond that act. But in freeing language from the actual intentionality of real subjects, writing is open to forgetfulness, the loss of meaning, and death. What is more, if the text were not dependent upon virtual intentionality nor *de jure* intelligible for a transcendental subject, then it would be no more "than a chaotic literalness" (*IOG*, 88). In other words, without the archive, the instituting act would not be readable.

The ideality of sense requires the very "binding" of written or scriptural space (*IOG*, 89). Derrida concludes that "the *ability* of sense to be linguistically embodied is the only means by which sense becomes nonspatiotemporal" (*IOG*, 90). The condition for the Objectivity and perdurability of truth is the possibility of its being said and written, otherwise ideal objectivity would be fully constituted "before and independently of its *ability to* be embodied" (*IOG*, 90). Writing authenticates the linguistic event: the intelligibility of language is guaranteed by the intentional synthesis of the ideality of sense and the reality of the sign.

We are not dealing with the opposition between the sensible and intelligible, because the graphic sign is the condition for the internal completion of Objectivity. Moreover, Husserl is concerned with possibility and not the factual embodiment of truth because truth endures "without being thought in act or in fact": "Truth depends on the pure possibility of speaking and writing, but is independent of what is spoken or written, insofar as they are in the world" (*IOG*, 92). The embodiment of truth in language is not a fall into the worldly because truth may reside in the sign, graphic or vocal, and remain unthought. Truth's mode of perduring liberates it from worldly existence or empirical subjectivity. "But since, in order to escape worldliness, sense *must* first *be able* to be set down in the pure world and be deposited in sensible spatiotemporality, it must put its pure intentional ideality, i.e., its truth-sense, in danger." Philosophy's other, empiricism (or nonphilosophy), appears *in* philosophy as "the possibility of truth's *disappearance*," which is not simply the possibility of its annihilation "but also what ceases, intermittently or definitely, to appear *in fact* yet without affecting its being or being-sense" (*IOG*, 92–93).

For philosophy to preserve itself, it admits the possibility of truth's disappearance but only to occult it. Egological consciousness is somewhat like a coffin preserving the dead letter, a writing subject to chaotic literalness, that is, a writing deprived of transcendental significance. In Husserl's analysis, "once sense appeared in egological consciousness, its total annihilation becomes impossible" (*IOG*, 93). A world-wide destruction of libraries would not banish sense to the realm of nothingness because the virtual presence of sense can always *de jure* be reanimated within the monadic subject; however, as Derrida points out, absolute ideal Objectivity, which is dependent upon, but *not* constituted by, corporeal exteriority, is threatened as truth in this world by forgetfulness, "a historical category" (*IOG*, 93).

Husserl's concern is with historicity, which is always sense-history, and not history or facticity. Phenomenology cannot answer the question of the singularity or uniqueness of the event but is directed toward its sense-being, and it proceeds by reduction of sedimentary retention—ideal objects preserved by consciousness as tradition. This sedimentation is not simply to be discarded as if it obscured the origin—this would cut off the present from the past—but is the very possibility of inquiry into and reactivation of an origin. The present appears "as the retention of a present past, i.e., as the retention of a retention" (*IOG*, 57).

The destruction of corporeal traces of sense, retentions of retentions, would not threaten *de jure* reanimation of sense. For Husserl, then, a world-wide conflagration of libraries, the burning of the archive, does not mean the destruction of the being-sense of truth. Insofar as the being-sense is a bound ideality—that is, an ideality limited to the world—it is vulnerable to worldly accident, its absolute destruction in what Derrida would later call a *"brûle-tout,"* but the absolute destruction of actual writing would not, for Husserl, mean the destruction of absolute ideality, which, however altered by factual destruction, "would remain intact in itself" (*IOG*, 94).

I have turned to this early text on Husserl because it is the first to address the theme of the destruction of the library. It should be pointed out, however, that Husserl entertains the idea of the annihilation of ideal Objectivity or truth only to reduce it to an exterior threat, an empirical, but not philosophical, possibility. Such a thinking would characterize destruction within the pole of the finite and infinite. Insofar as destruction is limited to the corporeal body, it is an accident of empirical finitude. The destruction of truth, on the other hand, would be an infinite destruction, an annihilation of the infinite thought as "absolute ideality . . . the correlate of a possibility of indefinite repetition" (*SP*, 52). However threatening to bound cultural idealities, "[d]eath is possible for them alone and has the transcendental signification we just now granted it [i.e., the disappearance of the subject in general ensures the intelligibility of bound idealities beyond any factual accident], but only insofar as the 'bound' ideality is animated or traversed by a transcendental intention, only insofar as it is guided by the Telos

of an absolute freeing which has not been fully attained" (*IOG*, 94).
The ideality of absence—an ideality because it is indifferent to the
empirical absence of the subject—means that for Husserl the perdurability of truth does not depend on factual writing but would
remain intact in "its sense-of-being as truth" even if there were a
world-wide destruction of all libraries. Ideality must, therefore, be
infinitely repeatable, which for Husserl means infinitely deferred
(see *SP*, 101). That the Idea is identical throughout its alteration
in the visible sign—the being-sense of the Idea is otherwise not
locatable in the world apart from writing—means that truth can
be "fully objective, i.e., ideal, intelligible for everyone and indefinitely perdurable" only if it can "be said *and* written" (*IOG*, 90).
The repeatability of truth is possible only through representation.
Consequently, the appearance of the Ideal is dependent on iterability—repetition and alteration. The ideality bound to the graphic
sign is animated, then, by death, the non-identity that makes repetition possible and defers the coming to presence of truth.

The possibility of absence is not, as Husserl would have it, an
accident that befalls an infinite truth but is the structural possibility of the appearing of the Ideal. Rather than deriving difference
from ideality as the permanence of the same, ideality is a possibility of repetition. If the being-sense of truth is not, according to
Husserl, subject to destruction, then death is not an accident
arresting infinite truth but is, as Gasché says, to be understood "as
the condition of iterability without which no unit could be
exchanged, transmitted, represented, referred to, reproduced,
remembered, and so on."[16] Death, the finitude of truth, is the condition of truth, the internal doubling or remarking of self and
other that makes any idealization possible. Therefore, rather than
derive difference from identity, Derrida will say, in the beginning
is *différance*:

But this appearing of the Ideal as an infinite *différance* can
only be produced within a relationship with death in general.
Only a relation to my-death could make the infinite differing
of presence appear. By the same token, compared to the ideality of the positive infinite, this relation to my-death becomes
an accident of empirical finitude. The appearing of the infinite *différance* is itself finite. Consequently, *différance*, which
does not occur outside this relation, becomes the finitude of

life as an essential relation with oneself and one's death. *The infinite* différance *is finite*. It can therefore no longer be conceived within the opposition of finiteness and infinity, absence and presence, negation and affirmation (*SP*, 102).

Death or finitude does not oppose the infinite but is its possibility. The destruction of the archive, for Husserl, may be said to be the condition of the sign in general. The apocalypse would not be an infinite destruction of truth but would be the possibility of its pure presence:

> Since absolute self-presence in con-sciousness is the infinite *vocation* of full presence, the achievement of absolute knowledge is the end of the infinite, which could only be the unity of the concept, logos, and consciousness in a voice without *différance. The history of metaphysics therefore can be expressed as the unfolding of the structure or schema of an absolute will-to-hear-oneself-speak.* This history is closed when this infinite absolute appears to itself as its own death. *A voice without différance, a voice without writing, is at once absolutely alive and absolutely dead* (*SP*, 102).

If the closure of history means the realization, the "presentation [*Gegenwärtigung*] of Being," then to say the "infinite absolute appears to itself as its own death" is tantamount to saying the closure of this history (the history of the metaphysics of presence) has already taken place. This closure of history does not coincide with revelation—closure is not apocalypse—but is the metaphysical desire for presence, a deathly desire that would consume itself in its realization.[17] Yet we can say that such a realization is not possible—a voice without *différance* would be no voice at all or would be pure voice—the difference is less than minimal—it will be "absolutely alive and absolutely dead," a condition that is conceivable only as infinite desire (for death).

IV

Derrida seems dangerously close to answering the call for a new language; indeed, he appears to anticipate the apocalypse. The future that announces itself "'beyond' absolute knowledge" requires *"unheard-of* thoughts . . . sought for across the memory of old signs" (*SP*, 102). A kind of reinscription of the old signs is required. The "history of presence is closed" not because we have finally freed ourselves from metaphysics but because this history has always meant the presentation of Being, the desire for the full realization of self-presence. The concept of differing can no longer be understood as infinite deferral of presence, which is well within the bounds of a history of presence, but should "be heard in the openness of an unheard-of question that opens neither upon knowledge nor upon some nonknowledge which is a knowledge to come" (*SP*, 103). Instead it would be beyond the system of meaning, that is, something "older" than Being. It would be a protowriting, a "retention and protention of differences" or "a kind of writing before the letter" (*M*, 15).

This archê-writing "originates" in the genetivity *of*—a written origin or *inscription*, "an origin which has no meaning before the *of*, an origin inseparable from genetivity and from the space that it engenders and orients: an *inscribed* origin. The *inscription* is the written origin: traced and henceforth *inscribed in* a system, in a figure which it no longer governs" (*WD*, 115). As inscribed, the origin must necessarily relate to the other if it is to be an origin *of* (something). Commenting on this passage, Gasché writes, "In a certain way one could speak of an inscription as an *epochê* of the origin; but it would be the opposite of a phenomenological *epochê*, since it would represent a bracketing of the function of origin and of the meaning that origin confers on what derives from it."[18]

The phenomenological *epochê* is a bracketing of the natural attitude in order to neutralize our convictions or judgments about the world so as to get at our natural convictions (this does not mean adopting a naive viewpoint toward the world but would require taking up a critical standpoint toward this naiveté).[19] As Husserl defines it in *Ideas* I, it is a parenthesizing or putting out of action the positing that belongs to the natural attitude.[20] Revealed to us in the *epochê* is the transcendental consciousness which "subsists as the sole object of our judgments."[21] Derrida's "inscription" opposes position, the thetic act of consciousness, in order to get at the "problem of the concept of the concept, and the problem of the relationship between the concept and the other" (*P*, 96). In contrast to Husserl's concept of writing as what emancipates sense from the factual or worldly realm, Derrida's notion of inscription confounds the opposition of infinite and finite, same and other, being-sense and the graphic sign. Whereas phenomenological reduction is aimed at essences; an inscribed origin exceeds any notion of a singular or pure source. Therefore, *"in the beginning there will have been speed,"* writes Derrida for his first "nuclear aphorism" (*NA*, 20). In the beginning there will have been a doubling and overtaking (*doublant*).

This excursion into Husserl allows us to approach the question of literature in the nuclear *epochê*. We have seen how writing, for Husserl, ensures the ideal Objectivity that constitutes a transcendental field. This means that writing ensures the essence of communication independent of actual subjects. Indeed, the possibility of the absence of all actual subjectivity is a necessary condition for the absolute ideal Objectivity of sense, and writing is what frees sense from the temporal and spatial limits of the speaking subject to create an "autonomous transcendental field" (*IOG*, 88). The question Derrida raises concerning this subjectless transcendental field is that as an absolute Objectivity, the field of writing has no need for any actual reading in general. Consequently, the text is haunted by the transcendental sense of death insofar as it is no more than illegible marks devoid of a transcendental function, which leaves us with the paradox that truth is free from actual subjectivity by virtue of its being exposed to the changeableness of written and spoken language. The danger is "the possibility of truth's *disappearance*" (*IOG*, 93). We have already seen that as long as truth does not depend on spatiotemporal events, even universal destruction would not involve the transcendental sense of death. Husserl opposes an intrinsic historicity to an actual or external historicity in order to preserve the absolute ideality of truth from worldly catastrophe.

A fundamental ambiguity persists in Husserl's concept of writing as that which constitutes absolute ideal Objectivity and which, as sensible body, can undergo corporeal disaster. Derrida argues that Husserl must dissociate *Körper* (sensible body) from *Leib* (constituting body) and preserve the "intention of writing (or of reading) in itself and in its purity." To do so means setting aside as inessential *"Körper* as such" (*IOG*, 97) in order to preserve the ideal identity of language, its univocity, from empirical history and consequently, equivocity. Husserl removes sense from the realm of historical change and secures it in historicity, which always concerns origins and traditions of ideal objects. We have seen that absolute Objectivity can be grasped only in the instituted object, writing. The Idea of the Absolute must expose itself in order to be, but it does not first exist and then enter history. "The Absolute of the Idea . . . is the Absolute *of* intentional historicity." Derrida goes on to note that the "*of*" does not designate an objective or subjective genetivity. "Rather, this 'of' concerns the intentional Absolute of *Objectivity*, the pure relation with an object—a relation in which subject and object are reciprocally engendered and governed. If the *of* announces neither an objective nor a subjective genitive, that is because it concerns the Absolute *of genetivity* itself as the pure possibility of a genetic relation" (*IOG*, 142–43). Husserl's unity of the constituted and constituting in which sense appears is historical *and* rational (see *IOG*, 143–46). Following from intentionality as the movement of consciousness from a sedimented tradition to an origin, a telos governs Husserl's reciprocal concept of history as rational and reason as historical. Derrida concludes, "In all the significance of this term, historicity is *sense*" (*IOG*, 150).

We are now ready to ask, what is threatened by apocalypse if the destruction of the library does not affect pure transcendental historicity? This is a question "of the *possibility of* historical factuality appearing" (*IOG*, 150). Apocalypse threatens the unity of sense and being: it is not limited to external history but would effect historicity itself. "History as institutive would be the profound area where sense is indissociable from being, where the de facto is indissociable from the de jure" (*IOG*, 46). To the extent that writing is necessary for the constitution of sense, Husserl's phenomenology does not leave the realm of factuality, but it is not an empiricism; it is a science of origins insofar as it insists that the historical habitat authenticates truth. History is where instituting *fact* is singular, irreducible, and invariable. In seeking the primordial constitution of truth, phenomenology proceeds from the sedimentation of tradition, from history, to the institutive act, an origin, "the unique fact of the *first time*" (*IOG*, 48). We may venture that this sedimentation constitutes an archive.

With an "inaugural signification that is always reproducible," we are dealing with the "non-fictive irreality of the essence" (*IOG*, 48): "*we call irreal every determination which . . . is founded with regard to its spatiotemporal appearance in a specifically real thing but which can appear in different realities as identical*—not merely as similar" (the real is *"essentially individualized by its spatiotemporal position"*). Husserl's example of the irreal is the literary work of art, which may be embodied in a book but is not individualized by it (unlike the painting, whose ideality, nonetheless, is, *"in principle . . .* indeed repeatable").[22] Thus, we can destroy Raphael's *Madonna*, but only insofar as it is a sense dependent on its spatiotemporal factuality is it threatened by destruction. *In principle* it would be repeatable. Annihilation would be the destruction of factual life but not of *sense.*

In light of Husserl's understanding of historicity as sense, we may ask along with Derrida, *"Is there, and why is there, any historical factuality"* (*IOG,* 150)? This question follows upon phenomenology's articulation of historicity as sense, and it is at this moment that phenomenology, in an ideal sense, anticipates "the end of its inquiry" in ontology. The question of historical factuality recalls Husserl's distinction between free and bound idealities, but here the questions ask us to distinguish ontology, "the *possible . . .* nonbeing of historical factuality," from phenomenology, the teleological consciousness of "nonbeing *as* nonhistory." The appearing of what is valid "'once and for all' and 'for everyone'" is the passage of the ideality of ideality,[23] that is, the passage that is historicity itself, the being-sense of factuality. "Intentionality is the root of historicity" (*IOG,* 150).

Herman Rapaport comments that "Derrida is raising not only the issue of what an event is but of its temporal significance in terms of the 'correspondences' of beginnings and ends."[24] For Husserl, the end is the constituted object of an intentional act. Therefore, the *primordial* sense is the *final* sense. "That is why only a teleology can open up a passage, a way back toward the beginnings" (*IOG,* 64). As Rapaport says, Husserl can only question the event on the basis of teleological consciousness. To move to the question of historical factuality is to move from the questioning of sense, which, insofar as sense need not be incarnated, derives its authority from phenomenology, to a questioning of an event's being, which derives from ontology. "The ontological question, then, seems able to arise only out of a teleological affirmation, i.e. out of freedom" (*IOG,* 151). That is, the ontological question is guided by the Telos of a freeing of sense from spatiotemporal restrictions, a freeing of "bound" ideality. This "judicative stipulation," as Husserl calls it, binds sense and being. Derrida continues, "Teleology is the threatened unity of sense and being, of phenomenology and ontology. However, this teleology . . . cannot be *determined* in a philosophical language without provisionally breaking this unity for the benefit of phenomenology" (*IOG*, 151). Insofar as phenomenology sets aside facticity, we can ask, knowing sense is historicity, "why there would be any history rather than nothing" (*IOG*, 151). Echoing Heidegger's initial question in his *Introduction to Metaphysics*, Derrida assumes the responsibility of taking "factuality seriously," which "is no longer to return to empiricism or nonphilosophy. On the contrary, it completes philosophy. But because of that, it must stand in the precarious openness of a question: the question of the origin of Being as History. . . . In the always open breach [*brèche*] of this question, Being itself is *silently* shown under the negativity of the *apeiron*" (*IOG*, 151). In an early text, "Philosophy as a Rigorous Science," Husserl writes, "For phenomenology, the singular is eternally the *apeiron*."[25] Appearing as the *apeiron*, the unlimited or indefinite, the Fact cannot be reduced in the phenomenological operation: "The Fact is *always more* or *always less*, always other, in any case, than what Husserl defines it as" (*IOG*, 152, n. 184).

The silent showing of Being under the *apeiron* means that the Fact, addressed in ontology, cannot be exhausted in a teleological determination originating in a primordial Logos.

> Being itself must always already be given to thinking in the pre-sumption [*présumption*, a neologism meant to be nearer "anticipation" rather than *présomption*, "conjecture" or "hypothesis"]—which is also a resumption—of Method. And undoubtedly access to Being *and* Being's arrival must always already be *contracted* or *drawn together*, when phenomenology begins by claiming the right to speak [*droit à parole*] (*IOG*, 151–152).

Being is given in an anticipation that is simultaneously a taking up again and a taking back (*résumption*). Being's arrival is a drawing back, an *epochê*, in Heidegger's sense of the term as sending-withdrawal. Derrida writes, "because historicity is prescribed for Being . . . delay [of "Discourse *after* the showing of Being"] is the destiny of Thought itself as Discourse" (*IOG*, 152). The delay or lateness of Discourse does not follow from Being as an accident but is "the philosophical absolute, because the beginning of methodic reflection can only consist in the consciousness of the implication of *another* previous, possible, and absolute origin in general" (*IOG*, 152). Consequently, the discovery in the reduction of a path between primordial Logos and polar Telos can begin only in the consciousness of the delay of the Absolute. The Telos of intentional historicity consists in the origin as delay because consciousness must "await" the showing of Being to the extent that access to Being must pass through Discourse. Husserl's inquiry into the origin of geometry as a first time has to proceed by a return inquiry (*Rückfrage*) that moves from the constituted object through tradition back to an intentional act, but if "the Reduction is only pure thought as that delay," then the Absolute is present only in/as *différance*.

Reduction is not, as Derrida says, a mere technique but "pure thought as that delay." Rapaport rightly draws attention to the introduction here of transcendental difference; to this we can add the theme of anticipation as *Rückfrage*, the return inquiry or the reactivation of origin in phenomenological inquiry:

> Since this alterity of the absolute origin structurally appears in *my Living Present* and since it can appear and be recognized only in the primordiality of something like *my Living Present*, this very fact signifies the authenticity of phenomenological delay and limitation. In the lackluster guise of a technique, the Reduction is only pure thought as that delay, pure thought investigating the sense of itself as delay within philosophy (*IOG*, 152–53).

The *Rückfrage* denotes, Derrida writes, a "postal and epistolary reference or resonance of communication from a distance" (*IOG*, 50). The possibility of inquiry into the primordial Absolute can only occur by way of a reduction of tradition. As the "technique" for answering the question of Being, the Reduction can only *ask again* about the primordial Absolute. A difference is introduced into the Living Present of the primordial Absolute "because the Absolute is *present* only in being *deferred-delayed* without respite [*qu'il n'est présent qu'en se* différant *sans relâche*]" (*IOG*, 153/ *LOG*, 171).

The threat to the unity of sense and being would be the appearance, without delay, of an Origin that no longer reserves itself and a Thought that finds its Telos has already come (cf: "Thought's pure certainty would be transcendental, since it can look forward to the already announced Telos only by advancing on (or being in advance of [*en avancant sur*]) the Origin that indefinitely reserves itself. Such a certainty never had to learn that Thought would always be to come" [*IOG*, 153]). This would amount to the unity of sense and being, the reduction of sense to an event's being, which would expose sense to pure presence, that is to say, pure absence. The "authentic thought of Being *as* History, as well as an authentic historicity of thought," means that consciousness of the delay cannot be reduced: "Now a primordial consciousness of delay can only have the pure form of anticipation. At the same time, pure consciousness of delay can only be a pure and legitimate, and therefore a priori, presumption, without which (once again) discourse and history would not be possible" (*IOG*, 153). This consciousness that is anticipation and apriori presumption is a consciousness of *différance*. Anticipation is always directed toward another origin, an origin as other, hence the melancholy of the archivist, for his work is one of mourning, the consciousness of delay as the possibility of history. The "strange procession of a '*Rückfrage*'" comes to resemble the occultation of the absolute referent.

V

We might ask, why No Apocalypse, Not Now? Nuclear war precipitates us toward "the uniqueness of an ultimate event, of a final collision or collusion" (*NA*, 21). An "absolute acceleration" would leave no time for repetition, the very condition of presence, of consciousness, of historicity. The collision/collusion of the intraworldly, the totality of objects of experience, and of phenomenology, a science of essences, would mean that consciousness itself would undergo annihilation along with the world. Nuclear war, to the extent that it is not located in the world but has existence "only where it is talked about," might be called a fable, as Derrida argues, not in its conventional sense as a fictive narrative, but as a "fabulous speculation" or what Husserl would call a pure object of consciousness (*NA*, 23).

For Derrida, the nuclear age brings phenomenology to a crisis. Because phenomenology begins with the parenthesizing of the natural attitude—that is, the exclusion of the positing of the natural world in its actuality, of the world as it is given to experience—and distinguishes experiential sciences or matters of fact from eidetic science, which concerns universal essences, nuclear war, as a phenomenon that is both technical and rhetorical, leaves, as Derrida says, "no more room for a distinction between belief and science" (*NA*, 24). Consequently, if Husserl's regressive inquiry (*Rückfrage*) should seek to establish the priority of ideal objects over the empirical determination of fact, then nuclear war is "fabulous" to the extent that it blurs any distinction between sense and actuality. This is not simply a matter of the rhetoric surrounding nuclear weapons but lies more precisely in its putting in crisis the phenomenological parenthesizing of the natural attitude.

Whereas the neutralizing of the thetic or naive belief in the given world would provide access to the world as a pure object of consciousness, nuclear war does not sustain this distinction precisely because, like literature, it exists only once—i.e., it has an ideal objectivity—*and* is finite.[26] There can be no essence of nuclear war, no absolute suspension of the natural attitude that is the condition of our talk of nuclear catastrophe. The reduction that goes under the name of nuclear war—the reality that comes to us as an event that is yet to happen—is a suspension of "reality." This is the fable of nuclear war. In the critical place of the nuclear age there is "[n]o truth, no apocalypse" (*NA*, 24). We might say, there is no essence of war—it is textual both in the colloquial sense and the broader sense Derrida gives the term. Therefore, to say we cannot oppose *doxa* and *epistemé* or the natural attitude and the phenomenological attitude means that the distinction between the idealization of anticipation, which authorizes the passage to the infinite Idea, and "ideation as an intuition of an essence" (*IOG*, 134–35) can no longer be maintained. Creation and production, truth and simulacrum, are crossed. As a result, the distinctions that are predicated by phenomenological reduction are not dismissed but are "folded." We can no longer think in terms of opposition but must recognize that these "distinctions" have no distinct boundaries; they contaminate one another.

What announces itself in nuclear war—and so far, it has only announced itself—never gives itself as such, that is, in its essence. Derrida's title, "No Apocalypse, Not Now," echoes his statement, "there is no—or hardly any, ever so little—literature" (*D*, 223). The threat of apocalyptic destruction, destruction without revelation, is echoed in the epochal character of literature. Literature belongs to the nuclear epoch to the extent it is exposed to destruction without revelation. In its character as the bracketing of transcendental authority, of Being, literature has not a real but a signified referent (cf. "The terrifying reality of the nuclear conflict can only be the signified referent, never the real referent (present or past) of a discourse or text" [*NA*, 23]). If "literary writing has, almost always and almost everywhere, according to some fashions and across very diverse ages, lent itself to this *transcendent* reading, in that search for the signified which we here put in question" (*OG*, 160), it does not do away with transcendent reading altogether, just as it does not do away with literature or philosophy. Derrida makes this point when questioned about this passage from *Of Grammatology*. Turning to a phenomenological language, Derrida denies that "literarity is . . . a natural essence, an intrinsic property of the text. It is the correlative of an intentional relation to the text. . . . There is therefore a literary *functioning* and a literary *intentionality*, an experience rather than an essence of literature (natural or ahistorical). The essence of literature, if we hold to this word essence, is produced as a set of objective rules in an original history of the 'acts' of inscription and reading" (*SIL*, 44–45).

In borrowing from phenomenological discourse, Derrida reminds us of the instituted, posited, or thetic character of the text. Literature is at once an "instituted *fiction* but also a *fictive institution* which in principle allows one to say everything" (*SIL*, 36). In addition to having a purely textual or linguistic existence, nuclear war is bound by a historically specific set of rules governing its discourse. Finally, there is the precarious position of the referent. Nuclear war, like literature, does not have a real referent. This does not mean it does away with reference nor that it can be reduced to the status of a mere fable. "One has to distinguish between the 'reality' of the nuclear age and the fiction of war. . . . 'Reality,' let's say the encompassing institution of the nuclear age, is constructed by the fable, on the basis of an event that has never happened (except in fantasy, and that is not nothing at all)" (*NA*,

23). Nuclear war would be the epochal determination of the nuclear age: as the ultimate referent, nuclear war multiplies discourses, produces the set of rules by which this anticipated entirely-other, nuclear catastrophe, is set aside or determined. Nuclear war, we might say, gives us to think the thesis as such. As a fable, an invention, it is a nonthetic experience of the thesis. Nuclear war does not annul the positing that Husserl calls the natural attitude but sets it aside, parenthesizes it, to allow us to speak seriously about the fiction of absolute catastrophe. Whereas for Husserl the consciousness that is reached in the *epochê* would not be touched by the annihilation of the physical world, the absolute destruction of nuclear war is "real," if we can use this term to describe a fiction whose referent is contained within itself.

It is the possibility of a nonthetic experience of the thesis, the "naive belief in meaning or referent," that links literature and the nuclear age. The suspension of a thetic relation to meaning or the referent does not eliminate reference nor, as Derrida points out, does it constitute "the object as a literary object. . . . In any case, a text cannot avoid lending itself to a 'transcendent' reading. A literature which forbade that transcendence would annul itself" (*SIL*, 45). Such a literature would be a chaotic literalness of defunct signs (see *IOG*, 88, cited above). Yet by providing a nonthetic experience of the thetic, literature dislodges the moment of transcendental consciousness, the pure thought that would be unaffected by the annihilation of the world. Literature is the expression of consciousness as delay and, therefore, a displacement of the reflexive appropriation of the Logos in the reduction. The "fold" in the moment of transcendence is not annulment but a remarking or spacing that accounts for the experience of the transcendental. The "fold is not a form of reflexivity," if one means by it the movement of self-presence (*D*, 270). The fold or folding back is a placing in reserve, a setting aside of Being in the margin or at the threshold of the text. It is a polysemic structure of "dehiscence, dissemination, spacing, temporalization, etc." (*D*, 271) that announces itself as literature, which, characterized by the fold, holds itself back and thereby escapes the phenomenalization that makes an intuition of the essence possible. "If there is no essence of literature—i.e. self-identity of the literary thing—if what is announced or promised as literature never gives itself as such, that means, among other things, that a literature that talked only about literature or a work that was purely self-referential would immediately be annulled" (*SIL*, 47).

A purely self-referential literature promises us the totality of that which is constituted in itself, constituted as producing its referent in and by itself. This would mean a literature indissociable from the nuclear epoch as "the absolute *epochê* . . . the *epochê* of absolute knowledge. Literature belongs to this nuclear epoch, that of the crisis and of nuclear criticism, at least if we mean by this the historical and ahistorical horizon of an absolute self-destructibility without apocalypse, without revelation of its own truth, without absolute knowledge" (*NA*, 27). The experience of nuclear war would be the "experience of the nothing-ing of nothing that interests our desire under the name of literature" (*SIL*, 47). In the self-referential work, literature (without essence) "experiences" itself as a nullity; it experiences the essential finitude wherein its relation to reference is suspended—i.e. held back, neutralized, as having no essence of its own, dependent on something other than itself (cf. *SIL*, 48).

Literature enables us to think the possibility of appearing (of Being), not in the sense of an a priori condition or as the phenomenological absolute but insofar as its status as writing or textuality suspends the relation to meaning or reference and thereby places it "on the edge of everything, almost beyond everything, including itself" (*SIL*, 47).

In reminding us that literature annuls neither reference nor transcendental reading, while simultaneously complicating these functions, Derrida observes that literature is characterizable by the formalizing powers of bracketing or parenthesizing (Husserl points out in *Ideas* that in parenthesizing "[w]e do not give up the positing [i.e., the general positing of the natural attitude] we effected"[27]). There would be no more literature if it were to be fully comprehended as the object of intentional consciousness, which would place it under the rule of Being and make it a product of history as the history of Being. Literature, "literary writing or reading, puts phenomenology in crisis as well as the very concept of institution or convention" not solely by the suspension of "the thetic relation to meaning or referent" (this is a possibility of non-literary texts) but in allowing one "to think the thesis," in a "nonthetic experience of the thesis" (*SIL*, 45–46). Because the thesis is a positing, the "'transcendental reduction,'" the "condition of literature," removes literature from the category of mimetic activity or mimesis in general. The bracketing or parenthesizing of the positing activity, mimesis itself, is a setting aside of the positioning power, the power of *Setzung*, which can be said to have been the philosophical determination of literature from Plato to Heidegger. Derrida is not suggesting, after Plato, the expulsion of the mimetic arts but is situating mimesis, in Heidegger's sense as *poiesis* or installation, within phenomenology, thereby revealing how literature puts phenomenology in crisis to the very extent that the reduction is central to phenomenological method. It must be stated that Derrida is not denying the mimetic function or aspect of literature, but is calling literature a nonthetic experience of the thesis; he resituates mimesis, removing it from the category of Being in which it functions as the re-presentation of the *eidos*, and reinscribes it on the other side of the mirror, the tain.[28] Rather than reflect or posit, literature is a fictioning, an act or experience of what makes a thesis a thesis *as such*, thereby dislodging the certitudes of self-presence, the *cogito*, transcendental consciousness that make up phenomenological language (*SIL*, 46).

This fictionality is anything but a removal from the world or aestheticism, a charge that has been leveled against deconstruction since the seventies. No greater evidence of this misunderstanding of fiction can be found outside the fable of nuclear war; indeed, the threat of nuclear war poses the question of the "outside" because of its status as the signified referent. The "fabulous textuality" or fictionality of nuclear war means it has existence only in language, in what is said about it (Derrida refers to the bombings of Hiroshima and Nagasaki as the ending of a conventional war). We can/do/must speculate on nuclear war; in fact, nuclear war is, Derrida says in an allusion to the contemporaneous essay "Psyché: Inventions of the Other," "a fable . . . a pure invention. . . . It may also be called a speculation, even a fabulous specularization. The breaking of the mirror would be, finally, through an act of language, the very occurrence of nuclear war" (*NA*, 23).

Why a breaking of the mirror? Would the end of speculation, through an act of language, yield reality? Perhaps not, since no remainder would be left. As a fable, nuclear war constructs "reality" not only because it consists of the rhetoric that guided much of U.S. foreign policy during the cold war, including technical assistance to underdeveloped nations and domestic scientific research, but "everything that is named by the old words culture, civilization, *Bildung, scholè, paideia*. 'Reality,' let's say the encompassing institution of the nuclear age, is constructed by the fable, on the basis of an event that has never happened" (*NA*, 23). The breaking of the mirror would not constitute a movement outside speculative discourse toward reality but would be a repetition of what was already invented in the fable.

Such is suggested by Derrida's allusion to "Psyché" and his reading of Francis Ponge's "Fable":

> Fable
> Par le mot *par* commence donc ce texte
> Dont la première ligne dit la vérité,
> Mais ce tain sous l'une et l'autre
>
> Peut-il être tolére?
> Cher lecteur déjà tu juges
> Là de nos difficultés . . .
>
> (APRÈS *sept ans de malheurs*
> *Elle brisa son mirroir.*)
>
> Fable
> By the word *by* begins this text
> Whose first line says the truth,
> But this tain under one and the other
> Can it be tolerated?
> Dear reader already you judge
> There as to our difficulties . . .
>
> (AFTER *seven years of bad luck*
> *She broke her mirror.*) (PIO, 30; trans. modified)

The misfortune would not be the breaking the mirror but "the mirror itself" (*PIO*, 37). The impossibility of moving outside the infinity of reflection is grounded in language, a language, such as the rhetoric of nuclear war, that does not allow us to distinguish constative from performative, the very condition of literature, as Paul de Man proposed. The breaking of the mirror (of speculation) through an act of language would not lead us to identity or to a real referent, transforming the fable of nuclear war into a reality, because the mirror itself is an act of language. The reality is already "here," in the mirror, but at a distance. This may be called the "temporal predicament" of the mirror (as well as of the missile/missive), which Derrida finds to be similar to a passage by de Man on irony:

> The act of irony, as we now understand it, reveals the existence of a temporality that is definitely *not organic*, in that it relates to its source only in terms of distance and difference and allows for *no end, for no* totality [this is indeed the technical and nonorganic structure of the mirror]. Irony divides the flow of temporal experience into a past that is pure mystification and a future that remains harassed forever by a relapse within the inauthentic. It can know this inauthenticity but can never overcome it.[29]

De Man might well be talking the language of deterrence, which follows a "logic of deviation and transgression" (*NA*, 29), a logic of the postal discourse of missiles/missives and a logic of invention, of act and archivization. It tells a story that does not take place and has no place outside language, a story about nuclear war.

VI

We should be cautious against granting to language a comprehensiveness that restores to it a transcendental significance. Derrida's notion of general writing or textuality runs contrary to such totalizing concepts, as can be seen in "The Double Session," where he describes Mallarmé's *Mimique* as "a sort of handbook of literature . . . because the necessity of that metaphor [i.e. of writing], which *nothing* escapes, makes it something other than a particular figure among others. What is produced is an absolute extension of the concepts of writing and reading, of text, of hymen, to the point where nothing of what *is* can lie beyond them" (*D*, 223). Mallarmé's "handbook of literature" suggests the self-constituting act of archivization. Nothing escapes the metaphor of writing not because writing is an idea in a transcendental sense nor because everything is reducible to writing as a material form of significa-tion. Writing is the name for the structural unity of ideality and repetition, the latter making possible and marking the limits of the former.

The unity of self-reflexive ideality must pass by way of the other. Derrida's figure of the hymen belongs to a series of "terms," including the "re-mark" and the "fold," that recall a difference without polarity, such as that between image and thing, imitation and imitated, that cannot be assimilated to reflexivity (see *D*, 209–210, 270). The hymen is the "between," the work of any for-malization that, in accounting for reflexivity and its other, marks the limits of ideality. Derrida writes, "Everything is reflected in the medium or speculum of reading-writing, *'without breaking the mirror.'* There is writing without a book, in which, each time, at every moment, the marking tip proceeds without a past upon the virgin sheet" (*D*, 223). This would be writing as pure act, the ideal-izing act of creation as opposed to the secondary act of reading. But if in the "speculum of reading-writing" the mirror is unbroken, reading is no more secondary than writing. Whereas writing as idealizing act of creation, an act or pure idea free from the past, starts from anticipation, the corporeal writing of the mime pro-duces the fold (*le pli*), the re-plying or repetition that makes possi-ble the recognition of primordial writing as an effect of the fold.

Idealization as creation is possible on the basis of a recogni-tion, a re-collection or repetition that allows the living present of an inaugural act to distinguish itself from the past. Therefore, the inaugural act of writing—"writing without a book"—proceeds because "there is also, *simultaneously*, an infinite number of book-lets enclosing and fitting inside other booklets, which are only able to issue forth by grafting, sampling, quotations, epigraphs, refer-ences, etc. Literature voids itself in its limitlessness" (*D*, 223). The self-affection of literary writing, the infinitization of the concepts of writing and reading to the point where nothing escapes them, is possible only on the basis of a supplementary grafting of another writing onto the virgin page. The specular structure of reading-writing is possible by virtue of the hymen, the between or fold, a mark, margin, or limit operating within the text (*D*, 270), which shows the virgin page to be an origin that writing goes toward rather than proceeds from. As the writing without a book, literature is a synthesis of spacing/temporalization, that is, the synthesis of self and other, not in a unitary structure, but in an originary difference that makes appearance possible. The condition for the first and last time of writing lies in repetition.

Literature has a peculiar relation to the distinction between purely formal laws of logic and their material forms or singularities, or in terms closer to Husserl, between pure ideality and its intentional fulfillment. Derrida's deconstruction of Husserlian ideation and the production of an irreal essence, such as the pure forms of geometry, reveals that this primordial ideation that constitutes an object as a pure act of creation is guided by a secondary ideation, one that is the intuition of an essence (*Wesensschau*).[30] Consequently, the primordial passage-to-the-limit in ideation has the structure of repetition (see *IOG*, 134–35).

When we turn to Mallarmé's "handbook," we find the pure act of writing simultaneously involves a repetition, a doubling in advance that supplements the lack of actuality in the pure ideality of a primordial or virgin writing. The limitlessness of literature does not lie in infinitization in Husserl's sense as a passage beyond the sensible limit to expose the aprioriness of an instituting act or what we may call the pure Idea that owes its existence to thought alone (see *IOG*, 127–28). Rather, literature voids itself, proclaims "that there is no—or hardly any, ever so little—literature; that in any event there is no essence of literature, no truth of literature, no literary-being or being-literary of literature" (*D*, 223). Whereas the fulfilled intention of the geometer is subjugated to the origin or essence—at least, this is what Husserl sets out to demonstrate— literature is without essence.[31] It remains to come, like a monstrous event, like nuclear war.

VII

The rhetoric of nuclear war founds an original reflexivity that divides itself into a first *and* last event. It constitutes itself as an archive, a stockpiling of missiles and missives (policy statements, treaties, threats, etc.). Nuclear catastrophe would be absolute death, not in terms of unprecedented mass destruction, although it certainly would embrace this, but in its annihilation of the basis for the symbolic work of mourning—i.e., the archive or the material basis of memory. Therefore, the threat of a remainderless destruction allows us, Derrida says, to rethink the referent because it is only in the face of the possibility of the end of all symbolizing, which entails the strategies of deterrence necessary for survival, that the absolutely real can be approached. "This absolute referent of all possible literature [i.e., "absolute nuclear catastrophe"] is on a par with the absolute effacement of any possible trace; it is thus the only ineffaceable trace, it is so as the trace of what is entirely other, *'trace du tout autre'*" (*NA*, 28). In other words, the nuclear age beckons toward this "remainderless and a-symbolic destruction of literature": the arrival of the absolute referent, the effaceable/ineffaceable trace, is the end of literature and its only subject because literature's survival depends on its character as the *epochê* of the *epochê*, that is, its capacity for suspending "the encounter with the wholly other." This suspension, however, is not absolute. "Capable of speaking only of that, literature cannot help but speak of other things as well, and invent strategies for speaking of other things, for putting off the encounter with the wholly other. . . . This is the only invention possible" (*NA*, 28).

The threat of nuclear catastrophe resides in the destruction of the basis for the symbolizing capacity of literature, the capacity to limit death through the work of mourning. In other words, literature is sustained by its avoidance of its only subject, the real or absolute presence/absolute absence. Literature requires the horizon of the absolute referent as an always-already there of a future that sustains the anticipation of death. That is, what we call "literature" is the symbolic work of monumentalization, the spatialization of memory. To say that nuclear catastrophe, as the ultimate referent, would be the only subject of literature is to say that literature survives by speaking of everything but its subject, the occulted thing that can never be named, the phantasm of the proper name.[32] We *sur-vive* by such inventions.

The uniqueness of nuclear war, therefore, does not lie in the extent of its powers of destruction—conceivably people, property, and much of the environment could be destroyed through "conventional" means—but in the possibility of a death that is not transcendental, that is, of a destruction that would not leave the truth intact. It would be the absolute destruction, the epochal destruction, destruction of the *epochê*, that is, the destruction of the archive: "Now what allows us perhaps to think the uniqueness of nuclear war, its being-for-the-first-time-and-perhaps-for-the-last-time, its absolute inventiveness . . . is obviously the possibility of an irreversible destruction, leaving no traces, of the juridico-literary archive—that is, total destruction of the basis of literature and criticism" (*NA*, 26).

Irreversible destruction need not necessarily encompass the "human habitat" or "other discourses" because they have a real referent external to the archive. Quite simply, the annulment of what is, the total destruction of the archive, is predicated upon the notion of the self-constituting power of the archivizing act. To the extent that the referent is external to the archive, the archive is not literary. Fictive or fabulous referents are what Husserl calls "irreal objectivities"—that is, they are "not bound to objective time and objective temporal points."[33] Irreal objects, such as the principles of geometry, can appear in individual acts or moments but are the same at all times. They are not bound to concrete lived experience and the unity of temporal connection and horizon of intentions. They sustain "no temporal differentiation" because they "can 'be' the same in any time."[34] If we consider language as an objectivity of the human, cultural world, we find that the sense intended by words is "itself a component of the object." Husserl calls this a "*sense of sense*" to distinguish it from "*sense as the determination of an object.*" Irreal objectivities are included as "second-level sense" or objectivities of sense, which remain the same in real embodiments.[35] We have already looked at how this applies to works of literature and art. There is, ideally, one *Ulysses* (to choose one of the most vexed examples) that has one identical signification in many exemplars.

The destruction of the archive would affect the exemplars but not the ideal objectivities. Derrida's deconstruction of ideality in Husserl would suggest that these idealities, insofar as they are constituted by an act that is simultaneously an archivization, or even a delay, would not survive nuclear catastrophe because the possibility of reconstruction depends upon an external referent. Yet this hardly seems to justify his insistence that literature gives us to think the totality of what is threatened by nuclear catastrophe. This would be possible only if by nuclear catastrophe we mean something beyond technological mass destruction to include irreal objectivities and that means inventions of the other, for one of the characteristics of irreal objects is that after they make their appearance in the world, "after having been discovered, they can be thought of anew and as often as desired and, in general, can be objects of experience according to their nature. But afterwards we say: even before they were discovered, they were already 'valid.'"[36] The destruction of the world, "the universe of realities," would not, according to Husserl, affect irreal objectivities, which have no world-reality. For instance, a mathematical proposition is producible at any time and, having an omnitemporal existence, its "invention" would be a first time, a last time, and iterable. In other words, the discovery of an irreal objectivity gives it a worldly reality, but it is not dependent on this spatiotemporal localization for its identity.

The point that must be emphasized is that the exemplar of an ideal objectivity, such as a copy of *Ulysses*, does not individualize it. The destruction of the literary-juridico archive, therefore, does not amount to the burning of all books, documents, papers, etc., but affects the "structural possibilities of what goes by the name literature" (*NA*, 27). Literature gives us to think the "absolute self-destructibility without apocalypse," a destruction without revelation, on the basis of its relation to the (fictive) referent. In the absolute epoch of the nuclear age, literature experiences its "death menace," something it has always done insofar as the "movement of its inscription is the very possibility of its effacement" (*NA*, 27). As this double movement of inscription/effacement, literature constitutes itself in a doubling movement of reference and withdrawal, an opening of its space to what makes it possible—the other. Literature cannot exist as a self-referential totality; the literary experience consists in the neutralizing or suspension that allows one to think the thesis, the positing of the world. Literature's status as writing—as self-deferring, self-effacing, iterable—means that it disappears in appearing as what it is not—as mimetic or referential, as thetic, as fictive. Literature has always belonged to the nuclear epoch because it has always been the suspension of the *epoché*. Hence, Derrida will note, "If we are bound and determined to speak in terms of reference, nuclear war is the only possible referent of any discourse and any experience that would share their condition with that of literature" (*NA*, 28). To the extent that nuclear war leaves no remainder that can be subjected to the work of mourning, to archivization, it is "the absolute referent, the horizon and condition of all others." It permits no evading by symbolization of the reality of death.

At stake here in the absolute destination is the status of the referent. In asking what remains after nuclear war, we anticipate the utterably unanticipatible, we can say the wholly other, "an encounter with which, however, this relationless relation, this relation of incommensurability cannot be wholly suspended, even though it is precisely the epochal suspension" (*NA*, 28). This is the experience of literature, what literature can only speak about—suspension, the absolute *epochê*. However, it must be realized that novels or other writings that seek to represent nuclear catastrophe are the last and the least literary thing being referred to here. If literature has always belonged to the nuclear age, it would not be a matter of prescience but of literary "being" as *epochê*, its inventiveness in speaking about other things and putting off, deterring, the absolute referent.

This "destinerrance," as Derrida calls it, is a suspending of the "ontico-ontological difference itself. The dissemination epochalizes the difference in its turn" (*NA*, 29). This *epochê* to the second degree does not even leave difference in place but dispatches—everything. "The aleatory destinerrance of the *envoi* allows us to think . . . the age of nuclear war" (*NA*, 29–30). As I have indicated, this *envoi* does not follow as a product of the nuclear age but has already been sent before nuclear technology. It is a question of the event as such, a question of singularity and generality, first and last times, of the question, why is there something rather than nothing? It is all a matter of chance. The other as other can only come in an aleatory encounter. This means the other does not first exist in an absolute plenitude and enter history nor is it the product of a transcendental historicity. As we have seen, this *of*—of the Absolute, of historicity, of the Telos, of intentionality—concerns the "relation in which subject and object are reciprocally engendered." It is the "Absolute of *genetivity* itself as the pure possibility of a genetic relation" (*IOG*, 142–43) and it is this genetivity that must be deconstructed if the other is to come (see *PIO*, 56).

Having no standing in Being, having no "foundation outside itself[,] [l]iterature is at once reassured and threatened by the fact of depending only on itself, standing in the air, all alone, aside from Being" (*D*, 280). Literature is characterized not by possessing an essence but by its setting aside or bracketing of essence and Being. As long as we think of literature conceptually, think of it as determined by the concept—preeminently that of mimesis in the sense of imitation—we are thinking it as (a) subject of/to philosophy. Consequently, the special relationship Derrida claims for literature and nuclear war would not hold because literature would have its possibility for being outside itself. However, if literature, harboring its referent within itself, is aside from Being, without any foundation outside itself, it "gives us to think the *totality* of that which, like literature and henceforth in it, is exposed to the same threat [i.e. of total destruction]" (*NA*, 27).

Were nuclear catastrophe to happen, there would be nothing—outside the text. Derrida's famous sentence "*il n'y a pas de hors-texte*" (*OG*, 158) implies that because there is no essence of literature, it does not constitute a totality. As the *epochê* of the *epochê*, literature's function of setting aside allows for the experience of the natural attitude or thesis but is itself nonthetic. Literature is, in other words, fiction, a being-suspended that neutralizes the metaphysical assumptions it cannot totally escape (*SIL*, 49). Literature is "at once the exception in the whole, the want-of-wholeness in the whole, and the exception to everything, that which exists by itself, alone, with nothing else, in exception to all. A part that, within *and* without the whole, marks the wholly other, the other incommensurate with the whole. Which cuts literature short: it doesn't exist, since there is nothing outside the whole. It does exist, since there is an 'exception to everything,' an outside of the whole, that is, a sort of subtraction without lack" (*D*, 56).

Literature, then, is all *and* nothing at all. Having no essence of its own, "literature," is aside from Being; it is epochal in character and, hence, indissociable from the nuclear epoch, "at least if we mean by this the historical and ahistorical horizon of an absolute self-destructibility without apocalypse, without revelation of its own truth, without absolute knowledge" (*NA*, 27). This absolute destruction does not concern a formal structure, called "literarity," which is "extended to any possible archive," but is literature's experience of "its own precariousness, its death menace and its essential finitude. The movement of its inscription is the very possibility of its effacement" (*NA*, 27). Literature and nuclear destruction are bound by the absolute referent, the only real referent being that absolute catastrophe that would destroy the entire archive and all symbolic capacity. Both nuclear warfare, to the extent that it belongs to rhetoric and still is to come, and literature share the

space of an instituted fiction, a fictive institution. And like literature, nuclear warfare is not to come, in the sense that it may occur
tomorrow or whenever, but has the status of a promise, a to-come
(*à-venir*) that never arrives but is already here, like a "memory
which produces the event to be told and which will never have been
present" (*SIL*, 42). The future is the work of literature.

4

Monstrous Writing:
The Gift of Literature

L'avenir ne peut s'anticiper que dans la forme du danger absolu. Il est ce qui rompt absolument avec la normalité constituée et ne peut donc s'annoncer, *se présenter*, que sous l'espèce de la monstruosité. Pour ce monde à venir et pour ce qui en lui aura fait trembler les valeurs de signe, de parole et d'écriture, pour ce qui conduit ici notre futur antérieur, il n'est pas encore d'exergue.

—*De la grammatologie*

The future can be anticipated only in the form of absolute danger. It is that which breaks absolutely with constituted normality and can thus announce itself, *present itself*, only under the species of monstrosity. For this world to come and for what in it will have shaken the values of the sign, speech, and writing, for what is guiding here our future anterior, there is no exergue as yet.

—Of Grammatology

I

When Jacques Derrida closes the "exergue" to *Of Grammatology* with a prediction of catastrophe, he anticipates the postal effect that puts in circulation the letter, destiny, and the event. As the space in a coin reserved for receiving an inscription, as well as the inscription itself, and as that which explicates or presents, the exergue anticipates the text it stands outside of and which it serves as epigraph. Here an exergue on the absence of the exergue that would guide "our future anterior" announces a birth in

143

the world, the arrival of the monstrous. This thinking of the dis-aster presupposes that "as soon as there is, there is *différance* . . . and there is postal maneuvering, relays, delay, anticipation, des-tination, telecommunicating network, the possibility, and there-fore the fatal necessity of going astray, etc." (*PC*, 66). Perhaps there is nothing more important to Derrida's work than the notion or quasi-transcendental of *différance*. In the turn from the search for origins, Derrida proposes that the aboriginal event, that event or thing, beyond which we cannot go, is already a differing and deferring. For something to be, there must be what he calls here the "telecommunicating network," what he elsewhere calls the "text." That is to say, as soon as there is, there is no presence, no absolute self-identity in a punctual now and here. And just as the possibility of going astray is a condition of sending, so the possibility of the end may be nearer than we think. "The end is near, they seem to say, which does not exclude that it may have already taken place" (*AT*, 125). Although we might be tempted to say the end precedes or is coeval with the beginning, we would be more accurate to think the apocalyptic event as folded: it has neither beginning nor end nor does it come from outside, but it produces beginning and end as an effect of the *envoi*, the apocalyptic sending from *envoi* to *envoi*, from one tone or destination to an other that promises to be there before the coming of the event and is "not yet there in the present of the *récit*" (*AT*, 156). This internally divided event displaces the present of the call (of Being). We can no longer speak of the event within the coordinates of gathering and sending in the manner of Heidegger.[1] Starting from the other, being already a response, the call, "Come," as distinct from the Heideggerean "*Schuld!*" describes in advance the retreat or erasure of the event. Therefore, the apocalyptic event has the structure of the divisible missive or *envoi*.

We are speaking here of the problematic singularity of an event to come. This singularity or uniqueness of the event, in its character as a divisible *envoi*, belongs to literature, which, as we have seen, asks us to think singularity and repetition together. It must take part in the generality of meaning that we traditionally associate with historico-institutional conditions (genre, context, culture, etc.).[2] Were the text not open to or originally constituted by iterability, it would not be readable or historical. The singular text must be repeated in its singularity—in this it participates in or belongs to history.[3] The literary may well be crucial to the understanding of singularity because a work occurs just once and, in its singularity, commands a response: "My law, the one to which I try to devote myself or to respond, is *the text of the other*, its very singularity, its idiom, its appeal which precedes me. But I can only respond to it in a responsible way (and this goes for the law in general, ethics in particular) if I put in play, and in guarantee [*en gage*], my singularity, by signing, with another signature" (*SIL*, 66).[4] The literary event gives itself as a "first" signature that affirms itself as singular only in calling forth another signature, a countersignature. The reading solicited by the signature is not free to say what it wants about the text but affirms it in a new way. The very iterability of the text, its structure as divisible and repeatable, means that a text would not be readable, would not be translatable into different contexts, were there not this "original" divisibility. This means that the text is not absolutely determined by its context. (If it were, it would be so rooted to the conditions of its existence as to be both unreadable and utterly without singularity. For knowledge would depend upon one's having an identical context, an obvious impossibility even for the work's contemporaries, and the work would be entirely determined by what is outside it, and so could not be said to be unique.) Both readability and singularity depend upon *différance*. This means that if reading is not free to "make up" the text, it also cannot, ought not, aim to reproduce the text. This would amount to becoming the text and violating its otherness, its singularity.

In his interview with Derek Attridge, Derrida repeats his position: "We have available contextual elements of great stability (not natural, universal and immutable but fairly stable, and thus also destabilizable)" (*SIL*, 64). Derrida may sound like a pragmatic hermeneutician, but this impression misses how the conditions of readability compromise the relation between singularity and repetition that permits reading in the "first" place. As an event, literature demands a response, a "yes," that affirms the status of the signature as a gift prior to any exchange. The prearchaic character of the donative, its being there before any exchange, is the condition of the singularity of the signature, its guarantee as unique. To think the singularity of the event requires us to think the "transcendental condition" of performativity whether it is verbalized or not: *"Yes* indicates that there is address to the other. . . . *Yes*, the condition of any signature and of any performative, addresses itself to some other which it does not constitute, and it can only begin by *asking* the other, in response to a request that has always already been made, *to ask* it to say *yes*. Time appears only as a result of this singular anachrony" (*UGE*, 298–99). *Yes* exemplifies the performative to the extent that it must begin in an address to an other in response to a request that has already been made; therefore, *yes* has no essence or being in itself but is presupposed in a performative insofar as it is divided from the start as address and response or a future saying and a past said. That is to say, it initiates from after. The first *yes* is a response to an other or second *yes* that precedes the first: "as a minimal event, a *yes* demands *a priori* its own repetition, its own memorizing, demands that a *yes* to the *yes* inhabit the arrival of the 'first' yes, which is never therefore simply originary" (*UGE*, 304). As a performative, the *yes* is neither a pure act nor a product but is characterized by a heterogeneity that more than any simple alterity exceeds the present relation between same and other as it is embodied in the donative or in responsibility.

We are not speaking here of dialogue or dialectic but of the conditions that open the possibility of the signature, the "I," and alterity. As a response to an other, the *yes* itself commands a response, but it says nothing in itself—it is a word used to express an affirmation but can be implied without being said or written.[5] "In short," Derrida says, *"yes* would be transcendental adverbiality, the ineffaceable supplement to any verb" (*UGE*, 297). *Yes* is the "minimal, primary" mark signifying address to an other in a self-positing that is neither tautological nor self-identical but divided. The "singular anachrony" of the *yes* lies in its being a "response to a request that has always already been made" (*UGE*, 299). One *yes* always recalls another, even when it says "yes" to itself: "The self-affirmation of the *yes* can address itself to the other only in recalling itself to itself, in saying to itself *yes, yes*" (*UGE*, 303). It is, Derrida says in words that echo the deconstruction of the Living Present in Husserl, a dispatch marked by a consciousness of delay in the form of anticipation (see *IOG*, 153): "The circle of this universal presupposition . . . is like a dispatch to oneself, a sending-back [*renvoi*] of self to self, which *both never leaves itself and never arrives at itself"* (*UGE*, 303). The *"yes"* is non-speculative; there is no gathering of self and other in the singular moment of an "I" who says, *"yes."* In asking only for another *yes*, it entrusts itself to the memory of the other, the second *yes* to which it responds in advance.[6]

As the minimal condition for any signature or performative, the *yes* belongs to the singular anachrony of the response to the other: "This countersigning response, this countersignature which is responsible (for itself and for the other), says 'yes' to the work, and again 'yes, this work was there before me, without me, I testify'. . . . The countersignature of the other text is held under the law of the first, of its absolute pastness. But this absolute pastness was already the demand for the countersigning reading. The first only inaugurates from after, and as the expectation of, the second countersignature" (*SIL*, 70). *Yes* is a differential mark, a mark that refers only in differing from itself. It defers self-relation (it responds to an other, even if that other is its "self") and is the trace of the other in itself: it can say "yes" to itself only by referral to an other.

Derrida situates literature, saying "yes" in *Ulysses*, within the postal discourse of a letter or missive that may not reach its destination. In the singular anachrony of the *yes*, the anticipatory event is at once the event still to come and the sending or *envoi* itself.[7] The "absolute danger" of a radical event, called the "future" in the exergue to *Of Grammatology*, is the "monstrosity" of an absolute referent, that which is without precedent and which can be figured as nuclear catastrophe, the "only referent that is absolutely real" (*NA*, 28). An absolute referent would be on a par with absolute erasure. An unerasable trace, would be "an indestructible and monumental substance" (*M*, 24). The erasure of any possible trace, the effacement of the general structure of reference, would constitute thinking what is outside the text, what escapes the very movement of deferral and delay that Derrida calls *"survivance."*

The possibility of thinking an event outside the text, for we are speaking of what exceeds Derridean textuality, of an event that has no origin outside itself, is itself a product of textuality, of the fold, "the non-sense of spacing" or "a repetition-toward-itself of the text" (*D*, 257, 238). The fold is the spacing of *a priori* repetition. Because nothing precedes the fold or exists outside the text, "there will never be . . . any theology of the Text. And yet the structural site of this theological trap is nevertheless prescribed: the mark-supplement produced by the text's workings, in falling outside of the text like an independent object with no origin other than itself, a trace that turns back into a presence (or a sign), is inseparable from desire (the desire for reappropriation or representation). Or rather, it gives birth to it and nourishes it in the very act of separating from it" (*D*, 258). The fold produces the desire for the reappropriation of presence—that is, for representation, monumentalization, archivization, idealization, which is the work of literature, the work of putting off the encounter with the wholly other, the a-symbolic destruction of the archive.

An individual death leaves a remainder, a "work of mourning, with memory, compensation, internalization, idealization, displacement, and so on. In that case there is monumentalization, archivization and *work on the remainder, work of the remainder*." This remainder softens the "reality" of every individual death "in the realm of the 'symbolic.'" The only referent that is absolutely real is nuclear catastrophe, the remainderless destruction of the entire archive and the very "'movement of survival.'" (*NA*, 28). This absolute referent amounts to a monstrosity, precisely that which does not have an exergue—a site, inscription, and presentation. As I argued in the previous chapter, it would be the destruction of literature insofar as literature is constituted by the "archivizing act" (*NA*, 27), an event that entrusts itself to memory.

The archive consists of a stockpiling and the positive law of copyright that distinguishes original from copy. Without the archive there would be no literature, which does not mean that the archive is the essence of literature—literature is without essence. There is literature wherever the signature leaves a trace, a remainder that is the condition of readability; which is to say, as soon as there is a trace, direct intuition is no longer possible. (I am not proposing that literature is the exemplary form of the trace, but the trace in general is a condition of literary writing and other forms of textuality.) Nor is this an argument that "readability" is a hermeneutic principle but that the archive belongs to the condition of what Derrida variously calls the "text" or "trace." It is more akin to the problem of the gift than to interpretative rules.

In thinking of literature according to the problem of the gift— that is, outside the circuit of exchange and debt—Derrida attempts at once to think its singularity and to think singularity through/in literature. This is evident when he says literature puts in crisis the distinction between use and mention so important to speech act theory. The functions of use and mention imply the singularity of the act, on the one hand, and citation, exemplification, or bracketing, on the other. The "exemplary" status of literature rests in this capacity to be something other than itself, that is, in its freedom to play with exemplarity itself. That there can be no determination between use and mention, singularity and repetition, means that literature's destiny is something monstrous, a possibility of the impossible event, act, thing, which is why, as I have been arguing, Derrida writes that the ultimate referent of literature, its only possible subject, is its remainderless destruction.

This is why literature can say anything—its transcendental condition is apocalyptic destruction without remainder. The possibility of a-symbolic destruction may be said to make literature delirious—it is the delirium of an original reflexivity, an inaugural act that is derailed, shattered, as in Ponge's "Fable," "before" it begins: "Par le mot *par* commence donc ce texte." Literature can only speak of apocalypse and is *already* speaking of apocalypse the moment it speaks. Apocalypse is not the origin or the end of the literary *envoi* but there are *envois* because the end is what opens the possibility of any sending to a destination still to come, which is to say the apocalypse starts without us. All literature presupposes it—the only subject possible for literature is the relationless relation with its end in the absolute referent.[8] Consequently, to speak of the absolute referent is to miss it, necessarily and by chance. The singularity of the literary work must annul itself in offering itself to be read. In giving itself to be read, it preserves the date, the signature of its event or timely occurrence, and annuls it.[9]

The literary work is conditioned by the structure of the date, which makes it readable and marks the singularity that it would preserve.[10] This is the delirium of literature—it gives itself and consumes itself from within; hence, as singular it gives itself as unreadable and is readable only as a singular event: "The unreadable is readable as unreadable, unreadable insofar as readable; this is the madness or fire which consumes a date from within" (*SPC*, 43). In offering itself as unique, it effaces itself; we are left to address the trace, the ash, of the singular remains.[11] As soon as the text is there, unique and repeatable at once, it betrays itself, offers itself in the *envoi* without return: "as soon as one no longer knows who speaks of who writes, the text becomes apocalyptic. And if the *envois* always refer [*renvoient*] to other *envois* without decidable destination, the destination remaining to come, then isn't this completely angelic structure, that of the Johannine apocalypse, isn't it also the structure of every scene of writing in general" (*AT*, 156)?

Literature's strange status as an *envoi* without a decidable destination situates it *"in place of the secret [au lieu du secret],"* as he puts it in a "confessional" moment in "Passions" (*ON*, 28), one of a series of texts, including "Sauf le nom" and "Khôra," that form "a sort of *Essay on the Name"* or what might be called the secret name or absolute name that cannot be revealed because it is of an order that is other than truth, *alêtheia*, or apocalypse.[12] We might say the name is like a gift, an *es gibt* of what remains, not withdrawn in Heidegger's sense of the *epochê* of Being, but like a promise, a date, the law, a yes, and a signature.[13] All these terms appear in various works by Derrida since the 1980s—*Of Spirit, Shibboleth, Before the Law, Ulysses Gramophone, Signsponge*— which are, in various ways, concerned with literature and the singular. The signature is the work of the text as a whole. It operates as the idiomatic mark that links the work to the proper name. Moreover, the "general signature, or signature of the signature" produces the thing as other—by inscribing the signature in the text the author (here Derrida is discussing Francis Ponge) monumentalizes it, "erect[s] it into a thing or a stony object. But in doing so, you also lose the identity, the title of ownership over the text: you let it become a moment or a part of the text, as a thing or a common noun." It is the text, "the thing as other, that signs" (*SS*, 56, 54). In other words, the signature is not confined to the act of inscribing my name but is the mark of appropriation, what we often call "style," that individuates a text. The signature assumes a proper name that is bound by law to the text.

If it can be said that the signature appropriates the name for myself, identifies me as me, it does so by virtue of its iterability, that is, the possibility of being readable in my absence, even, as in the case of forgery, repeatable in my absence, which is why the signature is attached to the law. This parasitical relation to the authentic signature is a part of its authenticity (see "Signature, Event, Context"). By virtue of its iterability, the signature, like the proper name, may detach itself from what it designates—it can only function if it announces in itself the possibility of my absence. Every signature, therefore, is a countersignature, a confirmation of the identity of the bearer, of his/her singularity and otherness. For the singularity of the text, its signature, calls for a countersignature that confirms "the signature of the other . . . by signing in an absolutely new and inaugural way, both at once" (*SIL*, 67). Every signature confirms by repetition the unrepeatable, the absolute idiom of the inaugural act. The signature marks itself by effacing itself *a priori*. It is both unique *and* repeatable at once. The countersignature testifies to the singularity of the signature event and, at the same time, confirms its repeatability by responding to the text of the other or the call of the signature. For the signature, the absolutely idiomatic, to be readable, it has to be divided, a differing from itself so that it always is compromised *and* constituted by the possibility of death.

Similarly, the promise that promises what will be announces what has taken place—a promise, in other words, cannot guarantee a future (requital of a debt or an act that incurs a debt) without asserting that it would be a fulfillment of what has already taken place as soon as there is language.[14] A promise is an act *and* an archive; what is promised in the promise is an act or performance that will recall the contractual verbal deed. Yet a promise does not fit readily into the opposition between performative and constative, to use J. L. Austin's terms, or act and non-act. The promise can never appear in a present without being annulled; after all, it would not be a promise if it did not evoke or convoke a future. A promise fulfilled is no longer a promise. But the promise is not a pure future, because it not only is always haunted by the possibility of not being fulfilled, but it is already engaged by an other that precedes it. A promise, no matter what form it takes, is a response to an other. In discussing the aporia of the promise, Derrida cites Paul de Man, who says this "noncoincidence of the theoretical statement with its phenomenal manifestation implies that . . . time is the phenomenal category produced by the discrepancy."[15] The promise is, therefore, at once a future—it is to come—and a "promised memory"—it is, already dated. The promise, as Derrida concludes in his essay on de Man, "cannot be kept, it cannot even be made in all its purity." Like the gift, the promise is annulled in the present; consequently, the promise only has meaning "on the condition of death" because only then is it assured the necessary impossibility of its fulfillment: the promise "will not have been made, but as a trace of the future it can still be *renewed*. . . . I prefer to call this an *act*, only an act, quite simply an act. An impossible act, therefore the only one worthy of its name, or rather which, in order to be worthy of its name, must be worthy of the name of the other, made in the name of the other" (*Mem*, 150). The promise is an act because it is impossible, impossible because it is an act. The act that is worthy of its name bears within itself witness to the other—that is, as a trace of the future, its end "precedes" its beginning, a beginning that is already taken over, ruined, by its end.

Like the gift, the *yes*, and the signature, the promise announces a temporality that is not defined by succession, duration, or extension. In other words, it announces an interpretation of time different from that "which has ruled over our *representation* at least since Aristotle" (*OS*, 91; my emphasis). In this notion, illustrated in our discussion of the signature, the *yes*, and the promise (the law in Kafka and the date in Celan are other examples), we have a notion of time as effraction, as a promise that engages me before I make it: "I do not master it because it is older than me; language [*la langage*] is there before me and, at the moment where I pledge myself in it, I say *yes to it and to you* in a certain manner. To say *yes* is also to promise, to promise moreover to confirm the *yes*. There is no *yes* that is not a promise to confirm itself. It is before me. As soon as I speak, I am in it. . . . And it is there that I am responsible before even choosing my responsibility" (*Points*, 384).

The event the promise institutes is of a structure that comes to be only in repeating or doubling itself. The difficulty in describing this event and the recourse to definition by negation—it is not this or that, neither linear nor circular—signal that it has a temporality different from that "which has ruled over our representation." Whatever is both possible and impossible, such as a promise or a signature, gives rise to a future, an *à-venir*, a date, which is also a gift or a promise, to come. "But to speak of it, one must make it readable, audible, intelligible *beyond the pure singularity* of which it speaks" (*SPC*, 11). At the risk of being reductive, I would simply say that to speak of the singular act or event is not to efface its singularity but to mark or accentuate that the act as pure singularity is, according to its structure, wedded to its other.

Consequently, to make it intelligible beyond what it is does not violate the purity of the idea but answers the call of its impossible demand.

What I wish to emphasize is the positive nature of the response instead of defending it as paradox or aporia, for it is related to the *yes*, the signature, and the promise. If we compare Derrida's notion of singularity with Heidegger's concept of the *epochê* of Being, we find that when Heidegger says Being holds itself back in sending itself, he suggests that Being, like time, is burdened by representation.[16] Derrida, on the other hand, suggests that time is the condition of possibility of representation or, preferably, the impossible condition of possibility, whence such formulations that are variations on "as soon as there is [*es gibt, il y a*] . . . there is . . ." (we might fill in the first ellipsis with "*différance*" or "trace"). In deconstructing the metaphysical tradition that holds writing to be a representation of a representation, Derrida rehabilitates writing not as a first representation nor as Heidegger's Being, but as the name for what puts phenomenology in crisis. Writing is there already at work *before* the phenomenon.

Literature, therefore, is "the most interesting thing in the world, maybe more interesting than the world" because literature, as fictionality, "stands on the edge of everything, almost beyond everything, including itself" (*SIL*, 47). Literature's "exemplary" status lies as "a nonthetic experience of the thesis, of belief, of position, of naivety, of what Husserl called the 'natural attitude'" (*SIL*, 46). It is not that literature does without the thesis; quite the contrary, it could be said that the thetic act of positing is the condition of literature. However, as nonthetic experience of the thesis, literature, in Derrida's special sense of the word, is what allows us to experience the event, say the event, as such. This puts literature on the edge or margin of metaphysics.

II

Derrida's pursuit of the singular leads to the aporias of judgment, responsibility, spirit, apophatic discourse, and literature. Although language may be said to unite these and other topics of Derrida's writings of the eighties and nineties, Derridean textuality and writing cannot, as Rodolphe Gasché and John Llewelyn among others have amply demonstrated, be reduced to language in a conventional sense. Instead, judgment and responsibility belong, as I have argued, to the aporia between singularity and institution or generality.

We might, however, say judgment, responsibility, the promise are a matter of time—"I" will be responsible if *given time*. I allude to *Donner le temps*, a work that gathers together, as the title indicates, problems addressed in earlier works: the gift, economy, and time. Derrida takes up the thread of the anthropological discourse of Marcel Mauss and the late thinking of Heidegger.[17] Derrida's argument turns upon the singularity of the gift—the gift is not a gift if it is duplicated, exchanged, reciprocated.[18] In Mauss's notion of exchange, the gift is confused with the presence of the phenomenon and, consequently, is annulled in the economic exchange of an object between subjects. If we entertain the possibility of the gift's singularity, we may ask how would the gift be recognized as a gift if it were not iterable—that is, always already constituted by the possibility of repetition and difference? In other words, what would the gift be if it were absolutely singular? An answer points toward the effraction of time, the breaking of the circle of temporal synthesis or the disruption of the present (see *GT*, 9).

Noting the verbal conjunction of the gift and the present, Derrida asks us to think the impossibility of the gift, which is never present, never a present thing, nor does it mean to present a thing. In "this gap between the impossible and the thinkable a dimension opens up where *there is* gift—and even where *there is* period, for example time, where *it gives* being and time" (*GT*, 10). Alluding to Heidegger's *es gibt Sein*, Derrida situates the gift in the aporia between the condition of possibility—one gives a gift to some other—and impossibility—to give or even intend to give is a gesture of self-appropriation and, therefore, not a gesture of giving. There is gift only where the gift does not appear as such. *"At the limit, the gift as gift* ought *not appear as gift: either to the donee or to the donor."* The very perception of the gift that opens the symbolic order of exchange leads us to consider the gift within the phenomenological frame of intentionality and the "temporalization of time (memory, present, anticipation; retention, protention, imminence of the future; 'ecstases,' and so forth)" (*GT*, 14). The economy of the gift includes its destruction—the intentional motive of the gift destroys the gift as such. The gift event, therefore, must take place outside intentionality, recognition, memory, or retention "in a time without time, in such a way that the forgetting forgets, that it forgets *itself*. . . . For there to be forgetting in this sense, there must be gift" [*"Pour qu'il y ait oubli en ce sense, il faut qu'il y ait don"*] (*GT*, 17 / *DT*, 30–31).

The impossibility of the gift, its tie to an absolute forgetting that absolves, "should accord with a certain experience of the *trace* as *cinder* or *ashes*" (*GT*, 17). The thinking of the gift as forgetting is a thinking outside of causality, intentionality, or even what is. If the *es gibt Sein* of Heidegger is the opening for beings or what is, then the gift remains unthought, an event other than the gift of Being (*es gibt Sein*). The gift is "older" than Being—to think the gift is to think a difference anterior to the ontico-ontological difference. The gift belongs to a thinking—if we still call that which is before the determination of the difference between Being and beings "thinking"— of a difference before Being, a self-differing/deferring that is unthought.[19] This *différance* is not subject to phenomenologization; hence Derrida, following Heidegger, speaks of the gift giving itself because the gift is not "the presence of its phenomenon" (*GT*, 29). The gift cannot be determined as present because it annuls itself in presenting itself. The gift is nothing present, but it is not nothing. There is gift, but the "gift, like the event, as event, must *remain* unforeseeable" (*GT*, 122). The tautological language of the gift, of Being, of difference, all point to a thought (perhaps "notion" would be the better word here) that does not belong to metaphysical thinking and the possibility of phenomenologization.

The time without time of the gift event, a time in which the gift is nothing present, presentable, or sensible, would be the extreme of finitude, an event that is without history, without memory, because the gift would be aligned with the forgetting that Heidegger called a condition of Being. It is experienced as a trace or ash, as that which erases itself in presenting itself.[20] If the gift were present, a present, it would extinguish itself as gift. The gift is the condition of forgetting and forgetting the condition of the gift. "We are not talking therefore about conditions in the sense of conditions posed (since forgetting and gift, if there is any, are in this sense unconditional), but in the sense in which forgetting would be in the *condition of the gift* and gift in the *condition of forgetting*" (*GT*, 17–18). The gift, which is never a present phenomena, is experienced as that which gives itself as something other than the gift. We can never experience the gift as gift. The truth of the gift annuls the gift. The gift, then, "gives nothing that is and that appears as such—determined thing, object, symbol" (*GT*, 28). Neither a present being nor a being present, the gift gives time.

We are confronted with the double aporetics of time and the gift. If the gift appears as such, as gift, it annuls itself. Time, according to convention, is apprehended on the basis of the present and, therefore, is not; it is modified so that past and future are a past-present and a present-to-come. What passes in time or happens is not time (see *GT*, 28). If time is nothing, the gift does not give time as a present phenomenon. "If the gift," Derrida says, "is another name of the impossible, we still think it, we name it, we desire it. We intend it" (*GT*, 29). To think the gift "according to the measureless measure [*mesure sans mesure*] of the impossible" belongs to a "logic" of the other that unsettles the law of the same governing the economy of exchange and the representation of time.

The gift and time give themselves to be thought on the basis of nothing that is, but there is gift; there is time and from this comes the singular responsibility to the other, that which is not given but makes itself felt as the call "come" (see *PIO*, 60–61). We are in the realm where there is exchange without sender and receiver, donor and donee, or as Derrida says, "The event of this 'Come' precedes and calls the event" (*AT*, 164). The "Come" is without content or identity; "[it] is apocalyptic" (*AT*, 167), a matter of sending or giving without any decidable destination or origin. "Come" is the unnameable name, "*le pronom d'un sans-nom*" (*Par*, 71), for something older than Being, forgetting. It "names" an absolute forgetting beyond Being: "The gift *comes* is, gives rather, gives itself in forgetting itself beyond being: *pas au-delà de l'être*" (*Par*, 101). The gift gives itself in a forgetting that is not attached to an origin. This forgetting is not simply negative, the contrary of Platonic *anamnêsis* or recollection, because insofar as memory is not to be thought within the confines of origins and ends, it is less an act of consciousness, a retrieval of the past, and closer to a promise that engages me before I speak. Forgetting opens the possibility of a memory of the future, a thought no longer attached to Being or being present.[21]

With the thinking of the gift, the motif "come," and the thing as something given, as given time, we are in the realm of narrative, of the *récit*, as that which puts in relation without relation, a gift that "arrives, if it arrives, only in narrative." As soon as there is the gift, there is time. The gift gives time, the interval inscribed in the given thing that obliges the recipient to give in exchange—after a time. The gift gives *différance* (see *GT*, 40). However, the truth of the gift annuls the gift, putting in crisis any possibility of exchange, reciprocation, presence, the present, and phenomenology. At stake in the gift, the given thing, is *what is* there, Being and time, the being of time: *"There where there is gift, there is time"* (*GT*, 41). This does not mean the thing is in time or has time or whatever conventional locution one may resort to when thinking of the thing as present, but the gift gives time. "To give time, the day, or life is to give nothing, nothing determinate, even if it is to give the giving of any possible giving, even if it gives the condition of giving" (*GT*, 54).

According to Mauss' logic of the gift, the given thing demands restitution. What is given, consequently, is not a determinate thing but the possibility of giving, the temporization of the thing: "It demands time, the thing, but it demands a delimited time, neither an instant nor an infinite time, but a time determined by a term, in other words, a rhythm, a cadence" (*GT*, 41). The gift has time or takes time as rhythm, which implies structuring by differentiation. In Plato, rhythm is what allows us to "distinguish the powers of elementary and then of compound sounds" (*Cratylus*, 424c). Rhythm is nothing in itself but difference. If the thing demands time as rhythm, if the thing gives or takes time, then time is inscribed in it as *différance*, hence the impossibility of restitution, a concept that depends upon the thing as a present, in both senses of the English word. The gift, because it demands time, is "linked to the—internal—necessity of a certain narrative [*récit*]" (*GT*, 41). As nothing determinate, the thing of the gift is not something in time, but it is time, the rhythm of a certain *destinnerance*, for there can be no gift that is not already in narrative and that is not already a promise of repetition.

III

The promise of the gift forms a narrative; it is narrative. As soon as there is a promise, a gift, there is the possibility of literary fiction, the possibility of a secret, the unreadable. In an analysis of Baudelaire's "Counterfeit Money" from *Paris Spleen*, Derrida writes, "The *interest* of 'Counterfeit Money,' like any analogous text in general, comes from the enigma constructed out of this crypt which gives to be read that which will remain *eternally* unreadable, *absolutely* indecipherable, even refusing itself to any promise of deciphering or hermeneutic" (*GT*, 152). The inviolability of the text "says the (non-) truth of literature, let us say the secret *of* literature: what literary fiction tells us about the secret, of the (non-) truth of the secret, but also a secret whose possibility assures the possibility of literature" (*GT*, 153). There is literature wherever there is the gift, that which manifests without there being revealed something—a gift, we might say, that unveils the non-truth of its end, a presentation without presentation. Literature is the possibility of revelation of non-truth, a simulacrum wherein every truth is held or kept secret. It is, as Derrida says, like counterfeit money that produces the effect of money as long as it passes for real (*GT*, 153).

Literature, then, is linked to the very possibility—not of "Being,"—but of the secret, the passion for secrets, a non-phenomenality that is not in opposition to or the negative of the phenomenal, that is not simply the inaccessible (truth) but is the impossible possibility that there is—the gift, the promise, singularity. We refer here not to that which represents the unrepresentable but to the possibility of representation and of mimesis. Literature shares with the gift the condition of a certain unconditionality; it must be irruptive, given to chance or the aleatory, which makes it possible for literature to say anything.

Literature, like negative theology, holds an attraction for Derrida in its power to destabilize, to put in crisis, the principle of phenomenology, as well as ontological and transcendental critique.[22] When Derrida confesses to his "taste (probably unconditional) for literature, more precisely for literary writing (*ON*, 27)," he does so in the context of a request to write a response to a "Critical Reader" (Derrida will play upon the double meaning of this term as a collection of essays on his work and as an individual respondent on his writings). In presuming that in a response one "claims to measure up to the discourse of the other . . . [t]he respondent presumes, with as much frivolity as arrogance, that he can respond to the other and before the other because first of all he is able to answer for himself and for all he has been able to do, say, or write." Responsibility assumes self-possession, self-identity, an I that accompanies all "I" think, say, or do. As Derrida points out, this Kantian notion of the subject supposes "that deconstruction is of the same order as the critique whose concept and history it precisely deconstructs" (*ON*, 20). In offering a non-response as a response to the demand for responsibility, Derrida rejects the dogmaticism of a principle of self-identity with its faith in a totalizing memory and the priority of the subject. In choosing not to respond, he opens himself, as he acknowledges, to the charge a non-response is a response and an inadequate one at that. Nor can the aporia of the non-response—it is and is not a response—be overcome in a performative, which invites the accusation of simultaneously claiming mastery and aestheticizing "serious" discourse (*ON*, 23).

Such a discourse of responsibility rests upon the phenomenality of the example, which explains this discourse's frequent, if not inevitable, recourse to the language of sacrifice, particularly as it pertains to the example of the passion of Christ (see *ON*, 140–41, n. 10). "What," Derrida asks, "could escape this sacrificial verification and so secure the very space of *this very discourse, for example?*" He answers, "**There** *is something secret. [Il y a là du secret]*" (*ON*, 23–24). The secret is neither phenomenal nor noumenal, but "no discussion would either begin or continue without it" (*ON*, 27). It is mute, impassive; it is neither sensible, nor intelligible, but there is a secret; we may even say that without it, there could be no ethics, no demand for a response.

What, then, is this secret? Derrida suggests that as the intractable, the secret is what must be respected, what cannot not be respected insofar as it is there, which is to say it is neither a present being nor *eidos*, neither ontological nor transcendental in character. Instead, it can be said to be "older" than Being insofar as its call precedes any ethics, any debt heard in the call "*Schuld*" ("guilt" and "debt"). The secret is what makes possible an absolute non-response because it allows one to say everything rather than nothing.

This is Derrida's secret—he likes literature or, rather, literary writing. What he likes about it is not some aesthetic pleasure it may give—he is, after all, not speaking of literature in its conventional sense—but something that "would be *in place of the secret* . . . there where nevertheless everything is said and where the remainder is nothing [*où le reste n'est rien*]—but the remainder [*que le reste*], not even of literature" (*ON*, 28 / *Pas*, 64; trans. modified). What is "in place of the secret?" As the remainder, the secret is what authorizes the possibility of saying everything and saying nothing, of an "absolute nonresponse" (*ON*, 29). The secret is an anarchic event anterior to all narrativity but which affirms itself in narrative. It shares with the gift, the law, the promise, the yes, and the signature, the condition of singularity—the moment the secret or the gift or the signature, etc. comes into its own, is exposed, exchanged, or repeated, it ruins the very conditions of its possibility, necessarily. The logic of the secret, as of the signature, is that it appears as a result of a singular anachrony—it comes into being in response to the other, an other for which it is the singular condition. The secret is a basis for the performative; it is there as soon as there is some *yes*, "the transcendental condition of all performative dimensions" (*UGE*, 298). The *yes* is the minimal "act" (the opposition of act and non-act or place no longer stands) that is never simply originary but demands from the start, as its own condition, its repetition: "We cannot say *yes* without promising to confirm it and to remember it, to keep it safe, countersigned in another *yes*, without promise and memory, without the promise of memory" (*UGE*, 304–305). In other words, the Derridean quasi-transcendental is a condition of possibility and impossibility that announces its non-identity with itself. As neither identical nor non-identical, the quasi-transcendental is knowable only in its effects, what it makes possible on/as the ruined grounds of its own condition (by ruin, here, I mean the necessarily divided or differential status of the "originary" condition). The trace, which is constituted by self-effacement, is perhaps the most familiar example of the quasi-transcendental, but the *yes* is a self-positing affirmation that "can address itself to the other only in recalling itself to itself, in saying to itself *yes, yes*" (*UGE*, 303). As self-sending, the *yes* says "*yes*" to itself only by referral to an other. Iterability belongs to the "possibility" of saying "*yes*."

Therefore, when Derrida says that all literature is fiction or narrative, he refers to its neutrality or independence, its being-suspended, which is not to say it is removed from the "real" world but to insist upon the literary as that which allows us to think such oppositions in the first place, allows us to think the thesis in general. Literature's fictionality is not to be confused with illusion or some naive notion of a purely imaginative product, but "there is fictionality in all literature. . . . And it is through this fictionality that we try to thematize the 'essence' or the 'truth' of 'language'" (*SIL*, 49). Literary writing permits this thematizing by virtue of "its *right to say everything*" (*ON*, 28). Rather than submit literature to a moral imperative, such as the capacity to represent the other, Derrida argues literature is characterized by a non-responsibility: "This authorization to say everything (which goes together with democracy, as the apparent hyper-responsibility of a 'subject') acknowledges a right to absolute nonresponse, just where there can be no question of responding, of being able to or having to respond. This nonresponse is more original and more secret than the modalities of power and duty because it is fundamentally heterogeneous to them" (*ON*, 29). Literature is the right not to respond to the call of Being.

At stake here is the experience of the other. In rejecting the dogmatic certitude of a call for ethics and by insisting on the possibility of an absolute nonresponse, Derrida suggests that nonresponse is the unthought of responsibility. Responsibility assumes a mastery of the other and of oneself, thus the linkage of power and duty. This presumption of responsibility is that of exemplarity, that the "moral" or responsible act is "moral" in itself and, therefore, repeatable, imitable, insofar as the example is at once singular and the same through its repetitions. But, Derrida writes, "The example itself, as such, overflows its singularity as much as its identity. This is why there are no examples, while at the same time there are only examples. . . . The exemplarity of the example is clearly never the exemplarity of the example" (*ON*, 17–18). The example has to be unforeseeable if it is to serve as example. Otherwise, it would be possible to be moral without reason; one would merely mimic the law or rules (see *ON*, 140, n. 10). The example remains an example insofar as it remains singular, inimitable, yet there is no example if it is purely singular. Derrida acknowledges this play of undecidability associated with deconstruction is interminable, and we may well ask, who will deliver us from this example? Christ, for example?

The exemplarity of Christ's passion serves Kant, as we saw in the first chapter, as the example of the impossibility of an example to serve as a model for morality since it would invite us to ignore the "'true original which lies in reason'" (*ON*, 141, n. 10; quoted from Kant, *Foundations of the Metaphysics of Morals*). In other words, not even Christ can serve as the example of morality if we do not first possess the idea of moral perfection. Otherwise, we would be merely imitating a model or example and not acting according to the Idea. Derrida concludes, the exemplarity of Christ's passion "demonstrates *in an exemplary way*, singularly, par excellence, the inadequacy of example, the secret of divine invisibility and the sovereignty of reason. . . . The example is the only visibility of the invisible" (*ON*, 141, n. 10). The structure of exemplarity is tied to that of the trace—it has no identity in itself but depends upon referral, iterabilty. Having no identity in itself, the example, reveals, exemplifies, the insecurity of the *as such*: there is no example *as such* but there are examples, only examples. This non-exemplary structure of the example ties it to the secret. To the extent that the example exemplifies the "secret of divine invisibility," not even God can serve as example. The example impassions us to say everything without touching upon the secret, which is why literature is always exemplary: "There is in literature, in the *exemplary* secret of literature, a chance of saying everything without touching upon the secret" (*ON*, 29). The non-phenomenality of the secret, therefore, is what authorizes nonresponse, a possibility of saying everything because it is not linked to a determinable subject nor regulated by law—of exemplarity we might say. The nonresponse ties its destiny to that of the secret. Because the secret is nonphenomenolizable, it calls for no response. There is something secret that is without content or interiority, nothing to unveil or reveal. The secret "exceeds the play of veiling/unveiling, dissimulation/revelation. . . . It does not belong therefore to the truth, neither to the truth as *homoiosis* or adequation, nor to the truth as memory (Mnemosyne, *alêtheia*), nor to the given truth, nor to the promised truth, nor to the inaccessible truth" (*ON*, 26). Thus, when Derrida writes, "no finite being will ever provide an economy of these figures, nor of mimesis in general, nor of anything that iterability contaminates" (*ON*, 141, n. 10), he rejects finitude as the basis of exemplarity and mimesis. Were it otherwise, the example would be singular and *not* repeatable.

Derrida's "example" of literature's exemplariness is the impossibility of deciding whether when I say "I" if "I write in the first person or that I write a text," if I am writing about myself or the "I" in general. This dissociation between use and mention of an "I," he says, is "already valid for every trace in general" and not even in need of words at all. I can say "I" because "I" am already an example: iterability allows me to say "I." Indeed, as a function of every trace, this difference is pragmatic, not linguistic. The difference between the two values is merely thematized by language and is experienced as time, as the non-coincidence of meaning and usage. The originary repetition that constitutes the "I" permits signification independent of an object. Mortality, therefore, is the possibility of taking "I" for example. Indeed, the sentence "I am dead" is the example of intelligibility independent of any possible object: "Therefore, 'I am dead' is not only a possible proposition for one who is known to be living, but the very condition for the living person to speak is for him to be able to say, significantly, 'I am dead.'"[23] "I" am already an example of the unthought, that which is not relational but *is*, which is why the person of Christ exemplifies the impurity of exemplarity—finite being can serve as the visible figure of the invisible *and* no finite being can govern the economy of these figures. One can never be done with the secret because the "secret never allows itself to be captured or covered over by the relation to the other, by being-with or by any form of 'social bond'" (*ON*, 30). This is not to say literature presumes in analogical fashion that Being is like a hermetic secret, an invisible source, or hidden truth but that literature does not answer to the other, does not allow itself to be gathered into relation with the other, to answer its call. It is not responsive. "Shall we call this death? Death dealt? Death dealing? I see no reason not to call that life, existence, trace. And it is not the contrary" (*ON*, 31).

The exemplary secret of literature tells us that the secret can never be rendered visible, which is why there is no contradiction between the secret and no secret. The secret is what we can never be finished with. It impassions us but is not rendered visible, which would amount to it being captured by the other in what Derrida calls "a *pure* thought of *pure* difference," a heterological thought of the absolutely Other (*WD*, 151). Recalling that Derrida writes in his first essay on Levinas that "the other cannot be what it is, infinitely other, except in finitude and mortality (mine *and* its)," we are reminded that the infinitely Other maintains itself in the negative: it is finite "as soon as it comes into language" (*WD*, 114–15). To think the absolutely Other would risk not to think at all. We cannot think positive infinity as absolute presence because to do so would be to do away with all determination. Therefore, the non-responsiveness of the secret, its being as "what does not answer," may be called death and, without contradiction, life. The secret can be spoken of, made use of, cited, but this playing with the secret "bears witness to a possibility which exceeds it," a solitude that makes possible consciousness, intersubjectivity, Being-with-others, but "does not answer to them." It is what Derrida calls "the absolute solitude of a passion without martyrdom [*sans martyre*]" (*ON*, 31).

The secret bears witness to the impossibility of establishing an experience (of the other) that is realizable in an example, as demonstrated in the exemplarity of the Passion. The nonresponse of the secret is life/death, the remainder that makes it impossible to reduce one to the other. "The secret of the passion, the passion of the secret," demonstrates in an exemplary way the impossibility of the example of doing away with mimesis or the simulacrum, a possibility that would mean rendering visible the divine secret. The dream of the passion is that of bearing witness to what exceeds the example; it is the dream of an absolute trace.

In his reading of Levinas, Derrida remarks that positive Infinity cannot be infinitely Other if the Other must maintain within itself negativity (labor and death). "If one thinks, as Levinas does, that positive Infinity tolerates, or even requires, infinite alterity, then one must renounce all language, and first of all the words *infinite* and *other*" (*WD*, 114). What would it mean to exclude death from God but "that God is *nothing* (determined), is not life, because he is *everything*? and therefore is at once All and Nothing. Life and Death. Which means that God is or appears, *is named*, within the difference between All and Nothing. Life and Death. Within difference, and at bottom as Difference itself" (*WD*, 115–16). If, as Gasché says, God is exemplary of the trace and, thus, is "self-presentation" as the "non-exemplifiable structure that constitutes the structure of the example," then God, as the example of the trace, points thought in a direction where it would no longer be thought; it would be a thought of "pure difference," as Derrida calls it at the end of his essay on Levinas, a thought of the absolutely Other, of "a trace of which Being would be a trace."[24]

Literature would be that which keeps thought on the side of thinking, of *différance* and the trace. If we can say God is the example of the trace, then literature is there (where?) thanks to God: it is exemplary of what happens each time there is some trace, some gift, before any speech act. The difference between God and literature, if I can be allowed such an extravagant (let us hope not blasphemous) formulation, is that as an effect of the trace, God is "beyond all gifts"; he is the necessary possibility of the erasure of the trace and is, thus, the dream of absolute erasure (An unerasable trace would not be a trace but a monument, a "son of God" [*WD*, 230]).

Literature begins the moment it becomes impossible to decide between use and mention, performative and constative, between the trace and what it exemplifies. Literature's exemplarity, its exemplary secret, bears witness to the secret that impassions us— the impossibility of ever doing away with or finishing with what Derrida calls the oblique and the trace or the remainder (*restance*) that makes possible responsiveness, and the right to a nonresponse. The trace is not a permanent substrate; it has nothing to do with permanence but is the anarchic condition of repeatability and idealization. Literature's exemplarity lies in its gift of "a chance of saying everything without touching upon the secret" (*ON*, 29). This gift is the possibility of a nonresponse, the very condition of responsibility, a passion for what never allows itself to be named or absolutely determined.

Derrida's secret is structurally infinite, the secret of the interminable, the inexhaustible, responsibility to the other. This responsibility is inexhaustible not because it possesses a telos that extends beyond our capacity to act in the here and now, nor because it represents an unattainable goal. Our responsibility is infinite because it is a gift, a given difference that allows for no decision between response and nonresponse. An infinity that would decide this difference would be a totalizing infinity, one that would be dependent on its self and not the Other.[25] Nor is Derrida's infinite an infinite regress or a transcendental; it is intractable. And lest we should confuse the undecidability between response and nonresponse with quietism, I would venture to say responsibility is an act, is definable as act.

The differential constitution of the trace, mark, or fold means that the space of their production, the "secret" place, is not identifiable, not meaningful, because it is a minimal structure without (self)identity. This space or receptacle, this *khôra*, is not a *mise en*

abyme, a representational concept for infinite regress, nor a principle of non-identity, but that which accounts for identity and difference, infinite and finite, without itself being either infinite or
finite. It deflects the philosophical infinite from within, foiling
infinity's movement toward totality. The secret, therefore, is
"intractable" (*intraitable*); in other words, it cannot be drawn into
discourse, let alone into the discourse of ethics, but there would be
no discourse without it. The secret is the stroke, line, missive—the
trait—that makes the "ethics of discussion" possible and "remains
there impassively, at a distance, out of reach" (*ON*, 27). The
abysmal structure of the secret disrupts the totalizing gesture of
an ethics to command a response by encompassing all discourse.
The secret allows the right to "absolute nonresponse," a possibility
that can exist only if we have a right to say everything, which is to
say only if there is literature.

Derrida concludes his essay "Passions" with a disclosure of a
secret, his taste for literature. Literature's "authorization to say
everything makes the author an author who is not responsible to
anyone, not even to himself" (*ON*, 28). In calling this nonresponse
"a condition of democracy" and in saying there is "No democracy
without literature; no literature without democracy," Derrida ties
the destiny of literature to the nonresponse, the possibility of challenging every dogmatism and every presupposition, including that
"of the ethics or the politics of responsibility." Literature is the preserve of the nonresponse, a secret that is more original than any
duty or responsibility because in its heterogeneity, the secret cannot be appropriated by any totality or subjectivity nor point toward
"some ideal community" (*ON*, 28). The secret makes possible a
relation to the other, which is not an absolute other, or otherwise it
would have to answer to the call for responsibility, thereby assuming a mastery that contradicts the demand for responsibility. The
secret remains secret, even to the point of our being able to ask if
there is one.

As the absolute nonresponse, literature is what "would be *in
place of the secret*" (*ON*, 28). Hence, the secret is the "unsignifi-
able" referent, "the "only 'subject' of all possible literature" because
literature or literary writing consists in the "strategic maneuvers"
that would "assimilate that unassimilable wholly other" (*NA*, 28).
Literature, we can say, suspends the encounter with the wholly
other. It says "yes" to the other, a *yes* that does not confirm the

absolute priority of the other but announces the coming of the unforeseeable. The singularity of this other is unimaginable without this *yes*; it is the only invention possible because it is not inventable. The other invents us; we invent the other—this is the dissymmetrical relationship of the performative—we can say *yes* to the other only because the "first" yes is already a repetition. This "first" *yes* is a *renvoi*, a sending that *"both never leaves itself and never arrives at itself"* (*UGE*, 303). It is a matter of destinnerant indirection.

The circuitous or, rather, destinnerant path of the *renvoi*, wherein an other says, "come," is the apocalyptic itself, the opening of the possibility of the coming of the absolutely other. This other comes back to the same—the minimal event, whether it be the call "come," the invention of the other, "a *yes* [that] demands *a priori* its own repetition" (*UGE*, 304). This event is breached, opened, by an originary specter, a mark or trait that haunts the event. Constituted on the basis of its fictive referent, literature can address this fabulous referent only be speaking of other things as well. That is, attuned to the absolute referent that would consume literature in an apocalypse without revelation, literature suspends its encounter with the absolute referent, the wholly other, by dispatching itself in sendings that may not reach their destination. Therefore, Derrida carefully avoids suggesting that this event cannot be imagined or that it will come from outside, a first and last missive/missile. The event, we might say, is already here in the archive as a kind of gift.

IV

The eschatological tone of much of Derrida's writings on literature, the other, and responsibility is marked by laughter, "the yes-laughter of a gift without debt, light affirmation, almost amnesic, of a gift or an abandoned event, which in classical language is called 'the work,' a lost signature without a proper name that reveals and names the cycle of reappropriation and domestication of all the paraphs only to delimit their phantasm, and does so in order to contrive the breach necessary for the coming of the other, whom one can always call Elijah" (*UGE*, 294–95). This laughter that announces the coming of the other is apocalyptic, but it is an apocalypse of the other, and as such, it is nothing verifiable, for it is always to come—it is a repetition from the start.

Literature is the experience of the apocalyptic coming, the coming of the apocalypse. The apocalyptic fold (*pli*) that he speaks of at the conclusion of the "Apocalyptic Tone" would be an apocalypse of apocalypse, a temporal effraction that makes the catastrophe of apocalypse something external to apocalypse—a cataclysm of the apocalypse—and internal to it—an apocalyptic catastrophe (*AT*, 167–68). Derrida's deconstruction of the apocalypse takes the form of an overturning of the sense of apocalypse or what we might call an apocalyptic sense—the advent of the end, the fulfillment of Being, the revelation of truth, the presencing of the present. These thoughts bear witness to the coming of the absolutely Other, the only thing literature can address, but addresses always too late. Hence, literature is always saying *yes* to the other's *yes*, entrusting itself to the memory of the other, to all that Derrida calls a "gramophone in the grave"—that is, the singular anachrony of what may best be called *ashes*—in the beginning there will have been ashes, the withheld apocalypse, the presencing of an other still to come. These ashes belong to the history of Being: "the gift, the sacrifice, the putting into play or the setting on fire of everything, the holocaust are under the power of ontology [*l'holocauste, sont en puissance d'ontologie*]. Without the holocaust the dialectical movement and the history of Being would not open themselves, engage themselves in the annulus [*l'anneau*] of their anniversary, could not annul themselves in producing the solar course from Orient to Occident" (*C*, 46 / *G*, 269; trans. modified). The holocaust would be the fulfillment of dialectic in the self-totalizing return of history, in the convergence of origin and end. The gift before exchange, on the other hand, is a holocaust of holocaust; the irruptive event sends thought on the way of its destinnerance.

This is the holocaust of pure light, of the fire that leaves no trace of itself. This "pure play of difference" that is without essence, without example, is nothing. "This example without essence, devoid of self (*Selbst*), is also a sort of signifier without signified, the wasting of an adornment without the body proper, the total absence of property, propriety [*propriete*], of truth, of meaning [*sens*]. . . . It is a One at once infinitely multiple and absolutely different, different from self, a One without self, the other without self that means (to say) nothing, whose language is absolutely empty, void, like an event that never comes about itself" [*un Un sans soi, l'autre sans soi qui ne veut rien dire, dont le langage est absolument vide, comme un événement qui ne s'arrive jamais*] (*Glas-E*, 239, left hand column / *G*, 266; trans. modified). The history of metaphysics is the determination of this pure play, this pure Being or essenceless example— ontology is the strange effort to reduce this limitless play by erecting monuments, pyramids and even crematoriums, Derrida says, that guard over the "trace of death" that haunts the history of the West (of metaphysics), the sending of the Being of pure difference as something other than itself (see *Glas–E*, 238–40, left hand column).

The gift of the *es gibt*, the gift before exchange, is a holocaust,

a holocaust of the holocaust, [that] *engages* the history of Being but does not belong to it. The gift *is not*; the holocaust *is not*; if at least *there is some such*. But as soon as it burns (the blaze is not a being), it must, burning itself, burn its action [*opération*] of burning and begin to be. This reflection (in both senses of the word) of the holocaust engages history, the dialectic of sense, ontology, the speculative. The speculative is the reflection (*speculum*) of the holocaust's holocaust (*Glas-E*, 242).

The holocaust is without Being; it *is* not, but there is holocaust. This means that it is an event that cannot be explained, and therein determined, by Being or ontology. It is not, therefore, an event whose truth unfolds in the movement toward totality. Such an argument reduces the Nazi genocide to an example without singularity. But if seen as an example of the trace, an action of burning itself, it presents itself as example in consuming itself as example. Rather than think it as the destination of radical evil, which would be a metaphysical determination, the ontic determination of an ontological category, Derrida suggests that it is an event without essence—it cannot fit within a calculable program that would allow us to bypass the undecidable (see *LI*, 116). Undecidability does not absolve us of responsibility; to the contrary, it is what demands it. Therefore, if the holocaust is unique— and each holocaust is—then as that which burns in order to be, it makes possible the thinking of unforeseeable disaster, an event without essence that allows us to think absolute consumption, a *brûle-tout*.

Derrida gives the name "cinder" to that which is beyond Being or presence but is there, "a name of the being that there is there but which, giving itself (*es gibt ashes*) is nothing [*c'est un nom de l'être qu'il y a là mais qui, se donnant* (es gibt ashes), *n'est rien, reste au-delà de tout ce qui est*], remains beyond everything that is (*konis epekeina tes ousias*), remains unpronounceable in order to make saying possible although it is nothing" (*C*, 73).[26] The reflection of the holocaust is the self-producing/self-consuming "*coup de don* [the gift's blow, stroke, time, etc.] as/in holocaust" (*Glas-E*, 242). The pure gift figures itself as holocaust, an all (*holos*) burning (*caustus*) wherein the fire consumes its own blaze. The holocaust engages the history of Being insofar as it is the speculative origin of the dialectic, the annulus of the anniversary. The all-consuming blaze is the law of referral without essence. Hence, the holocaust, like God, is "without example." It is the law of example, the impossible condition of the possibility of exemplification. The word "holocaust" designates a sacrifice to God—it is the law governing the exemplification of the non-exemplifiable. It is also an inappropriate name, for as the exemplary name for genocide, it would both confuse the Nazi genocide with sacrifice and turn Jews into an example.

As essence without example, the holocaust cannot be thought by philosophy, yet it gives birth to "the annulus of the exchange," "the solar course from Orient to Occident" that in Hegel is the pathway of the gift of a God who leaves himself and determines himself in his finitude, as passion: "The gift can be only a sacrifice, that is the axiom of speculative reason" (*Glas-E*, 242, 243). The irruptive event of the gift, however, does not let itself be thought by dialectics and the history of Being, but as soon as there is something, the holocaust burns, it engages the history of Being in the annulus of its anniversary, that is, in the finite time of the date that consigns itself to forgetfulness. The holocaust "is at work everywhere that a date inscribes its *here* and *now* within iterability," in self-effacement. "Trace, or ash" (*SPC*, 43).

The holocaust, the gift, does not let itself be thought by the history of Being to which it gives rise. The holocaust names the nonrecurrence in recurrence, the forgetting in memory itself. "If one can speak of the gift in the language [*langue*] of philosophy or the philosophy of religion, one *must say* that the holocaust, the pure gift, the pure *cadeau*, the cake [*gâteau*] of honey or fire hold on to themselves in giving themselves, are never doing anything but exchanging themselves according to the annulus. The gift for (it)self. . . . The annulus, the chain of the annular anniversary, is not one gift among others; it hands over the gift itself, the very gift of the self (*Selbst*) for (it)self, the present for (it)self. The gift, *cadeau*, names what makes itself present" (*Glas-E*, 243).

The gift does not let itself be circumscribed by the dialectical process of reappropriation of the same or by Heidegger's gathering of the sending of Being but is kept open as a date to come, a trace that is at once singular and iterable, readable at every moment as unreadable—the impossible possibility of what is—ashes without origin. Everything bears witness to the remainder without origin. We are haunted by these spectral remains, this trace or ashes, not in the form of lost presence, which would mean the incorporation of the dead through the work of mourning, but in the impossible experience of a singular event, like a promise or a gift, that institutes and annuls in a single stroke, in *Un coup de don*. It is the impossible experience of the temporality of the instant, the demand of an absolutely singular that is not (something present).

In contradistinction to Heideggerean debt, wherein Dasein temporalizes by assuming its debt/guilt (*Schuld*) in answering the call, Derrida's notion of responsibility involves keeping a secret in the form of a shibboleth, a secret which sounds but is "the absolute of invisibility" (*GD, 89 / DM*, 85). It would be the "secret" without secrecy, a differential mark of a maternal language and of an invisible God. As a mark that is without meaning, *Shibboleth* signifies that there is something incalculable, an other commemorated like a date—it is readable only in the effacing of its singularity, as in the annulus of the anniversary: "In a language, in the poetic writing of a language, there is nothing but *shibboleth*. Like the date, like a name, it permits anniversaries, alliances, returns, commemorations" (*SPC*, 36). The date, a cipher that gives access to memory and assigns a moment or place a future anterior, "always functions as a *shibboleth*. It shows that there is something not shown, that there is ciphered singularity" (*SPC*, 35). As readable, the date recalls a singularity that it annuls and thereby risks becoming "no one's and nothing's date, the essence without essence of ash." Like the determinate secret of the shibboleth, a signifier that shows something secret, the date consumes the other's singularity by making it available to all. In the date, the commemorated is available to all and no one (see *SPC*, 39).

I can only respond to the other in sacrificing ethics, that is, my obligation to all the others: "I cannot respond to the call, the request, the obligation, or even the love of another without sacrificing the other other, the others others. *Every other (one) is entirely other*" [*Je ne peux répondre à l'appel, à la demande, à l'obligation, ni même à l'amour d'un autre sans lui sacrifier l'autre autre, les autres autres*. Tout autre est tout autre.] (*GD*, 68 / *DM*, 68). This responsibility before the other is the impossible demand of the temporality of the instant, a responsibility/instant that can only be met by violating it. It is the impossible economy of the absolute singularity of the other, every other, that makes the singular unique when it should have been universal. It is the experience of literature: "there is no literature without a work, without an absolutely singular performance, and this necessary irreplaceability again recalls what the man from the country [in Kafka's "Before the Law"] asks when the singular crosses the universal, when the categorical engages the idiomatic, as literature always must. The man from the country had difficulty in grasping that an entrance was singular or unique when it should have been universal, as in truth it was. He had difficulty with literature" [*Il avait du mal avec la littérature*] (*BL*, 213 / *Préjugés*, 131).

The mad experience of singularity is figured among Jews as the rite of passage that occurs on the eighth day following birth, that is, as circumcision.[27] This is what Derrida calls elsewhere the madness of an instant that cuts and decides. It is the madness of the desire for justice (see *FL*, 965–67). In his reading of the tropes of circumcision in Paul Celan, the circumcised word, the wound "is tied to both the differential marks and the destination of language: the inaccessibility of the other returns there in the same, dates and sets turning the ring [*l'anneau*]. To say 'all poets are Jews' is to state something which marks *and* annuls the mark of a circumcision. It is tropic. All those who deal with or inhabit language as poets are Jews—but in a tropic sense. . . . What the trope . . . comes to, then, is locating the Jew not only *as* a poet but also in every man circumcised by language or led to circumcise a language" (*SPC*, 59 / *S*, 98). This circumcision of the word, the mark that defines and decides, like the shibboleth, is a doorway, a promise that is at once singular and dated, and therefore universal. It is a wound, a cipher of the covenant, and what distinguishes the community. But if all poets are Jews, then it is as much universal as singular, a trope or mark naming the wound of singularity.

Wherever the singular is given to be read, experienced, there is circumcision, the unique event that comes about as the relation between the singular and its repetition. Circumcision is the cipher of singularity, the promise of the unique and its recurrence, "offering and recalling its time at the risk of losing them in the holocaustic generality of recurrence and the readability of the concept, in the anniversary repetition of the unrepeatable. Wherever a signature has entered into an idiom, leaving in language the trace of an incision which is *at once* unique and iterable, cryptic and readable, there is date" (*SPC*, 52).

This wound of the differential mark of language, circumcision, marks "the breach necessary for the coming of the other, whom one can always call Elijah, if Elijah is the name of the unforeseeable other for whom a place must be kept" (*UGE*, 295). This unforeseeable other, a future for which there is no exergue, "can only announce itself in the form of monstrosity, beyond all anticipated norms, beyond all genres or kinds. . . . Here in this very place, in the poem, the monster, or Elijah, the guest or the other, stands before the door, at the poem's first step, on the threshold of the text" (*SPC*, 62). He stands before the door and the law—Elijah is present at all circumcisions. The passage through the door, the door marked by the wound of circumcision, the mark of belonging and exclusion (see *SPC*, 67), is the passage through the undecidable, the necessary condition for every decision, "when the categorical engages the idiomatic." It is this crossing of the unconditional or categorical with the determinate or idiomatic that designates literary writing as deconstructive; it is the partition, *parage*, that divides "itself along two sides of a limit," erasing it in the process of marking it. Derrida describes this as the structure of a context without closure. The outside is the inside: "it intervenes in the determination of a context from its very inception, and from an injunction, a law, a responsibility that transcends this or that determination of a given context" (*LI*, 152).[28] It is a *circumcision*, the manifest sign of a secret, a shibboleth, that "must take place once, precisely, each time one time, the one time only. This time awaits its coming, as its vicissitude. It awaits a date, and this date can only be poetic, an incision in the body of language. It remains to come, always" (*SPC*, 68).

We who are circumcised (and as a writing for the body, circumcision must be understood as the opening of the limits of what it delimits or defines, as "conferring on it a singular indefiniteness" [*SPC*, 64]) are like the man from the country who waits before the door; we are called upon to be faithful to a secret, the impossibility of the *as such*, irreplaceable singularity, what Heidegger calls "death": "*death* is always the name of a secret, since it signs the irreplaceable singularity" (*Aporias*, 74). It is what menaces the history of Being, the epoch of representation, as soon as there are *envois*, that which puts in place, gathers, and sends what governs the history of Being.

As the secret that manifests that something is not shown, circumcision institutes law, which is not only the prohibition of representation, but what transgresses "the figure of all possible representation. Which is difficult to conceive, as it is difficult to conceive anything at all beyond representation, but commits us perhaps to thinking altogether differently" (*SOR*, 137). In observing and enduring the aporia of all decisions and responsibilities, we endure that which is without a name, that which is secret, what is everywhere and everyday at work inscribing the instant, the here and now, in iterability. It is irreplaceable singularity, a consigning of the gift to forgetting, the date to annulment, an effacing of the border between the unique and iterable. We give the name *death* for this secret since it designates singularity: "It puts forth the public name, the common name of a secret, the common name of the proper name without name. It is therefore always a shibboleth, for the manifest name of a secret is from the beginning a private name, so that language about death is nothing but the long history of a secret society, neither public nor private, semi-private, semi-public, on the border between the two; thus, also a sort of hidden religion of the *awaiting* (oneself as well as each other), with its ceremonies, cults, liturgy, or its Marranolike rituals" (*Aporias*, 74). Hegel said that "the life of Spirit is not the life that shrinks from death . . . but rather the life that endures it and maintains it and maintains itself in it. It wins its truth only when, in utter dismemberment, it finds itself."[29] The *Phenomenology* is a text written by a Marrano, one "who remains faithful to a secret he

has not chosen. . . . In the unchallenged night where the radical
absence of any historical witness keeps him or her, in the dominant culture that by definition has calendars, this secret keeps the
Marrano even before the Marrano keeps it" (*Aporias*, 81). "All
poets are Jews," wrote Marina Tsvetaeva. We might say all poets
are Marranos, those who are born, without choice, to keep secrets
and be kept by secrets. Call it death; call it life. Call it literature.

The possible as impossible names an economy of the secret, a
dissymmetrical economy of sacrifice and the gift wherein the hand
that gives is always two: "The dissociation between right and left
again breaks . . . the symmetry between, or homogeneity of, two
economies [of gift and recompense]. In fact it inaugurates sacrifice
[*Elle inaugure en vérité le sacrifice*]" (*GD*, 107 / *DM*, 100). This dissymmetrical economy is a *coup de don*, a gift that is there, that is
not chosen, a gift we can only call a monstrous secret. As irreplaceable singularity, it manifests itself wherever there is a date that is
not calculable, that annuls itself in its recurrence: "there is a holocaust for every date, and somewhere in the world at every hour"
(*SPC*, 50). The gift, the date, God—all that belong to the secret,
the singularity that keeps us—manifest the non-manifest, the irreducible experience of justice, the experience of the instant, of
Abraham on Mount Moriah. It is the refusal to accede to a general
ethics. In being willing to sacrifice Isaac, Abraham must betray his
son in being faithful to God. In the instant God stops his hand, a
hand that is, indeed, monstrous, and a monstration of faith in God,
"it is as if Abraham had *already* killed Isaac" (*GD*, 72). It is also a
monstration of a secret, a secret whose name is "God." It is the
name for what, in producing the law transgresses the possibility of
representation; it is a secret that keeps me, impassions me, makes
possible the interiorization we call subjectivity *and* the relation to
the other, but it does not answer to them.

Notes

Introduction

1. The secondary literature on deconstruction and literary criticism is vast and is tangled up with the problem of distinguishing Derrida's deconstruction from Paul de Man's. Critics like J. Hillis Miller and Jonathan Culler have rightly been criticized for treating deconstruction, whether they are writing of Derrida or de Man, as another form of reflexivity. On another front of the debates surrounding deconstruction, Richard Rorty has argued that Derrida's early works were written within the field of philosophy but later works, like *Glas* and *The Post Card*, signify a turn to literature. See "From Ironist Theory to Private Allusions: Derrida," in *Contingency, Irony, and Solidarity* (Cambridge: Cambridge University Press, 1989), 122–37, as well as "Is Derrida a Transcendental Philosopher?" in *Derrida: A Critical Reader*, ed. David Wood (Oxford: Blackwell, 1992), 235–46. Rodolphe Gasché first criticized literary interpretations of deconstruction as another form of reflexivity in "Deconstruction as Criticism," which appeared in *Glyph* 8 (Baltimore: Johns Hopkins University Press, 1979) and has since been reprinted in *Inventions of Difference: On Jacques Derrida* (Cambridge: Harvard University Press, 1994), 22–57. In the introduction to this volume, Gasché replies to those writers, such as Rorty, who criticized his previous work on Derrida, *The Tain of the Mirror: Derrida and the Philosophy of Reflection* (Cambridge: Harvard University Press, 1986), for "philosophizing" him. My approach will make clear my agreement with Gasché and my debt to his work. More recently, Derrida has responded to Rorty's distinction between the public philosopher and private ironist in "Remarks on Deconstruction and Pragmatism," trans. Simon Critchley in Critchley, Derrida, Ernesto Laclau, and Rorty, *Deconstruction and Pragmatism*, ed. Chantal Mouffe (London: Routledge, 1996). Derrida respectfully rejects Rorty's distinction and says, "if I have tried to withdraw a dimension of experience—whether I call it 'singularity,' the 'secret' or whatever—from the public or political sphere . . . I would not call this private. In other words, for me the private

177

is not defined by the singular . . . or the secret" (78–79). He also says in this reply to papers presented at a symposium that he never confused literature and philosophy or tried to reduce philosophy to literature.

2. A good example of literary deconstruction is Jeffrey Nealon's *Double Reading: Postmodernism after Deconstruction* (Ithaca: Cornell University Press, 1993). Nealon's concern is with the problem that lies in the creation of a postmodern discipline of literary theory. For Nealon, literature clearly remains literature—novels and poetry—and deconstruction, while not a method, is a "theory" (Nealon is fully aware of the limited use of this word) of writing that situates the necessary impasses encountered by systems or disciplines and opens them to a radical otherness. Although I am sympathetic with much of Nealon's argument, his work can still be read as an application of deconstruction to the discipline of literary theory. As such, it is a useful book.

Despite his more explicit concern with philosophical issues, Timothy Clark's *Derrida, Heidegger, Blanchot: Sources of Derrida's Notion and Practice of Literature* (Cambridge: Cambridge University Press, 1992) also understands literature to be primarily poetry and fiction, and as his subtitle indicates, his study treats the "literary" character of Derrida's writings. He examines the practice or performance of his subjects' texts, particularly those that employ the dialogic form one finds in Blanchot's works like *L'Attente l'oubli* and Heidegger's "Conversations on a Country Path about Thinking," in *Discourse on Thinking*, trans. John M. Anderson and E. Hans Freund (New York: Harper & Row, 1966). Nonetheless, he offers a very good account of Derrida's argument against thematic criticism and of his concept of literature as something aside from being (116). Unlike Clark, I am less concerned with Derrida's sources than I am with demonstrating the importance of literature for most of his key notions, which can never be done unless one sets aside the conventional notion of literature.

3. Edmund Husserl, *Experience and Judgment: Investigations in a Genealogy of Logic*, ed. Ludwig Landgrebe, trans. James S. Churchill and Karl Ameriks (Evanston: Northwestern University Press, 1973), 266. I will return to this issue in my third chapter.

4. Speaking of literature in a more conventional sense, Derrida says, "Literature interests me, supposing that, in my own way, I practice it or that I study it in others, precisely as something which is the complete opposite of the expression of private life. Literature is a public institution of recent invention, with a comparatively short history, governed by all sorts of conventions connected to the evolution of law, which allows, in principle, everything to be said." This right to say everything makes literature inseparable from democracy and human rights. See "Remarks

on Deconstruction and Pragmatism," 79–80.

5. For Derrida's own assessment of the charges that deconstruction harbors secrets and resembles a negative theology, see "How to Avoid Speaking," 16–19.

6. Several times in this essay, Derrida cites Jean-Luc Marion, *L'Idole et la distance* (Paris: Bernard Grasset, 1977), who places a cross through "God" rather than "Being," as does Heidegger in "On the Question of Being" (in *Pathmarks*, ed. William McNeill [Cambridge: Cambridge University Press, 1998], 291–322), "to subtract the thinking of the gift, or rather the trace of the gift," from God (*HAS*, 70, n. 29). In this context, one should also see Marion's *God Without Being: Hors-Texte*, trans. Thomas A. Carlson (Chicago: University of Chicago Press, 1991). Marion's effort to think God outside onto-theological determinations, as the cause of Being rather than as an existent, is extremely important in this context, but his concept of distance as nonrelational communion between God and human being leads him to conclude that Derrida's *différance* remains ontico-ontological difference. See *L'Idole et la distance*, 280–94. For a discussion of Marion's relation to Derrida, see Rodolphe Gasché's "The Eclipse of Difference" and "God, for Example," in *Inventions of Difference: On Jacques Derrida* (Cambridge: Harvard University Press, 1994), 93–106, 153–58.

7. Gasché, "God, for Example," 162.

8. This is the argument of Philippe Lacoue-Labarthe's "Typography," in *Typography: Mimesis, Philosophy, Politics*, ed. Christopher Fynsk (Cambridge: Harvard University Press, 1989), 43–138.

9. For a reading of *"littérature"* as what provides a means to approach the other of philosophy, see Clark, *Derrida, Heidegger, Blanchot*, esp. 108–112.

10. Lacoue-Labarthe, "Transcendence Ends in Politics," in *Typography*, 297–98.

11. John Sallis, *Echoes: After Heidegger* (Bloomington: Indiana University Press, 1990), 180, 185.

12. Cf. Derrida, "Heidegger's Ear: Philopolemology (*Geschlecht* IV)," trans. John P. Leavey, Jr., in *Reading Heidegger: Commemorations*, ed. John Sallis (Bloomington: Indiana University Press, 1993), 187: "At bottom logocentrism is perhaps not so much the gesture that consists in placing the *logos* at the center as the interpretation of *logos* as *Versammlung*, that is, the gathering that precisely concenters what it needs to configure." I do not wish to suggest by these remarks that Heidegger remains

metaphysical while Derrida has passed beyond metaphysics. Such readings ignore the distinction between ending and closure, as well as Derrida's reminders that Heidegger's texts are never simply metaphysical. A good discussion of the relation between metaphysics and closure in Heidegger can be found in Robert Bernasconi's "The Transformation of Language at Another Beginning," in *Heidegger in Question: The Art of Existing* (Atlantic Highlands, N.J.: Humanities Press, 1993), 190–210.

13. Martin Heidegger, "The Origin of the Work of Art," in *Poetry, Language, Thought*, trans. Albert Hofstadter (New York: Harper & Row, 1971), 61–62.

14. Heidegger, "The Origin of the Work of Art," 63.

15. The literature on the *Kehre*, reversal, is large and was initiated by William Richardson, *Heidegger: Through Phenomenology to Thought* (The Hague: Martinus Nijhoff, 1963). Heidegger's response to Richardson's distinction between Heidegger I and II is to be found in his preface to this important work, "Letter to Father Richardson." My discussion is indebted to Otto Pöggeler's invaluable essay "Being as Appropriation," trans. Rüdiger H. Grimm in *Philosophy Today* 19 (Summer 1975) and reprinted in *Heidegger and Modern Philosophy*, ed. Michael Murray (New Haven: Yale University Press, 1978), 84–115.

16. Martin Heidegger, *On Time and Being*, trans. Joan Stambaugh (New York: Harper & Row, 1972), 9.

17. Martin Heidegger, *Identity and Difference*, trans. Joan Stambaugh (New York: Harper & Row, 1969), 62–63.

18. Heidegger, *Identity and Difference*, 50.

19. See Lacoue-Labarthe, "Typography," esp. pp. 77–80. Also see Samuel IJsseling, "Mimesis and Translation," in *Reading Heidegger: Commemorations*, 348–49. IJsseling argues that narrative is mimesis, "that there is a certain displacement of so-called reality that takes place so that reality can appear . . . at another place, namely, in the rendering" (349). *Lichtung*, *alêtheia*, and *Ereignis* are all names for mimesis, and translation, which is never simply a verbal activity for Heidegger, also is a mimetic displacement and relocation.

20. See Sallis, *Echoes*, 175.

21. Cf. Derrida, "The Law of Genre," trans. Avital Ronell, *Glyph* 7 (Baltimore: Johns Hopkins University Press, 1980), 212: "this supplementary and distinctive trait, a mark of belonging or inclusion, does not properly pertain to any genre or class. The re-mark of belonging does not

belong." Clark argues that this re-mark breaks with Heidegger's *Dichtung*. See *Derrida, Heidegger, Blanchot*, 120.

22. See Gasché, *The Tain of the Mirror* and "Joining the Text: From Heidegger to Derrida," in *The Yale Critics: Deconstruction in America*, ed. Jonathan Arac et al. (Minneapolis: University of Minnesota Press, 1983), 156–75. Also see in connection with art as the bringing forth of truth, John Sallis's *Echoes*, pp. 183–85. Heidegger, says Sallis, reinscribes mimesis: "The work of art does not imitate any being, whether individual or universal; it does not imitate anything that would simply *be* prior to the imitation, that would be set over against the imitation, which, then, would only double something already subsisting in itself" (184). Art as the setting in place or *Gestalt* of truth would still need to be distinguished from Derrida's literary writing, which is not a setting in place but a dissemination.

23. See Samuel IJsseling, "Mimesis and Translation," 349. IJsseling cites in this context John Sallis's essay "Heidegger's Poetics: The Question in Mimesis," in *Kunst und Technik: Gedächtnisschrift zum 100. Geburstag von Martin Heidegger*, eds. W. Biemel and F.-W. Von Hermann (Frankfurt a.M.: Vittorio Klostermann, 1989), which has since been incorporated into *Echoes*.

24. Lacoue-Labarthe, "Typography," 120.

25. See Peggy Kamuf's definition of literature as reserve in *The Division of Literature, or The University in Deconstruction* (Chicago: University of Chicago Press, 1997), 4–6. Her analysis of the deconstructive reserve called "literature" is incisive, as is her critique of the thesis literature equals ideology. Richard Beardsworth offers a similar definition of literature in *Derrida and the Political* (New York: Routledge, 1997), 34–40. In a reading of Derrida's essay "Before the Law," he argues that the aporia of the law—the law cannot account for what constitutes it as law—is the law of literature: The law can never appear to itself as an ideality but always re-marks itself in a judgment or decision that necessarily fails to repeat the law in a present. The impossibility of the concurrence of judgment and law in an absolute present is a consequence of iterability and is, therefore, a necessary failure and what gives rise to a future. The writing called "literature" witnesses the failure of the law: "all disciplines are *also* 'literary' (even the most formal logic, the most abstract mathematics) to the extent that they betray, in their very failure to achieve their accounts of law (their disciplinary origins and horizons), the aporia of origin" (38).

For example, J. L. Austin's speech act theory is literary precisely to the extent it must exclude literature in order to maintain itself as a theory; what it simultaneously recognizes and represses is that the possibility of the illocutionary speech act (a performance of an act in saying something, as when making a bet) rests upon the iterability he must exclude (that is, citationality, imitation, quotation, absence, etc.). The speech act is a speech act not because it is spoken in the first person in a present moment but because the possibility of the "first person" and the "present" rests upon the trait of repetition and absence, the *retrait*, necessary for a successful speech act or for the identity of a speech act. See *How to Do Things with Words*, ed. J. O. Urmson and Marina Sbisà (2nd ed.; Cambridge: Harvard University Press, 1975). Also see Derrida's analysis of Austin in "Signature, Event, Context," in *Margins*, 307–330, and his reply to John Searle's criticisms of this essay in *Limited Inc*. Searle's essay, "Reiterating the Differences: A Reply to Derrida," appeared in *Glyph* 1 (Baltimore: Johns Hopkins University Press, 1977), 198–208.

Finally, I should mention John Llewelyn's "Responsibility with Indecidabilty," in *Derrida: A Critical Reader*, ed. David Wood (Oxford: Blackwell, 1992), 72–96. Llewelyn asks, how can we respond responsibly without a criteria or rule that can assure validity? The first principle upon which all principles must rest is not a first. This is Derrida's "law of all law." The impossibility of grounding a decision in a law increases responsibility. Llewelyn approaches this law by comparing Derrida's re-mark to Bertrand Russell's theory of types. His argument focuses on Derrida's essay "The Law of Genre" and Russell's antinomy, which would exclude self-reflexive statements from classes he calls "normal" (that is, one that does not contain itself as a member). An example of a normal class would be the class of novels, for the class is not a novel and, therefore, does not include itself. Genre, on the other hand, is a non-normal class because a genre is a class. But the antinomy collapses when we say, "N" stands for all normal classes, because then it is a normal class that includes itself, which makes it non-normal at the same time. This is what Beardsworth calls the "literary." It is no coincidence that it involves the problem of self-reflexivity. My discussion does not do justice to these three works to which I am indebted.

26. The great Russian formalist Victor Shklovsky has indeed argued that *"Tristram Shandy* is the most typical novel in world literature" because it violates form in order to make form the subject of the novel. "Literariness" is the act of bearing witness to the formalizing of the very laws it violates. See "Sterne's *Tristram Shandy*: Stylistic Commentary," trans. Lee T. Lemon and Marion J. Reis, in *Russian Formalist Criticism: Four Essays* (Lincoln: University of Nebraska Press, 1965), 25–57.

27. See Beardsworth's discussion of *Totem and Taboo* in *Derrida and the Political*, 29–31, 34–37.

28. John Caputo, *The Prayers and Tears of Jacques Derrida: Religion without Religion* (Bloomington: University of Indiana Press, 1997), 112.

29. Caputo, *The Prayers and Tears of Jacques Derrida*, 103.

30. Caputo, 291. Again I would direct the reader to Jean-Luc Marion's *God Without Being* for a related effort to approach God outside onto-theology. Space precludes my discussing Emmanuel Levinas, whose philosophical works and Talmudic exegeses are crucial to any discussion of alterity and God. For a good discussion of the importance of Levinas for literary criticism, see Jill Robbins, *Prodigal Son / Elder Brother: Interpretation and Alterity in Augustine, Petrarch, Kafka, Levinas* (Chicago: University of Chicago Press, 1991), 100–132. Also see Ewa Plonowska Ziarek, *The Rhetoric of Failure: Deconstruction of Skepticism, Reinvention of Modernism* (Albany: State University of New York Press, 1996), 82–89 for a good account of Levinas's and Derrida's notions of alterity and the problem of representation. Her work also provides a powerful reply to misreadings of deconstruction as skepticism and pure textuality.

31. Caputo, *The Prayers and Tears of Jacques Derrida*, 290.

32. Caputo, *The Prayers and Tears of Jacques Derrida*, 289, 290.

33. See Caputo, *The Prayers and Tears of Jacques Derrida*, 339: "the passion for the impossible 'is'. . . where everything that 'is' means trembles in undecidability . . . the passion for God, the passion of God."

34. Caputo, *The Prayers and Tears of Jacques Derrida*, 195.

35. Caputo, *The Prayers and Tears of Jacques Derrida*, 338: "Faith is a passion for something to come, for something I know not what, with an unknowing, *non-savoir, sans savoir*, which is such that I cannot say what is a translation of what. I cannot say whether God is a translation of 'justice,' so whenever I pray and weep over justice I am praying and weeping over God." Caputo runs the risk that Jean-Luc Nancy warns against in "Of Divine Places," trans. Michael Holland, in *The Inoperative Community*, ed. Peter Connor (Minneapolis: University of Minnesota Press, 1991): "Try as it may, there is no theology that does not turn out here to be either ontological or anthropological—saying *nothing about the god* that cannot immediately be said about 'event,' about 'love,' about 'poetry,' and so on and so forth. Why not recognize, on the contrary, that thought in this age of ours is in the process of wresting from so-called theology the prerogative of talking about the Other, the Infinitely-other, the Other-Infinite. It is taking away from theology the privilege of expressing the *absconditum* of experience and discourse. In so doing, perhaps the modern age secretly corresponds to the true destination of a *theology:* for it indicates to theology that, in order to speak of God, we have to speak of something other than the Other, the Abstruse, and their infinite remoteness (if indeed it is still a matter of

'speaking of something')" (113). Although Caputo tries to wrest God from His position as prior entity and ground of what is, he must still speak of God as justice, love, passion, the secret, the limit; he converts God into the name for "our abysses," a double blasphemy, says Nancy, because it gives a ground to the abyss and makes the name of God the name of something.

36. Caputo, *The Prayers and Tears of Jacques Derrida*, 52.

37. Gasché, "God, for Example," 155, 156.

38. Gasché, "God, for Example," 161–62.

39. Gasché, "God, for Example," 168.

40. See Gasché, "God, for Example," 169. He refers to "Violence and Metaphysics": "in having recognized . . . that alterity had to circulate at the origin of meaning, in welcoming alterity in general into the heart of the logos, the Greek thought of Being forever has protected itself against every absolutely *surprising* convocation" (*WD*, 153).

41. Caputo, *The Prayers and Tears of Jacques Derrida*, 23.

42. Caputo, *The Prayers and Tears of Jacques Derrida*, 10, 52–53.

43. The reference is to Kierkegaard's interpretation of Abraham as the knight of faith in *Fear and Trembling*. Emmanuel Levinas's response to Kierkegaard, "Kierkegaard: Existence and Ethics," appears in *Proper Names*, trans. Michael B. Smith (Palo Alto: Stanford University Press, 1996), 66–74.

44. A very different criticism of Kierkegaard's reading of the *Akedah* (the binding of Isaac) can be found in Emil Fackenheim's *Encounters between Judaism and Modern Philosophy: A Preface to Future Jewish Thought* (New York: Schocken Books, 1980), 53–77. Rejecting Kierkegaard's Abraham as the isolated individual, as well as Kantian ethics, Fackenheim argues that the Jew reveres Abraham, not as the knight of faith, but "*[b]ecause of a perpetually reenacted radical surprise. . . . To receive the Torah on account of Abraham's merit is, first, to have called all things into question in the sight of Divinity, the intrinsic value of humanity included; second, it is to accept that some things are in question no longer; and third, it is to receive, in surprise as well as gratitude, the value of humanity as a gift that Divinity might have withheld and that is yet given forever" (70).

45. Beardsworth gives a succinct account of the aporia in *Derrida and the Political*, 31–33. In the Aristotelian aporia of time in *Physics*, Book IV, time is and is not: thought in terms of its divisibility, it is a *now*; thought

in terms of the *now*, it is robbed of being because the *now* is always already future or past. The contradiction lies in the single entity. "The Aristotelian aporetic of time is only possible through prejudging the nature of time. Time is and is not, because it is thought in terms of 'now.'" Heidegger would overcome this blockage by distinguishing two types of time, the "vulgar" and the authentic. "The aporia *remains* impracticable for Derrida. In other words, if the terms of the aporia of time are deconstructible, the aporia of time is not; it is absolutely irreducible" (33). Sacrifice is just such an aporia. Levinas would try to overcome it by distinguishing two infinite others, God and man, but every other is other.

46. See Caputo, *The Prayers and Tears of Jacques Derrida*, xx.

47. Clark, *Derrida, Heidegger, Blanchot*, 120.

48. Heidegger, *Being and Time*, trans. John Macquarrie and Edward Robinson (New York: Harper and Row, 1962), H. 143. I follow the practice of the translators and cite the pagination of the German edition, preceded by an "H," as given in the margin.

49. Heidegger, *Being and Time*, H. 133.

50. Heidegger, *Being and Time*, H. 135.

51. Beardsworth, *Derrida and the Political*, 105.

52. For Kant on the inner voice, see "On a Newly Arisen Superior Tone in Philosophy," trans. Peter Fenves, in *Raising the Tone of Philosophy: Late Essays by Immanuel Kant, Transformative Critique by Jacques Derrida*, ed. Peter Fenves (Baltimore: Johns Hopkins University Press, 1993), 51–81.

53. See in this context Derrida's "Before the Law": "one cannot reach the law, and in order to have a *rapport* of respect with it, *one must not* have a rapport with the law, *one must interrupt the relation*. One must *enter into relation* only with the law's representatives, its examples, its guardians" (203–204). For a reading of Kafka's interpretation of Kierkegaard's interpretation of Abraham's sacrifice as autobiographical allegory, see Jill Robbins, *Prodigal Son / Elder Brother*, 91–99. In Kafka's alternative to Kierkegaard's Abraham, he does not yet have a son and is already called upon to sacrifice him (95).

54. Speaking of "the problematic rapport with the boundary of metaphysics," Derrida says, it can only be "thought about from *another* topos or space. . . . Hence my attempts to discover the non-place or *non-lieu* which would be the 'other' of philosophy. This is the task of deconstruction." When asked if literature could be such a non-place, Derrida responds, "I think

so; but when I speak of literature it is not with a capital L; it is rather an allusion to certain movements which have worked around the limits of our logical concepts, certain texts which make the limits of our language tremble, exposing them as divisible and questionable." "Deconstruction and the Other," an interview with Richard Kearney in *Dialogue with Contemporary Continental Thinkers: The Phenomenological Heritage* (Manchester: Manchester University Press, 1984), 112.

55. Gasché, "God, for Example," 164.

56. On the infrastructures, see Gasché, *The Tain of the Mirror*, 185–251.

57. Caputo, *The Prayers and Tears of Jacques Derrida*, 290.

58. I refer, of course, to Hegel's preface to the *Phenomenology of Spirit*, trans. A. V. Miller (Oxford: Oxford University Press, 1977), 19: "the life of Spirit is not the life that shrinks from death and keeps itself untouched by devastation, but rather the life that endures it and maintains itself in it." But whereas death, as non-actuality or the negative, is but a moment in the life of Spirit that wins the truth only in this passage through the negative, the secret without secret is never sublated (*aufheben*) but is always already unknowable.

59. Cf. "Force of Law": "Justice in itself, if such a thing exists, outside or beyond law, is not deconstructible. No more than deconstruction itself, if such a thing exists. Deconstruction is justice" (945).

Chapter One

1. At the 1980 MLA Convention, Barbara Johnson presented a paper, "Nothing Fails Like Success," since reprinted in *A World of Difference* (Baltimore: Johns Hopkins University Press, 1987), where she announced that "what is loosely called deconstructionism is now being widely institutionalized in the United States" (11). If the amount of articles and books about Derrida or adaptations of his writings would be any sign of institutionalization, then this remark certainly holds true. However, citing sheer numbers is not adequate to the question of institutionalization.

2. See Derrida's discussion of "fresh judgment" in "Force of Law," 961. The phrase is borrowed from Stanley Fish's essay "Force" in *Doing What Comes Naturally: Change, Rhetoric, and the Practice of Theory in Literary and Legal Studies* (Durham: Duke University Press, 1989), 505. I should add the reminder that law is not to be thought in opposition to justice. Derrida emphasizes this when he proposes as a possible subtitle for "Force

of Law": "justice as the possibility of deconstruction, the structure of law (*droit*) or of the law, the foundation or the self-authorization of law (*droit*) as the possibility of the exercise of deconstruction" (*FL*, 945). John Caputo argues, "The deconstructibility of law is the enabling legislation of deconstruction; it gives deconstruction its charter, charges it with a task. . . . Derrida likewise insists that the undeconstructibility of justice—this is the scandal—is likewise a condition of deconstruction, also part of its enabling charter." See *Demythologizing Heidegger* (Bloomington: Indiana University Press, 1993), 193.

3. On the subject of deconstruction and institution, see Samuel Weber's *Institution and Interpretation* (Minneapolis: University of Minnesota Press, 1987), particularly the chapter "Reading and Writing—*chez* Derrida," 85–101. Also important is the afterword by Wlad Godzich, "Religion, the State, and Post(al) Modernism," 153–64, which has since been reprinted in Godzich's collection *The Culture of Literacy* (Cambridge: Harvard University Press, 1994), 233–46. Also see Peggy Kamuf's analysis of literature as institutional force in *The Division of Literature, or The University in Deconstruction* (Chicago: University of Chicago Press, 1997), 1–39.

4. A monster is what abuses a norm; it is catachresis. It is also a figure of the future, the coming of what surprises. In an interview, Derrida explains that "philosophy is literary, not so much because it is *metaphor* but because it is *catachresis*. The term metaphor generally implies a relation to an original 'property' of meaning, a 'proper' sense to which it indirectly or equivocally refers, whereas catachresis is a violent production of meaning, an abuse which refers to no anterior or proper norm. The founding concepts of metaphysics—*logos*, *eidos*, *theoria*, etc.—are instances of *catachresis* rather than metaphors." Interview with Richard Kearney, "Deconstruction and the Other," in *Dialogues with Contemporary Thinkers*, ed. Richard Kearney (Manchester: Manchester University Press, 1984), 123. A monster is not an absolute break with normality but is a graft that puts heterogeneous things together: "This in fact happens in certain kinds of writing. At that moment, monstrosity may reveal or make one aware of what normality is. . . . The monster is also that which appears for the first time and, consequently, is not yet recognized. A monster is a species for which we do not yet have a name, which does not mean that the species is abnormal, namely, the composition or hybridization of already known species [*à savoir la composition ou l'hybridation d'espèces déjà connues*]. Simply, it *shows* itself [*elle se* montre]—that is what the word monster [*monstre*] means—it shows itself in something that is not yet shown [*montré*] and that therefore looks like a hallucination, it strikes the eye [*vient frapper la vue*], it frightens precisely because no

anticipation had prepared one to identify this figure" (*Points*, 385–86 / *PdS*, 399–400). The monstrous is a *montre*, a display, and the action of showing (*montrer*) that which exceeds the boundaries of representation or violates the law. For more on the link between *montrer* and *monstre*, see "*Geschlecht* II: Heidegger's Hand," trans. John P. Leavey, Jr., in *Deconstruction and Philosophy: The Texts of Jacques Derrida*, ed. John Sallis (Chicago: University of Chicago Press, 1987), 166–69.

5. This last phrase is from David Wood, *The Deconstruction of Time* (Atlantic Highlands: Humanities Press, 1989), 372. Wood argues that the idea of the future must be approached through Derrida's notion of writing. The future is already "inside" the present, already at work in the text. In an interview, Derrida says of his use of the figure of the monster when speaking of the future in *Of Grammatology* and at the end of *Writing and Difference* that "the figure of the future, that is, that which can only be surprising, that for which we are not prepared, you see, is heralded by the species of the monster. A future that would not be monstrous would not be a future; it would already be a predictable, calculable, and programmable tomorrow" (*Points, 386–87*; translation modified).

6. I refer to *The Post Card* and Derrida's translation of Heidegger's *Geschick des Seins* as *envois* in his postal discourse. Derrida maintains this translation of the destining of Being is not simply a metaphor but serves "as the site of all transferences and all correspondences" (*PC*, 65). There is no singular departure for the *envoi* nor even a destination, but "as soon as there is, there is *différance* . . . and there is postal maneuvering, relays, delay, anticipation, destination, telecommunicating network, the possibility, and therefore the fatal necessity of going astray, etc." (*PC*, 66). Commenting on the disruptive power of repetition, Samuel Weber writes, "Presence is no longer an original point of departure but at best, one of arrival; not something that can be kept but something that must be gained; not something that can be posed, but rather that must be *imposed,* upon others" (*Institution and Interpretation*, 97).

7. Derrida, "Letter to a Japanese Friend," trans. David Wood and Andrew Benjamin, in *Derrida and Différance*, ed. David Wood and Robert Bernasconi (1985; rpr. Evanston: Northwestern University Press, 1988), 4. In the same letter, Derrida cautions, "It is not enough to say that deconstruction could not be reduced to some methodological instrumentality or to a set of rules and transposable procedures. Nor will it do to claim that each deconstructive 'event' remains singular or, in any case, as close as possible to something like an idiom or a signature. It must also be made clear that deconstruction is not even an *act* or an *operation*" (3).

8. For the notion of inscription, see *Of Grammatology*: "A new transcendental aesthetic must let itself be guided not only by mathematical

idealities but by the possibility of inscription in general, not befalling an already constituted space as a contingent accident but producing the spatiality of space. Indeed, we say of inscription *in general*, in order to make it quite clear that it is not simply the notation of a prepared speech representing itself, but inscription within speech and inscription as *habitation* always already situated" (290; translation modified). Derrida acknowledges that this could no longer be called a transcendental aesthetic. Gasché discusses general inscription in *The Tain of the Mirror: Derrida and the Philosophy of Reflection* (Cambridge: Harvard University Press, 1986), 157–58.

9. J. L. Austin, *How to Do Things with Words*, 2nd ed., ed. J. O. Urmson and Marina Sbisà (1962; Cambridge: Harvard University Press, 1975), 6.

10. In his thesis defense of 2 June 1980, Derrida says of *The Post Card*, *Glas*, and *Spurs*, that although they continue the "project of grammatology" and the "deconstruction of a certain hermeneutics," "I do not believe them to be simply presentable or acceptable to the university and I have not dared, have not judged it opportune, to include them here among the works to be defended." See "The Time of a Thesis: Punctuations," trans. Kathleen McLaughlin, in *Philosophy in France Today*, ed. Alan Montefiore (Cambridge: Cambridge University Press, 1983), 46.

11. For the importance of law for literature, see "Des Tours de Babel," trans. Joseph F. Graham, in *Difference in Translation*, ed. Joseph F. Graham (Ithaca: Cornell University Press, 1985), 190–200.

12. See Derrida's "Signature Event Context" in *Margins*, esp. 327–30, for the relation of the signature to repetition.

13. For an analysis that links the countersignature to the law, the thing, and singularity, see *Signéponge/Signsponge*, 48–54.

14. On the problem of the infinitely Other, see Derrida's "Violence and Metaphysics: An Essay on the Thought of Emmanuel Levinas," in *Writing and Difference*: "If one thinks, as Levinas does, that positive Infinity tolerates, or even requires, infinite alterity, then one must renounce all language, and first of all the words *infinite* and *other*. Infinity cannot be understood as Other except in the form of the in-finite. . . . The other cannot be what it is, infinitely other, except in finitude and mortality (mine *and* its)" (114–15).

15. I draw upon Derrida's remarks on the thing and law in *Signéponge/Signsponge*: "Thus the thing would be the other, the other-thing which gives me an order or addresses an impossible, intransigent, insatiable demand to me, without an exchange and without a transaction,

without a possible contract. . . . I owe to the thing an absolute respect which no general law would mediate: the law of the thing is singularity and difference as well. An infinite debt ties me to it, a duty without funds or foundation. I shall never acquit myself of it. Thus the thing is not an object; it cannot become one" (14).

16. See Derek Attridge's discussion of singularity and law in "Introduction: Derrida and the Question of Literature," in Jacques Derrida, *Acts of Literature*, ed. Derek Attridge (New York: Routledge, 1992), 15.

17. Richard Beardsworth, *Derrida and the Political* (New York: Routledge, 1997), 5, 24.

18. Beardsworth, *Derrida and the Political*, 24.

19. "Decisionism" is a concept associated with the Weimar legal theorist Carl Schmitt, who went on to give his support to the Nazi regime. In offering the term in his *Political Theology*, Schmitt addresses the problem that a legal decision always involves a question of authority. A decision "is rooted in the character of the normative and is derived from the necessity of judging a concrete fact concretely even though what is given as a standard for the judgment is only a legal principle in its general universality. Thus a transformation takes place every time." The problem Schmitt addresses is that "the legal idea cannot translate itself independently" of the act of judgment, and for him this is evident in the fact that it says nothing about who has authority to impose it. He seeks to resolve the problem in his theory of the state of exception: the challenge to the stability of the state is what gives it authority. See *Political Theology: Four Chapters in the Concept of Sovereignty*, trans. George Schwab (Cambridge: MIT Press, 1985), 31. Derrida writes on Schmitt's concepts of the enemy and the state in *Politques de l'amité* (Paris: Galilée, 1994), 93–193. Also see Samuel Weber, "Taking Exception to Decision: Walter Benjamin and Carl Schmitt," *Diacritics* (Fall/Winter 1992), 5–18.

20. See Derrida's *Specters of Marx*: "Repetition *and* first time: this is perhaps the question of the event as question of the ghost. *What is* a ghost? What is the *effectivity* or the *presence* of a specter, that is, of what seems to remain as ineffective, virtual, insubstantial as a simulacrum? Is there *there*, between the thing itself and its simulacrum, an opposition that holds up? Repetition *and* first time, but also repetition *and* last time, since the singularity of any *first time* makes of it also a *last time*. Each time it is the event itself, a first time is a last time. Altogether other. Staging for the end of history. Let us call it a *hauntology*" (10).

21. Beardsworth, *Derrida and the Political*, 39.

22. William Gaddis, *A Frolic of His Own* (New York: Poseidon Press, 1994), 11.

23. See Gasché, "Responding Responsibly," in *Inventions of Difference*, 235.

24. Gasché, *The Tain of the Mirror*, 274. Hereinafter cited in text as *TM*.

25. Martin Heidegger, *On Time and Being*, trans. Joan Stambaugh (New York: Harper & Row, 1977), 6.

26. Martin Heidegger, *Identity and Difference*, trans. Joan Stambaugh (New York: Harper & Row, 1969), 62.

27. See Edmund Husserl, *Experience and Judgment: Investigations in a Genealogy of Logic*, ed. Ludwig Landgrebe, trans. James S. Churchill and Karl Ameriks (Evanston: Northwestern University Press, 1973), 266.

Chapter Two

1. For Kant on testimony and the cognitive status of the secret, see "On a Newly Arisen Superior Tone in Philosophy," trans. Peter Fenves, in *Raising the Tone of Philosophy: Late Essays by Immanuel Kant, Transformative Critique by Jacques Derrida*, ed. Peter Fenves (Baltimore: Johns Hopkins University Press, 1993), 62.

2. Rodolphe Gasché, "God, for Example," in *Inventions of Difference: On Jacques Derrida* (Cambridge: Harvard University Press, 1994), 161.

3. John Caputo quotes Meister Eckhart's prayer "I pray God to rid me of God" in his discussion of deconstruction and negative theology in *The Prayers and Tears of Jacques Derrida: Religion without Religion* (Bloomington: Indiana University Press, 1997). For Derrida's fullest engagement with negative theology, see "How to Avoid Speaking: Denials," trans. Ken Frieden, in *Languages of the Unsayable: The Play of Negativity in Literature and Literary Theory*. Ed. Sanford Budick and Wolfgang Iser (New York: Columbia University Press, 1989), 3–70. This essay originally appeared in *Psché: Inventions de l'autre* (Paris: Galilée, 1987). In conjunction with my argument concerning the theological trap, I would refer to Derrida's comment that apophatic discourse can be avoided or escaped by the prayer that precedes it, but the risk is always there that prayer and invocation can be mimicked by apophatic discourse. This risk, he says, "is inevitable" and "need not be limited to the apophatic moment of negative theology. It may be extended to all language, and even to all

manifestation in general. This risk is inscribed in the structure of the mark" (5).

4. Gasché, "God, for Example," 162.

5. Gasché, "God, for Example," 168.

6. Friedrich Nietzsche, *Twilight of the Idols*, trans. R. J. Hollingdale (1968; rpr. New York: Penguin Books, 1990), 48.

7. When asked if this passage from *Of Grammatology* means that he operates, in relation to Hegel, on a totally different or exterior terrain, Derrida replies, "We will never be finished with the reading or rereading of Hegel, and, in a certain way, I do nothing other than attempt to explain myself on this point. In effect I believe that Hegel's text is necessarily fissured; that it is something more and other than the circular closure of its representation" (*Positions*, 77).

8. Edmond Jabès, *The Book of Questions*, trans. Rosemarie Waldrop (Middletown: Wesleyan University Press, 1976), 31. Hereafter cited in text as *BQ*. The French original is in *Le Livre des questions* (Paris: Gallimard, 1963), 33. Hereafter citations from French originals will be given in the text following citations of English translations where available. The following abbreviations will be used for the French originals, all published in Paris by Gallimard unless otherwise noted: *LQ—Le Livre des questions*; *LY—Le Livre de Yukel* (1964); *RL—Le Retour au livre* (1965); *Y—Yaël* (1967); *E—Elya* (1969); *A—Aely* (1972); *EL—.(El, ou le dernier livre)* (1973); *LM—Le Livre des marges* (Paris: Fata Morgana, 1975 and 1984). The following abbreviations will be used for the translations by Rosemarie Waldrop, all published by Wesleyan University Press unless otherwise noted: *BY—The Book of Yukel* (1977); *RB—Return to the Book* (1977; pub. in one volume with *BY*); *YEA—The Book of Questions: Yaël, Elya, Aely* (1983); *LB—The Book of Questions: .(El, or the Last Book)* (1984); *BM— The Book of Margins* (Chicago: University of Chicago Press, 1993). Where the English text is not given, translations are my own.

9. This association of deconstruction and Jewish writing is particularly strong in the essays collected in *The Sin of the Book: Edmond Jabès*, ed. Eric Gould (Lincoln: University of Nebraska Press, 1985). Although not all of the contributors refer to Derrida or explicitly claim to be "deconstructing" *The Book of Questions*, Jabès's fascination with what Gould calls "the language of ontological limits" (xiii) provokes his readers to treat his themes of absence, exile, and the holocaust within a metaphorics of writing that is loosely associated with deconstruction. In *Questioning Edmond Jabès* (Lincoln: University of Nebraska Press, 1990), Warren F. Motte, Jr. avoids a philosophical analysis of Jabès in favor of a thematic reading of key metaphors, but his discussion reveals the ease with which

even non-theoretical readings assume the postmodern and anti-metaphysical status of Jabès's writings.

The identification of Jewish writing with deconstruction has been reinforced by Geoffrey Hartman's inclusion, under the heading "Contemporary Midrash," of translations of Derrida's essay on Paul Celan, "Shibboleth," and a chapter from Jabès's *Le Parcours*, "The Key," in his volume co-edited with Sanford Budick, *Midrash and Literature* (New Haven: Yale University Press, 1986). Hartman is more cautious in pointing to similarities between Derrida's concept of writing and Hebrew tradition in his *Saving the Text: Literature, Derrida, Philosophy* (Baltimore: Johns Hopkins Press, 1981), 17–19. Susan Handelman has examined the parallels between Rabbinic interpretation and modern theory in *The Slayers of Moses: The Emergence of Rabbinic Interpretation in Modern Literary Theory* (Albany: State University of New York Press, 1982). She writes, "The work of Jacques Derrida is the latest in the line of Jewish heretic hermeneutics" (163). Perhaps the best essay on Derrida's relation to Judaism is Jill Robbins' review of "Circumfession," trans. Geoffrey Bennington, in Bennington and Derrida, *Jacques Derrida* (Chicago: University of Chicago Press, 1993). See "Circumcising Confession: Derrida, Autobiography, Judaism," *Diacritics*, 25 (Winter 1995), 20–38.

In France, Henri Meschonnic has attacked the "conjunction of the Jew and writing" in Jabès and Derrida (see *Le signe et le poème* [Paris: Gallimard, 1975], 462). Meschonnic's polemic centers on what he calls the "myth of writing." According to him, the theory of the arbitrariness of the sign is essentially theological and "anti-Jewish" because it links absence to the sacred. Like many readers of Derrida, Meschonnic cannot tell the difference between what Derrida deconstructs and what position he occupies. For instance, he argues that in *Of Grammatology* Derrida makes an absolute distinction between nature and culture, whereas Derrida is, in fact, deconstructing this opposition (see pp. 449–457). See also his essay, "Maurice Blanchot ou l'écriture hors langage" (in *Pour la poétique, Poésie sans réponse*, vol. 5 (Paris: Gallimard, 1978), 126–131), where he criticizes Blanchot and Derrida for accepting Jabès's alignment of Judaism and writing because Jabès departs from biblical Judaism, a criticism that disregards Jabès's own insistence on his distance from normative Judaism.

10. We should not assume that the rabbis, or even Yukel (this passage is attributed to him), speak for Jabès. In his interview with Marcel Cohen, he says, "I have never considered myself a Jewish writer. I am . . . Jewish and a writer, which is not at all the same." See *Du désert au livre: Entretiens avec Marcel Cohen* (Paris: Belfond, 1980), 89.

11. Space does not permit me to examine Paul de Man's work, but see my essay "*Libra* and the Assassination of JFK: A Textbook Operation,"

Arizona Quarterly, 50 (Spring 1994), 109–32, for an analysis of his theories of textuality and history.

12. Samuel Weber, "After Eight: Remarking Glyph," *Glyph* 8 (1981), 235.

13. Rodolphe Gasché, "Deconstruction as Criticism," in *Inventions of Difference*, 26. This essay originally appeared in *Glyph* 6 (1979), 177–215.

14. Alexandre Kojève, *Introduction à la lecture de Hegel*, edited Raymond Queneau (1947; rpr. Paris: Gallimard, 1968), 416–17.

15. In "'Torments of an Ancient Word': Jabès and the Rabbinic Tradition," Susan Handelman characterizes the "absence of God as a void *within* God" (71). In Handelman's reading of Jabès, the sacred text is simultaneously "word, presence, law" and "silence, absence, void." The word and the void exist in a primordial unity mimetically represented in the fragmentariness of *The Book of Questions*. The discontinuities of Jabès's texts bear witness to the irreducible otherness of the Jewish God. Like Handelman, Richard Stamelman, in "Nomadic Writing: The Poetics of Exile," equates Jabès's work with deconstruction and likewise invokes the breaking of the tablets, the withdrawal of God (*tsimtzum*), and the fragment. But all these tropes posit a transcendental totality recalled by and through ontic metaphor. My point is not to deny the perspicuity of these readings but to point out that according to them Jabès still remains within the confines of onto-theology. This is especially true of the essay by Beryl Lang, "Writing-the-Holocaust: Jabès and the Measure of History," criticizing Jabès for ignoring the positive side of Judaism present in the biblical Judaism that forms the reverse image of the diaspora. The question these readings raise concern the very claim for a Jewish writing distinct from the logocentric, and therefore metaphysical, writing of Christianity.

16. Gasché, "Deconstruction as Criticism," 55, 57.

17. This reading of Judaism has its precedent in Hegel's account of Abraham in *The Spirit of Christianity* and was developed in the *Phenomenology of Spirit*, but it is not fully articulated until the work of Alexandre Kojève and Jean Hyppolite. See Kojève, *Introduction à la lecture de Hegel*, and Hyppolite, "La critique hégéliene de la réflexion kantienne," in *Figures de la pensée philosophique*, vol. 1 (Paris: Presses Universitaires de France, 1971). In his outline to the *Phenomenology*, Kojève identifies the "Judaic attitude" in the passage where Hegel writes that the "simple Unchangeable" is taken to be the "*essential* Being" and consciousness takes itself to be changeable and merely unessential. In the text of his lectures, Kojève remarks cryptically, "1° l'Esclave cherche un Maître (terrible) dans l'au-delà, parce qu'il a peur de la mort. (Analogie

avec la première phase de la Lutte pour la Vie et la Mort (p. 160, l. 20 [in Hoffmeister; Miller, p. 128, l. 6]). Judaïsme. Dieu le Père. . . . 3ᵉ 'La conscience (malheureuse) se trouve elle-même dans l'Immuable.' Le Christianisme, l'Église, le Saint-Esprit. Ou: a) l'essential immuable condamnant la particularité (Judaïsme)." [1st the slave seeks a (terrifying) Master in the beyond because he is afraid of death. (Analogy with the first phase of the Struggle for Life and Death.)] (p. 68). Elsewhere, he refers to Hegel's "sole allusion to the Jewish religion" and says Judaism "is not a religion of masters" but one of nature, which is to say one of slaves (p. 248). The reference is to the opening paragraph of "The living work of art," a subsection of "Religion in the Form of Art." Again, Hegel makes no direct reference to Judaism: "The nation that approaches its god in the cult of the religion of art is the ethical nation that knows its state and the actions of the state to be the will and the achievement of its own self" (*Phenomenology of Spirit,* trans. A.V. Miller (Oxford: Clarendon Press, 1977), 435–36.

Hyppolite discusses this section in terms of Hellenism and Christianity: "That way the Jewish world, then Christianity, expresses a reflection which is properly the unhappy consciousness, the consciousness of the unhappiness of life radically separated from the Absolute, always beyond" (176). It is important to note that Kojève also writes, "The unhappy consciousness is the Christian consciousness; the psychology of the Christian, who is for Hegel the most perfect type of the Religious man" (204).

18. Hegel, *Phenomenology of Spirit,* 492. Hereafter cited in text as *PS.* The following abbreviations will be used for Hegel's texts, all published by the Clarendon Press, Oxford unless otherwise stated: *Aesthetics— Aesthetics: Lectures on Fine Art,* trans. T. M. Knox, 2 vols. (1975); *PM— Philosophy of Mind,* trans. William Wallace, *Zusätze* trans. A. V. Miller (1971); *PR—Lectures on the Philosophy of Religion,* ed. Peter C. Hodgson, trans. R.F. Brown, P.C. Hodgson, and J.M. Stewart, with the assistance of H.S. Harris. 3 vols. (Berkeley: University of California Press, 1984–87).

19. Georges Bataille, "Hegel, la mort et le sacrifice," *Deucalion,* 5 (Neuchâtel, 1955), 32.

20. Maurice Blanchot, "Literature and the Right to Death," trans. Lydia Davis, in *The Work of Fire,* trans. Charlotte Mandell (Stanford: Stanford University Press, 1995), 322: "The word gives me the being, but it gives it to me deprived of being."

21. Paul Auster, "Book of the Dead: An Interview with Edmond Jabès," in *The Sin of the Book,* 19.

22. Maurice Blanchot, "Interruptions," trans. Paul Auster and Rosemarie Waldrop, in *The Sin of the Book: Edmond Jabès,* 47. This

translation is comprised of two essays, "L'Interruption (Comme sur une surface de Riemann)," in *L'Entretien infini* (Paris: Gallimard, 1969), and "Le livre des questions," in *L'Amitié* (Paris: Gallimard, 1971). Both essays were first published as one in *La Nouvelle Revue Française* (May 1964).

23. Cf. Derrida, "The Ends of Man," in *Margins of Philosophy*: "It remains that Being, which is nothing, is not a being, cannot be said, cannot say itself, except in the ontic metaphor" (131). Also see John Llewelyn's commentary on this critique of Heidegger's concept of Being in *Derrida on the Threshold of Sense* (New York: St. Martin's Press, 1986), 38.

24. Maurice Blanchot, *The Infinite Conversation*, trans. Susan Hanson (Minneapolis: University of Minnesota Press, 1993), 128.

25. Blanchot, "Interruptions," 49.

26. Blanchot, "Interruptions," 49.

27. Cf. Rosemarie Waldrop, "Mirrors and Paradoxes," in *The Sin of the Book*: "There is a wound at the origin of self-reflection, of self-consciousness: the wound of existence, of individuation, of 'otherness'" (137).

28. See "Edmond Jabès and the Question of the Book," *WD*, 67: "Between the fragments of the broken Tables the poem grows and the right to speech takes root." Also see Blanchot, "Interruptions," 49: "There is the empty, desertlike waiting that holds back the writer who works at the threshold of the book. . . . Because, first of all, the Tablets of the Law were broken when still only barely touched by the divine hand . . . and were written again, but not in their original form, so that it is from an already destroyed word that man learns the demand that must speak to him: there is no real first understanding, no initial and unbroken word, as if one could never speak except the second time."

29. Paul de Man, "Hegel on the Sublime," in *Aesthetic Ideology*, ed. Andrzej Warminski (Minneapolis: University of Minnesota Press, 1996), 112.

30. Edmond Jabès, *Le Parcours* (Paris: Gallimard, 1985), 86–87.

31. Gasché, "Deconstruction as Criticism," 28.

32. Gasché, "Deconstruction as Criticism," 50. And see *The Tain of the Mirror*, 259.

Chapter Three

1. Immanuel Kant, "On a Newly Arisen Superior Tone in Philosophy," trans. Peter Fenves, in *Raising the Tone of Philosophy: Late Essays by*

Immanuel Kant, Transformative Critique by Jacques Derrida, ed. Peter Fenves (Baltimore: Johns Hopkins University Press, 1993), 59. Hereinafter cited in text as *RTP*. Derrida's address was first published, along with the proceedings of the conference, in *Les Fins de l'homme. A partir du travail de Jacques Derrida*, ed. Philippe Lacoue-Labarthe and Jean-Luc Nancy (Paris: Galilée, 1981).

2. Interview with Richard Kearney, "Jacques Derrida: Deconstruction and the Other," in *Dialogues with Contemporary Continental Thinkers: The Phenomenological Heritage* (Manchester, Eng.: Manchester University Press, 1984), 123.

3. "Deconstruction and the Other," 123.

4. Edmund Husserl, *Ideas Pertaining to a Pure Phenomenology and to a Phenomenological Philosophy. First Book: General Introduction to a Pure Phenomenology*, trans. F. Kersten (The Hague: Martinus Nijhoff, 1983), 116. See also section 49.

5. See *Ideas*, 110.

6. Jacques Derrida, "The Time of a Thesis: Punctuations," trans. Kathleen McLaughlin, in *Philosophy in France Today*, ed. Alan Montefiore (Cambridge: Cambridge University Press, 1983), 39.

7. "Time of the Thesis," 38. The notion that literary writing must erase itself in order to produce itself can be fruitfully considered in the context of Russell's theory of types. See John Llewelyn's discussion of the theory of types and undecidability in "Responsibility with Indecidability," in *Derrida: A Critical Reader*, ed. David Wood (Oxford: Blackwell, 1992), 75–80. The theory of types seeks to avoid the paradox of self-referential sentences (such as, "This sentence is false") "by asserting that no propositional function can meaningfully take itself as argument" (75). Llewelyn exposes the limitations of this theory in a reading of Francis Ponge's "Fable."

8. Gasché, *The Tain of the Mirror*, 259. Gasché's situating of Derrida's remarks on the being of literature within and against phenomenology is very important to my argument, as the ensuing discussion will show.

9. See section 84 of *Ideas*: "Intentionality is an essential peculiarity of the sphere of mental processes taken universally in so far as all mental processes in some manner or other share in it" (199). Intentionality is the property of consciousness to be the consciousness *of. . . .*

10. Paul Ricoeur, *Husserl: An Analysis of His Phenomenology*, trans. Edward G. Ballard and Lester E. Embree (Evanston: Northwestern University Press, 1967), 145. Citing this passage, Derrida praises Ricoeur

for recognizing "in the Idea 'the mediating role between consciousness and history'" (*IOG*, 137).

11. See Husserl, *Ideas*, 356. Husserl uses the term *"Eidos"* (German *"Wesen,"* "essence") to avoid confusion with the Kantian Idea (xxii).

12. Nevertheless, several works have appeared on nuclear war and criticism. Their major themes include the function of time, infinite deferral, and the rhetoric of deterrence. One of the better works is Peter Schwenger, *Letter Bomb: Nuclear Holocaust and the Exploding Word* (Baltimore: Johns Hopkins University Press, 1992). Christopher Norris has written on Derrida's essay "No Apocalypse, Not Now" on at least two occasions. In *Derrida* (Cambridge: Harvard University Press, 1987), he treats it in the context of his overall argument that deconstruction is a critique of the "paradoxes in the nature of reason" (163). In *Uncritical Theory: Postmodernism, Intellectuals and the Gulf War* (London: Lawrence & Wishart, 1992), he is more critical of the essay, charging that it invites a blurring of the distinction between the actual and the simulated necessary for judgment (38–47). This criticism strikes me as more pertinent to a work like William Chaloupka's *Knowing Nukes: The Politics and Culture of the Atom* (Minneapolis: University of Minnesota Press, 1992) than as a proper assessment of Derrida's argument. According to Norris, Derrida's work represents a radicalizing of Kant that continues the "critical engagement with the truth-claims and ethical values of Enlightenment thought" (*Uncritical Theory*, 47). Norris narrowly interprets the phenomenological suspension of judgment as a relinquishment of accountability and misses the point that Derrida's deconstruction of the *epochê* situates the possibility of judgment in literature's being without essence.

13. Richard Klein calls this godlike perspective the "nuclear sublime" after Frances Ferguson's article of this name (*Diacritics* 14, no. 2 [Summer 1984]: 4–10). He writes, "Nuclear Criticism denies itself that posthumous, apocalyptic perspective, with its pathos, its revelations, and its implicit reassurances; it supposes that the only future may be the one we project forward from the time when total nuclear war, for the time being, has not taken place" ("The Future of Nuclear Criticism," *Yale French Studies* 77 [1990]: 77–78). He goes on to say that what distinguishes this future would be the absence of a "posthumous perspective," the work of mourning (81). I believe he misreads Derrida to the extent that he treats the possibility of total destruction strictly within terms of a hypothetical or anticipatible future. The prospect of a future without repetition falls within the possibility of an origin without alterity: absolute absence is on a par with absolute presence.

14. Gasché, *The Tain of the Mirror*, 281.

15. See Derrida, "The Time of a Thesis," 37.

16. Gasché, *The Tain of the Mirror*, 214.

17. Simon Critchley offers a good account of closure in Derrida in *The Ethics of Deconstruction: Derrida and Levinas* (Oxford: Blackwell, 1992), 59–88. He distinguishes between a spatial sense of a finite territory and a temporal sense of bringing something to its conclusion. It is this latter meaning that requires that closure not be confused with end because "end signifies the completion of the act and not the act of completion. Thus, on a temporal level, closure signifies a state of being prior to the end" (61–62). Derrida's notion of closure is different from Heidegger's "end of metaphysics." Closure repeats and transgresses the logic of end and of a unitary history. Therefore, we are not trapped within metaphysics as if it were some spatial enclosure nor are we simply able to escape it either. Critchley writes, "The problem of closure does not enclose the space of a unitary history and foreclose the possibility of transgression, but rather traces the double necessity and double impossibility of both belonging to a history whose closure can be delimited and not belonging to a history whose closure we are unable to leave. There is no exit within a repetition, and there is no exit without repetition" (88). Much of Critchley's book is devoted to what he calls the logic of *clôtural* reading.

18. Gasché, *The Tain of the Mirror*, 159.

19. See the discussion of world-belief and *epoché* in Robert Sokolowski, *Husserlian Meditations: How Words Present Things* (Evanston: Northwestern University Press, 1974), 173–74. A useful discussion of the types of *epoché* can be found in Frederick A. Elliston, "Husserl's Phenomenology of Empathy," in *Husserl: Expositions and Appraisals*, ed. Frederick Elliston and Peter McCormick (Notre Dame: University of Notre Dame Press, 1977), 217–18.

20. Edmund Husserl, *Ideas*, 61: "*We put out of action the general positing which belongs to the essence of the natural attitude*; we parenthesize everything which that positing encompasses with respect to being: *thus the whole natural world* which is continually 'there for us,' 'on hand,' and which will always remain there according to consciousness as an 'actuality' even if we choose to parenthesize it.

"If I do that, as I can with complete freedom, then I am *not negating* this 'world' as though I were a sophist; I am *not doubting its factual being* as though I were a skeptic; rather I am exercising the 'phenomenological' *epochê* which also *completely shuts me off from any judgment about spatiotemporal factual being.*"

21. Emmanuel Levinas, *The Theory of Intuition in Husserl's Phenomenology*, trans. André Orianne (Evanston: Northwestern University Press, 1973), 148.

22. Edmund Husserl, *Experience and Judgment: Investigations in a Genealogy of Logic*, Revised and edited Ludwig Landgrebe, trans. James S. Churchill and Karl Ameriks (Evanston: Northwestern University Press, 1973), 265–66.

23. Husserl, *Experience and Judgment*, 267.

24. Herman Rapaport, *Heidegger and Derrida (Lincoln: University of Nebraska Press, 1989)*, 181. Rapaport points out that Derrida's early text on Husserl anticipates *The Post Card* and "Of an Apocalyptic Tone."

25. Edmund Husserl, *Phenomenology and the Crisis of Philosophy*, trans. Quentin Lauer (New York: Harper & Row, 1965), 116.

26. In "The Origin of Geometry" (written in 1936 and first published in 1939, it was included in *Die Krisis der eurpäischen Wissenschaften und die transzendentale Phänomenologie* [1954], translated as *The Crisis of European Sciences and Transcendental Phenomenology*, trans. David Carr [Evanston: Northwestern University Press, 1970]; I cite from this translation as reprinted in an appendix to Derrida's *Introduction*), Husserl defines ideal objects as a class of "spiritual products of the cultural world" that exist permanently for everyone, unlike either a mere psychic experience lying exclusively in an individual's mental space or a physical product, such as a tool, that is repeatable in exemplars. In a note he adds, "But the broadest concept of literature encompasses them all; that is, it belongs to their objective being that they be linguistically expressed and can be expressed again and again; or, more precisely, they have their objectivity, their existence-for-everyone, only as signification, as the meaning of speech" (160).

27. Husserl, *Ideas* 58–59.

28. In "The Double Session," Derrida summarizes the history of the interpretation of mimesis: "1. either, even before it can be translated as imitation, *mimêsis* signifies the presentation of the thing itself, of nature, of the *physis* that produces itself, engenders itself, and appears (to itself) as it really is, in the present of its image, its visible aspect, its face . . . . 2. or else *mimêsis* sets up a relation of *homoiôsis* or *adaequatio* between two (terms)" (*D*, 193).

29. Derrida, "Psyché: Inventions of the Other," 37, (translation modified) citing Paul de Man, "The Rhetoric of Temporality," in *Blindness and Insight: Essays in the Rhetoric of Contemporary Criticism*, 2nd ed.

(Minneapolis: University of Minnesota Press, 1983), 222. The bracketed remarks and emphasis are Derrida's.

30. See Husserl, *Ideas*, section 74.

31. See "'This Strange Institution Called Literature.'" In asserting that literature dissrupts phenomenology, Derrida denies there is an essence of literature but says there is "a literary *functioning* and a literary *intentionality*, an experience rather than an essence of literature (natural or ahistorical)" (45). He goes on to note the special relation of literature to phenomenology, suggesting that the "phenomenological conversion of the gaze, the 'transcendental reduction' he [Husserl] recommended is perhaps the very condition (I do not say the natural condition) of literature." The fictionality of literature, its capacity to allow one to say anything, lies in its function as the *epochê* of the *epochê*. As such, "[p]oetry and literature provide or facilitate 'phenomenological' access to what makes of a thesis a *thesis as such*" (46).

32. In one of his last essays, Eugenio Donato provides a brilliant reading of representation as a strategy for the occultation of the unnameable referent whose master metaphor is death. See "Bodies: On the Limits of Representation in Romantic Poetics," published posthumously in *The Script of Decadence* (New York: Oxford University Press, 1993), 191–208.

33. Husserl, *Experience and Judgment*, 254.

34. Husserl, *Experience and Judgment*, 259.

35. Husserl, *Experience and Judgment*, 268.

36. Husserl, *Experience and Judgment*, 260.

Chapter Four

1. An important discussion of gathering is to be found in Heidegger's 1951 essay "Logos (Heraclitus, Fragment B 50)," originally published in *Vorträge und Aufsätze* (Pfullingen: Verlag Günther Neske, 1954) and translated in *Early Greek Thinking*, trans. David Farrell Krell and Frank A. Capuzzi (New York: Harper & Row, 1975), 59–78. The essay proceeds as a reflection on the translation of the Greek *légein* by the German *lesen* (gathering, reading). The thinking of *légein* as "gathered-letting-lie-before" echoes and modifies the words on the "greatness" of the Greek beginning in the Rector's Address. He writes, "Since the beginning of Western thought the Being of beings emerges as what is alone worthy of thought.

If we think this historic development in a truly historical way, then that in which the beginning of Western thought rests first becomes manifest: that in Greek antiquity the Being of beings becomes worthy of thought *is* the beginning of the West and *is* the hidden source of its destiny. Had this beginning not safeguarded what has been, i.e. the gathering of what still endures, the Being of beings would not now govern from the essence of modern technology" (76).

Derrida says that gathering, *Versammlung*, is "always a matter of this gathering together, of this being-one with oneself . . . of indivisible individuality or of being always already with oneself, from the origin or at the finish line of some *Bestimmung* [destination]. I recognize the force and necessity of this motif of the *Versammlung* in Heidegger, all the more so in that it never excludes difference, on the contrary" (*Points,* 305).

2. When asked about the relationship between the uniqueness of the literary text and the historical act of reading, Derrida answers, "A work takes place just once, and far from going against history, this uniqueness of the institution, which is in no way natural and will never be replaced, seems to me historical through and through. It must be referred to as a proper name and whatever irreplaceable reference a proper name bears within it. Attention to history, context, and genre is necessitated, and not contradicted, by this singularity, by the date and the signature of the work" (*SIL,* 67).

3. Those who say deconstruction pays no heed to the text but indulges in wild interpretations have misunderstood Derrida, who was explicit on this point in *Of Grammatology* when he wrote, "To recognize and respect all its [i.e., critical reading's] classical exigencies is not easy and requires all the instruments of traditional criticism. Without this recognition and this respect, critical production would risk developing in any direction at all and authorize itself to say almost anything. But this indispensable guardrail has always only *protected*, it has never *opened*, a reading" (*OG,* 158).

4. Cf. "What is singular about this tyrannical *thou must* of the thing is exactly its singularity. The singularity of a command which is irreplaceable each time—its rarity—prevents it from becoming law. Or rather, if you prefer, it is a law that is immediately transgressed (let us say, more precisely, *freed up* [*franchie*]), the one who responds being placed, immediately, in a singular link with it, whereby he frees himself from the tyranny even as he experiences and approves it" (*SS,* 50).

5. The *OED* defines "yes" as "a word used to express an affirmative reply to a question, statement, command, etc." (*OED*). *Robert* offers a similar definition of *oui*. But in the definitions and examples we find that "yes" does not fit the dominant paradigms that commonly inform our

thinking about language—that is, it is not a noun, verb, or even a clearly recognizable part of speech (although it is designated as an adverb) but is typically a word whose meaning is more a matter of tone and occasion of use. Indeed, it is preeminently a word whose meaning is determined by use rather than by reference, meaning, or grammatical function. The *OED* defines "adverb" as "a word used to express the attribute of an attribute, which expresses any relation of place, time, circumstance, causality, manner, or degree, or which modifies or limits an attribute, or predicate, or their modification." It dates its earliest use from 1530: "It is harde to a lerner to discerne the difference bytwene an adverbe and the other partes of spetche."

6. John Llewelyn's discussion of "the first step" in the contestation of ontological difference in Levinas and Derrida is helpful here. He writes, "the first step is first only pedagogically. It is not true here that the first step is the only step that counts, for when the second step has been taken it takes with it the firstness of the other. This is the nature of the negativity of the *pas*. The trace will have retraced the distance covered by the first step before it was ever made." "Responsibility with Indecidability," in *Derrida: A Critical Reader*, edited David Wood (Oxford: Blackwell, 1992), 88.

7. Cf.: "One does not know (for it is no longer of the order of knowing) to whom the apocalyptic sending [*envoi*] returns; it leaps [*saute*] from one place of emission to the other (and a place is always determined *starting from* [*à partir de*] the presummed emission); it goes from one destination, one name, and one tone to the other; it always refers [*renvoie*] to the name and to the tone of the other that is there but as having been there and before yet coming" (*AT* 156 / *TA* 470).

8. I do not wish to be misunderstood as proposing that literature is somehow "about" the destruction of humanity or the world. This reading misses the crucial point that Derrida's conditions of possibility/impossibility constitute a rejection of a traditional concept of finitude, to which "nuclear criticism" still holds on. It makes no sense to write, as does Tobin Siebers in *The Ethics of Criticism* (Ithaca: Cornell University Press, 1988), that deconstruction attempts to draw literature into its own "sublime" destruction of knowledge and the humanities. Siebers's misunderstanding of Derrida is nowhere more evident than when he writes, "Derrida decides to write from the vantage of a postnuclear landscape in which humanity has accomplished its end; and the agent and expression of that end remains literature" (225). First, Derrida's essay denies the apocalyptic perspective that most discourse on nuclear catastrophe adopts. Secondly, literature serves no end, which, as Derrida suggests, is precisely what makes it necessary for democracy.

9. See Derrida's reading of the date in Paul Celan: "A date gets carried away, transported; it takes off, takes itself off—and thus effaces itself in its readability. Effacement is not something that befalls it like an accident; it affects neither its meaning nor its readability; it merges, on the contrary, with reading's very access to that which a date may still signify. But if readability effaces the date, the very thing which it offers for reading, this strange process will have begun with the very inscription of the date" (*SPC*, 22).

10. In an interview, Derrida responds to a question about his analysis of the date in Celan: "A date marks singularity: this happened in this place, not only at such a moment but in such a place. In French one says, '*daté de*,' dated from, and that also means the place of origination. So the date is the mark of a singularity, of a temporal and spatial 'this here.' And it is with the date that one wants to keep the trace of this irreplaceable uniqueness. . . . A date inscribes this singularity in a readability, that is, in reference to a calendar, to marks that are in any case repeatable, accessible to everyone. A date cannot be secret, can it? Once it is read, whether it makes reference to the calendar or not, it is immediately repeated and, consequently, in this iterability that makes it readable, it loses the singularity that it keeps" (*Points*, 377–78).

11. On the motif of ashes, see *Shibboleth*: "The poem's desire or gift, the date is borne, in a movement of blessing, toward ash. . . . The incineration of which I speak takes place prior to any operation, it burns from within. The date is consumed by incineration in that expiring which is its production, genesis, or inscription: its essence and its chance" (44–45). Also see *Cinders*.

12. Derrida, *Khôra* (Paris: Galilée, 1993), 1. *Sauf le nom (Post-Scriptum)* (Paris: Galilée, 1993) first appeared in English as "Post-Scriptum: Aporias, Ways and Voices," trans. John P. Leavey, Jr., in *Derrida and Negative Theology*, ed. Harold Coward and Toby Foshay (Albany: State University of New York Press, 1992), 283–323. *Passions* (Paris: Galilée, 1993), the third of the *Essays on the Name*, first appeared in English as "Passions: 'An Oblique Offering,'" trans. David Wood, in *Derrida: A Critical Reader*, 5–35. They have been published together as *On the Name*.

13. See "Passages—from Traumatism to Promise," in *Points*. After distinguishing the performative character of promises from constatives, he says, "Now, I believe that one ought to be able to say that, beyond determined promises, all language acts entail a certain structure of the promise, even if they do something else at the same time. All language is addressed to the other in order to promise him or her to speak to him or

her in some way. Even if I do so in order to threaten, to insult, to hold forth a scientific discourse, to do anything other than promise, there is in the simple fact that I am speaking to the other a kind of commitment to go to the end of my sentence, to continue, to affirm by making a commitment. . . . Before I even decide what I am going to say, I promise to speak to you, I respond to the promise to speak, I respond. I respond to you as soon as I speak and consequently I commit or pledge myself" (384).

14. See *Of Spirit*, 93–94 and *Memoires for Paul de Man*, 145–50.

15. Paul de Man, *Allegories of Reading: Figural Language in Rousseau, Nietzsche, Rilke, and Proust* (New Haven: Yale University Press, 1979). 273.

16. See the essay "Time and Being" in Heidegger's *On Time and Being*, trans. Joan Stambaugh (New York: Harper & Row, 1972), 6–24. The essay is an attempt "to think Being without regard to its being grounded in terms of beings" (2). This means thinking Being as *epochê*, the characteristic of sending, wherein what is sent, Being, holds itself back "in favor of the discernibility of the gift, that is, of Being with regard to the groundings of beings" (9). The impossible condition Heidegger proposes is that we think Being in terms of what blocks our thinking of Being, its grounding in beings. He concludes the essay by saying that the attempt to say Being as Appropriation (*Ereignis*), the gift of presence, "in the form of a lecture remains an obstacle of this kind" (24). I take this not to mean a confession of failure but a submission to the necessity of a thinking that enters into the very obstacles it would overcome.

17. Mauss's classic study, *Essai sur le Don*, was first published in 1950 and appeared in English translation in 1954. It has been newly translated as *The Gift: The Form and Reason for Exchange in Archaic Societies*, trans. W. D. Halls (New York: Norton, 1990).

18. When asked about the gift and sexual difference, Derrida responds, "In as much as a gift has an assignable destination, it is an exchange— therefore, it is not a gift. . . . Consequently, there is no gift except in that all determinations—particularly sexual determination as classically defined—are absolutely unconscious and random. And this randomness is the chance of the gift—the gift must be given by chance." See "Women in the Beehive: A Seminar with Jacques Derrida," trans. James Adner, originally published in *Subjects/Objects* (Spring 1984), 5–19; reprinted in *Discourses: Conversations in Postmodern Art and Culture*, ed. Russell Ferguson, William Olander, Marcia Tucker, and Karen Fiss (New York: The New Museum of Contemporary Art; Cambridge: MIT Press, 1990), 122–23.

19. See the conclusion of "Ousia and Grammê": "If Being, according to the Greek forgetting which would have been the very form of its advent, has never meant anything except beings, then perhaps difference is older than Being itself. There may be a difference still more unthought than the difference between Being and beings. We certainly can go further toward naming it in our language. Beyond Being and beings, this difference . . . this *différance* would be the first or last trace if one still could speak, here, of origin and end" (*M,* 67).

20. See Derrida, "On Reading Heidegger: An Outline of Remarks to the Essex Colloquium," *Research in Phenomenology,* 17 (1987), 177: "Of course, the word *trace* doesn't mean anything by itself. But the model of imprinting, mold, etc. of *tupos,* is one particular mode of determining the trace—and it is not mine, I would say. On the contrary, I am trying to deconstruct this model and even the model of the vestige, the footprint in the sand. I would prefer something which is neither present nor absent: I would prefer *ashes* as the better paradigm for what I call the trace—something which erases itself totally, radically, while presenting itself."

21. When asked if philosophy may not be "consumed" in anamnesis, Derrida replies, "Yes, if there is anamnesis, it is not just a movement of memory to find again finally what has been forgotten, to restore finally an origin, a moment or a past that will have been present. . . . To think memory or to think anamnêsis, here, is to think things as paradoxical as the memory of a past that has not been present, the memory of the future— the movement of memory as tied to the future and not only to the past, memory turned toward the promise, toward what is coming, what is arriving, what is happening tomorrow" (*Points,* 382–383).

22. Derrida's comments on apophasis ("a kind of an Irony, whereby we deny that we say, or do that which we especially say or do" [*Oxford English Dictionary*]) are pertinent here: "Apophatic statements represent what Husserl identifies as the moment of *crisis* (forgetting of the full and originary intuition, empty functioning of symbolic language, objectivism, etc.). But in revealing the originary and final necessity of this crisis, in denouncing from the language of crisis the snares of intuitive consciousness and of phenomenology, they destabilize the very axiomatics of the phenomenological, that is also, the ontological and transcendental, critique" (*ON,* 50–51).

23. These remarks are recorded in the discussion following Roland Barthes' "To Write: An Intransitive Verb?" in *The Structuralist Controversy,* ed. Richard Macksey and Eugenio Donato (1970; rpr. Baltimore: Johns Hopkins University Press, 1972), 156.

24. Gasché, "God, for Example," 168.

25. See Gasché, "Structural Infinity," in *Inventions of Difference*, 147.

26. For a valuable discussion of Derrida's use of cinder (*cendre*) or ash as the paradigm of the trace, or a residue that makes thinking and representation possible, see Ned Lukacher's introduction to his translation of *Cinders*, "Introduction: Mourning Becomes Telepathy," 1–19.

27. Derrida says of "the baffling structure of a date and the mark of a wound" in his essay on Celan: "Given that all experience is the experience of a singularity and thus is the desire to keep this singularity as such, the 'as such' of the singularity, that is, what permits one to keep it as what it is, this is what effaces it right away. And this wound or this pain [*douleur*] of the effacing in memory itself, in the gathering-up [*le recueillement*] of memory, is wounding, it is a pain reawakened in itself; the poetic in Paul Celan is also the thing of this pain [*le poétique chez Paul Celan est aussi de cette douleur-là*]" (*Points*, 378 / *PdS*, 392).

28. Simon Critchley, in *The Ethics of Deconstruction: Derrida and Levinas*, argues that this "*clôtural* logic" wherein the limit interrupts and exceeds the context it borders constitutes "the ethical moment in Derrida's thinking" (p. 32). "*Clôtural* logic" is a mode of reading that interrupts ontological closure.

29. Hegel, *Phenomenology of Spirit*, trans. A. V. Miller (Oxford: Oxford University Press, 1977), 19.

Index

Abraham, 194n. 17; and sacrifice of Isaac, 15–19, 22–24, 28, 175, 184nn. 43, 44; 185n. 53. *See also* Akedah

abyme, mise en, 79, 166

act, 8, 11, 16, 18, 28, 29, 50, 56, 64, 115, 123, 133–35, 137, 146, 160, 165; deconstruction as, 32–34, 188n. 7; Literature as, 6, 34–36, 73, 106, 112–13, 131, 148–49, 151–52

Akedah, 17, 184n. 44. *See also* Abraham

alêtheia, 9, 75, 88, 150, 162, 180n. 19. *See also* truth

alterity, 5, 14–17, 21, 25, 26, 36, 38, 48, 51, 57, 65, 69, 90, 115, 125, 146, 164, 184n. 40, 189n. 14, 198n. 13. *See also* other; otherness

analogical structure: of Being, 23; of thinking, 13, 14, 16, 23, 102; of the secret, 24, 25, 27

anamnêsis, 156, 206n. 21

apocalypse, 3, 12, 28, 49, 119, 122, 126, 127; and future, 33, 103, 105, 109, 111, 198n. 13; and God, 26, 84; and literature, 26, 69–70, 130, 149, 167–68, 203n. 8; and secret, 70; and sending, 144, 150, 167, 203n. 7; and tone, 71–72, 102; as transcendental condition of discourse, 26, 27, 70, 72, 128; without revelation, 128, 130, 140. *See also* nuclear catastrophe

apocalyptic. *See* apocalypse

apophasis, 5, 153, 191n. 3, 206n. 22

aporia, 58, 62; defined, 37; of the gift, 154, 156; and ethics,

15–17, 28, 29, 31, 39, 40, 153, 159, 174; of God, 25; of law, 11, 37, 42–44, 48–49, 53, 54, 181n. 25; of the promise, 151, 153; of the secret, 24, 48; of singularity, 38–39, 42, 154; of time, 184–85n. 25. *See also* decision; judgment

arche-trace. *See* trace

arche-writing. *See* writing

archive, 122; and act, 32–34, 36, 112–13, 151; and deconstruction, 34; and destruction, 32–33, 114–17, 119, 135–38, 122, 140, 148; and gift, 167; and literature, 1, 105, 106, 112–14, 137, 140, 148

Aristotle, 32, 74, 152, 184–85n. 25

Auerbach, Erich, 74

Auschwitz: and representation, 83

Austin, J. L., 33, 151, 181–82n. 25. *See also* speech act theory

Bataille, Georges, 82

Beardsworth, Richard, 40, 41, 181n. 25, 182n. 26, 184–85n. 45

Being, 1, 10, 31, 64, 76–78, 81, 84, 144; as appropriation (*Ereignis*), 7–9, 59, 61, 85, 150, 169, 171, 188n. 6, 205n. 16; and the Book, 72–75, 98–99; and God, 5, 12–18, 20–27, 72, 76, 86; and holocaust, 168–71, 174; of literature, 108, 128–31, 135, 140; and ontico-ontological difference, 8, 13, 21, 25, 27, 59–62, 111, 139, 155, 179n. 6, 203n. 6, 206n. 19

Bernasconi, Robert, 180n. 12

209